Theorizing Internal Security Cooperation in the European Union

Theorizing Internal Security Cooperation in the European Union

Edited by
Raphael Bossong and Mark Rhinard

OXFORD
UNIVERSITY PRESS

OXFORD
UNIVERSITY PRESS

Great Clarendon Street, Oxford, OX2 6DP,
United Kingdom

Oxford University Press is a department of the University of Oxford.
It furthers the University's objective of excellence in research, scholarship,
and education by publishing worldwide. Oxford is a registered trade mark of
Oxford University Press in the UK and in certain other countries

Published in the United States of America by Oxford University Press
198 Madison Avenue, New York, NY 10016, United States of America

British Library Cataloguing in Publication Data
Data available

Library of Congress Control Number: 2016942454

ISBN 978-0-19-873948-7

Contents

Part I. Introduction

Part II. Theoretical Perspectives

Contents

Part III. Concluding Remarks

List of Figures and Table

List of Abbreviations

AFSJ	Area of Freedom, Security and Justice
CEPOL	European Police College
CFSP	Common Foreign and Security Policy
CJEU	Court of Justice of the European Union
COREPER	Committee of Permanent Representatives
COSAC	Conference of Parliamentary Committees for Union Affairs of Parliaments of the European Union
COSI	Internal Security Committee
CS	Copenhagen School
CSDP	Common Security and Defence Policy
EASO	European Asylum Support Office
EAW	European Arrest Warrant
EC	European Communities
EC3	European Cybercrime Centre
ECHR	European Convention of Human Rights
ECJ	European Court of Justice
ECSC	European Coal and Steel Community
EEC	European Economic Community
EP	European Parliament
EPP	European People's Party
EPP-ED	European People's Party–European Democrats
EU	European Union
EU-LISA	Agency for the Management of Large Scale IT Systems
EURODAC	European Dactyloscopy Database
EUROJUST	The European Union's Judicial Cooperation Unit
EUROPOL	European Police Office
FIU	Financial Information Unit
FRONTEX	European Agency for the Management of Operational Cooperation at the External Borders

List of Abbreviations

GDP	Gross Domestic Product
HUM-INT	Human Intelligence
IGC	Intergovernmental Conference
IPS	International Political Sociology
IR	International Relations
JHA	Justice and Home Affairs
LIBE	Committee on Civil Liberties and Justice and Home Affairs
MEP	Member of European Parliament
NATO	North Atlantic Treaty Organization
PARIS	Political Anthropological Research of International Sociology
PES	Party of European Socialists
QMV	Qualified Majority Voting
RFID	Radio Frequency Identification
SCIFA	Strategic Committee on Immigrations, Frontiers and Asylum
SIG-INT	Signals Intelligence
SIS	Schengen Information System
SOCTA	Serious and Organised Crime Threat Assessment
SWIFT	Society for Worldwide Interbank Financial Telecommunication
TEC	Treaty establishing the European Community
TEU	Treaty on the European Union
TFEU	Treaty on the Functioning of the European Union
TFTP	Terrorist Finance Tracking Programme
TREVI	Working group on Terrorism, Radicalism, Extremism and International Violence
VIS	Visa Information System
UK	United Kingdom
UN	United Nations
UNHCR	United Nations High Commissioner for Refugees
UNODC	United Nations Offices on Drugs and Crime
UNSC	United Nations Security Council
US	United States

Author Biographies

Didier Bigo is Professor at King's College London, Department of War Studies, and Research Professor of International Relations at Sciences-Po Paris. He is a leading scholar in the field of critical security studies, Director of the Center for the Study of Conflicts, Liberty and Security, editor of the journal *Cultures & Conflits* and co-founder of the journal *International Political Sociology*.

Thierry Balzacq is Professor and Tocqueville Chair in International Relations at the University of Namur. He is also the Scientific Director of the Institute for Strategic Research, the French Ministry of Defense research center. He conducts research in the fields of security theories, IR, and EU security policies.

Raphael Bossong is Lecturer at the Europe University Viadrina. His research focuses on EU internal security policy, crisis management, and security governance. His recent publications include *European Civil Security Governance* (with H. Hegemann; 2015, Palgrave Macmillan) and *Explaining EU Internal Security Cooperation* (with M. Rhinard; 2014, Routledge).

Dora Kostakopoulou is Professor of European Union Law, European Integration and Public Policy at Warwick University, and a member of the editorial board of *Citizenship Studies*. Her research interests range across European public law, free movement of persons and European Union citizenship, the Area of Freedom, Security and Justice, citizenship, multiculturalism, and integration.

Sandra Lavenex is Professor of European and International Politics at the University of Geneva and regular visiting professor at the College of Europe (Natolin Campus). Her research centres on modes of governance and public policy in the EU and in international politics.

Valsamis Mitsilegas is Professor of European Criminal Law, Director of the Criminal Justice Centre and Head of the Department of Law at Queen Mary University of London. From 2001 to 2005 he served as legal adviser to the House of Lords European Union Committee. His research interests and expertise lie in the fields of European criminal law; migration, asylum and borders; security and human rights; and legal responses to transnational crime.

Jörg Monar is a Professor and Rector of the College of Europe. He is the author of over two hundred articles and books on the political and institutional development of the EU, EU Justice and Home Affairs and EU external relations. He is also a founding editor of the *European Foreign Affairs Review* and has been a consultant for numerous national and European political institutions.

Author Biographies

Arne Niemann is Professor of International Politics at the Department of Political Science of the Johannes Gutenberg University Mainz, Germany. He is co-director of the Jean Monnet Centre of Excellence 'Europe in Global Dialogue', which is jointly hosted at the Technical University Darmstadt and the Johannes Gutenberg University Mainz. His research focuses on European Union politics and policies, including the area of Justice and Home Affairs.

Ariadna Ripoll Servent is a Junior Professor of Political Science at the University of Bamberg. Her research focuses on EU institutions, decision-making processes, and EU internal security policies. Her latest publications include *Policy Change in the Area of Freedom, Security and Justice* (with Florian Trauner; 2015, Routledge) and *Institutional and Policy Change in the European Parliament—Deciding on Freedom, Security and Justice* (2015, Palgrave MacMillan).

Mark Rhinard is Professor of International Relations at Stockholm University and Senior Research Fellow at the Swedish Institute of International Affairs. His research examines international cooperation on complex threats, with a special interest in the European Union. His recent works include *The European Commission* (with Neill Nugent; 2015, Palgrave) and *Explaining EU Internal Security Cooperation* (with Raphael Bossong; 2014, Routledge).

The authors are grateful for research assistance and administrative help provided by Aras Lindh of the Swedish Institute of International Affairs.

Part I
Introduction

1

Alternative Perspectives on Internal Security Cooperation in the European Union

Setting the Scene

Raphael Bossong and Mark Rhinard

1.1 Introduction

Initiated almost four decades ago, European Union cooperation in the field of internal security can now be counted amongst the most established areas of European integration. Since 1975, when EU member states embarked on cooperation via the TREVI intergovernmental framework, progress has been slow but steady.[1] The 1992 Maastricht Treaty proved a watershed moment by drawing Justice and Home Affairs (JHA) formally into the EU's institutional framework, and the 1999 Amsterdam Treaty subjected many aspects of JHA, by then retitled—and given a normative goal—as the 'Area of Freedom, Security and Justice' (AFSJ), to the Community Method of decision-making. Subsequent policy frameworks, including the Tampere, Hague, and Stockholm programmes, set the agenda for cooperation as the 2010 Lisbon Treaty incorporated the remaining issues into the Community Method and built new institutional structures for cooperation. Even an 'EU Internal Security Strategy' has surfaced. The road has not been smooth or automatic: some countries have decided to 'opt out' of some elements of internal security, implementation gaps remain, and the 2015 refugee crisis in the Southern Mediterranean—the worse of its kind in post-war Europe—revealed serious cooperation problems. But the field has evolved empirically to the point that it can be considered an established and central field of European integration.

Academically, scholars were slow to follow suit, seeing cooperation in this field as arcane in content and unique in relation to other fields—the 'stuff' of lawyers and policing experts, it might be said. Yet the 1990s witnessed a mushrooming of interest as internal security cooperation 'normalized' because of empirical developments and in a gradual acceptance of research on this topic by conferences, publishers, and academic departments. The number of books and articles has increased, as has the number of graduate students focused on various elements of internal security cooperation. Naturally, much of the early scholarship in the field was empirical and descriptive in nature: mapping developments, describing trends, highlighting problems. The last few years have seen a move towards more developed, advanced applications of theory, which produce new insights but which also raise central questions as regards the state of theorizing: Where do we stand? What has been accomplished? Where might the field be going?

These questions animate the content of this volume. While encouraged by growing theoretical developments in the field, we are concerned about fragmentation. As our mapping exercise below shows, a number of fascinating but fairly narrow agendas have developed in relative isolation from one another. Some degree of isolation is normal. In the social sciences, research does not take place in a perfectly coherent stream of inquiry, and nor should it: precision and empirical accuracy require specialization. Yet theoretical diversity in this field is particularly pronounced, not only because it remains a fairly new field but also because it attracts scholars from many disciplines. Overly isolated agendas inhibit our ability to draw out general and cumulative insights in a complex field and preclude any benefits that might derive from theoretical dialogue. As this research field continues to mature, the time is right for theoretical reflection and consolidation. By drawing together the main theoretical and conceptual approaches currently in use, assessing their utility and identifying areas for dialogue, we aim at two goals. First, we hope to encourage further theorizing and a conscious reflection of theoretical positions and links to other developments in the research field. Second, we provide new scholars entering the field with a theoretical primer, helpful for signposting existing approaches and illuminating pathways for future work.

This is the first volume of its type to bring together the field's top theory-oriented scholars in the field of EU internal security cooperation. Divided into three sections, the book has a structure that reflects its goal. The first section provides an introduction to the book along with a timeline of developments in EU internal security cooperation. Both chapters make the case that the field has reached a point at which theoretical reflection is required. The second section includes chapters on different theories and conceptual approaches used in this burgeoning field, authored by their leading proponents. Each chapter presents an approach, discusses how it is typically applied, illustrates the points using a short empirical example, and concludes with a discussion of relationships with other theories. The third section concludes the volume, reviewing the contributions and highlighting areas in which theoretical dialogue and complementarity might be most productive.

This introductory chapter sets the scene for the subsequent discussion by defining terms, laying bare our assumptions, and delimiting our approach. We first describe how we define 'internal security', what we mean by 'theory', and what theories in this field are generally aimed at explaining. We then sketch research developments in the field from its early beginnings to the current diverse menu of approaches and agendas, organized in terms of their respective attention to the politics, polity, or policy aspects related to internal security cooperation. We then describe the structure of the book in more detail and introduce the chapters.

1.2 Theorizing Internal Security in the EU

The title of this book requires some untangling if we are to specify our focus and avoid misunderstandings. The first term likely to attract attention is 'internal security', a concept known in French and German parlance but lacking a functional equivalent in other languages. In the EU, internal security coexists in the institutional lexicon, past and present, alongside 'Justice and Home Affairs', 'Third Pillar', 'Police and Judicial Cooperation in Criminal Matters', and the 'Area of Freedom, Security and Justice'. Our pragmatic definition of internal security corresponds most closely with the latter term, officially used to denote the collection of policies focused on security, rights, and the free movement of people.[2] Concretely, this means border security, police matters, customs questions, and criminal justice. Some issues, such as civil protection, are not formally part of the EU's AFSJ but clearly seem to be part of any definition of internal security. The deeper normative and conceptual meanings and criticisms that can and have been raised in regard to the notion of internal security in contemporary Western societies are manifold (Loader and Walker, 2007), but cannot be pursued further here.[3]

Another complex term used in this volume is 'theory'. What is our definition of theory? And what role do we see theory playing in analysis? This book pushes no ontological, epistemological, or methodological agenda. We do not argue for objectivist or positivist research, for instance, nor do we counsel that theory testing is somehow more valuable than theory development. As intended by our use of the word 'theorizing', this book hopes to encourage a conscious, yet open-minded, approach to the use and evolution of theories. It seeks to stimulate reflections on their underlying assumptions, main alternatives and implications for the area of study as a whole. This leads us to a tripartite definition of three types of theory, each associated with a different kind of question. The first is explanatory theory, which asks why certain things happen. An example from AFSJ might include: why has internal security cooperation proceeded in a certain pattern? Or, why is implementation difficult in certain policy areas of AFSJ? Theory used to answer such questions may involve causal or non-causal (e.g. constitutive) explanations for certain outcomes.

A second type of theory asks what we should do, or what should we be doing. This is normative or prescriptive theory, and in the field of AFSJ could include: what should be the proper balance of rule of law versus the pursuit of security? A third type is interpretative theory, oriented to finding meaning. An example from AFJS might be: what is the meaning of 'security' and how are different conceptions deployed in language and action? These different kinds of theories allow us to not only allow for variation but also to bridge the oft-described gap between 'theoretical approaches' and what might be better described as 'conceptual approaches', the latter usually taking an interpretive perspective that highlights previously unknown or neglected aspects of a certain phenomenon.[4]

No matter which type is used, a theory consists of a number of assumptions, a set of definitions and concepts, and an explicitly described area of applicability. This last consideration leads us to a second question. If this is a book about 'theory in AFSJ', what particular area of AFSJ are we speaking of? Here we are torn by contending desires to encourage research questions of many shapes and sizes while still allowing for theoretical dialogue. On the one hand, the field of AFSJ is still relatively new and demands investigations of its many intriguing aspects, from national adaption to overlapping cognitive frameworks, and from member state power plays to the proliferation of certain speech acts. On the other hand, a common—even if general—'area of applicability' would enhance our ability to compare and contrast different theories and to understand where they may be complementary or contradictory in enlightening our understanding of certain phenomena. To bridge these concerns, we take the position that the theories discussed in this volume address, in one way or another, *the emergence and dynamics of cooperation on internal security issues in the European Union.*

With three different kinds of theory outlined, and a loose specification of the object of theorizing in this book, we are left with one more caveat. That caveat relates to the fact that theories incorporate assumptions about actors, structures, institutions, processes, and relations between these four basic components. We cannot hope—nor do we desire—that all the contributions to this volume share core assumptions. Theoretical approaches are useful precisely because they prioritize and highlight different aspects of phenomena to be studied. Indeed, the mapping exercise that follows this section demonstrates the numerous possible uses of theory and assumptions underlying each. Our goal is to trace the many small, medium, and large veins of theoretical work taking place, not only to set the scene for subsequent chapters but also as a mapping exercise to build awareness and to encourage scholars to be more explicit about their own theoretical perspectives and assumptions.

1.3 Development of the Field

There are many ways to map theoretical developments in a research field. None of them are perfect. This chapter will organize developments not in terms of their theoretical origins but in terms of their general focus: the politics, polity, or policies of internal security cooperation. We complement the mapping exercise with an introduction covering the early days of research in the field and a concluding discussion of the cross-cutting research agenda focused on the 'external dimension' of EU internal security cooperation.

1.3.1 *Early Days*

The first main analytical puzzle in the field of EU internal security cooperation was the growth of cooperation per se in this sensitive field. Theories associated with international relations and classical integration theory would not necessarily have predicted the steady pace of cooperation, since internal security was traditionally assumed to be one of the remaining core areas of national sovereignty (Knelangen, 2000). Yet integration theory did provide the kernel of at least one early explanation for cooperation in the field of internal security: spillover. Researchers used neofunctionalist perspectives to explain practitioners' justification for cooperation within the context of functionalist spillover. By this logic, the creation of the single market (especially its reinvigoration in the mid-1980s with the Single European Act) generated the impetus for the abolition of internal border controls (i.e. the Schengen agreement), which, in turn, called for common standards of external border security and for 'compensatory' measures taken cooperatively by police and customs officials (Cullen, 1996; Lobkowicz, 2001). Cooperation usually deepened following periodic crises, each of which appeared to underline the salience and necessity of joining forces (Monar, 2001). In so far as there were delays and setbacks to cooperation, those could be accounted for with reference to remaining sovereignty concerns and the mobilization of counter-interests (Guyomarch, 1995), as has been done in contemporary versions of neofunctionalism in order to address the critique that such approaches have an overly teleological and optimistic view of the European integration process.

At the same time, a more critical perspective on the development of internal security cooperation in Europe developed. This approach shined light on the rather hidden actions of security professionals and practitioners to exploit the opportunities for transnational cooperation that the European level provided (Bigo, 1992; Lodge, 1992; Bunyan, 1993; Bigo, 1994). Originally, this cooperation did not relate directly to the EU but rather originated in a bewildering array of specialized working groups, such as the Police Working Group on Terrorism, and informal venues, such as the Club of Berne. Over time, however, police networks came increasingly to be associated via the integration of the so-called TREVI groups and the Schengen framework into the EU framework. Beyond the issue of regular border security and customs, the activities of 'high policing' (Brodeur, 1983)—mainly the fight against terrorism and later against the increasingly accepted concept of 'organized crime'—were critical to the formation of these transnational professional networks at several political and professional levels (Benyon, 1996).

While these transnational cooperation explanations did not exclude functionalist arguments, its proponents mainly accentuated discursive threat constructions and the formation of unaccountable structures for agenda-setting and information exchange in the European setting (den Boer and Walker, 1993). Thus, there were suspicions of attempts by security professionals to 'shift up' security measures that were opposed at the national level (Guiraudon, 2000)—and assumptions of a broad (though not total) convergence of security interests between transnational elites, based on common world views or bureaucratically defined interests. This argument proved especially popular in analyses of migration and asylum policy, both of which could be interpreted as more restrictive, 'securitized' and repressive in the EU compared to many national regimes (den Boer, 1998; Huysmans, 2000). A related perspective looked less at actor incentives and more at structural trends, such as broad moves to 'modernize' police action through centralized structures, technological solutions, and task specialization (Aden, 1998). These trends were rationalized by arguments of functional efficiency but had the effect of generating elite cadres of officials with less control and oversight by democratic institutions.

The two agendas of neofunctionalism and critical sociological theory continue to structure the field and are often set at odds to one another (although they share various points in common, a theme we return to in the conclusion). A wider range of theoretically informed scholarship, however, has emerged in recent years, looking at a variety of different research questions. In this respect, the research field of EU internal security cooperation has evolved in a way not unlike more traditional EU policy fields. Starting with the analysis of historical origins and cooperation patterns, scholars eventually moved beyond these questions to study more specific dynamics, including but not limited to policymaking dynamics, policy effects, implementation and compliance, governance within individual subfields, and so on. Furthermore, the growth of internal security cooperation in the EU attracted scholars from a growing number of related disciplines, such as criminology, law, ethnography, and public administration, each with their own distinct concerns and questions.

A discussion of this literature requires selectivity while still emphasizing diversity; after all, the goal of this volume is to give readers a wider and more inclusive perspective on the diverse literature available. For the sake of clarity, we categorize this work according to its focus on the familiar categories of politics, polity, and policy, but we are aware that some works cited below span those boundaries.

1.3.2 Focus on Politics

Generally speaking, research on politics explores the 'who gets what, when, and how' of internal security cooperation: the relevant (political) actors, their motivations and constraints, and the resulting interactive dynamics that shape outcomes. What separates internal security research from broader EU research is an emphasis on the remarkable speed at which the politics of cooperation came together to drive developments—which thus requires special explanation. Incremental, functionalist explanations demanded updating and revision, while on the critical side, the very speed of developments had undesirable implications for transparency, accountability, and the overall balance between norms.

Critical analyses of EU internal security evolved in close association with the field of critical security studies, which gained particular weight after the events of September 11 (Collective, 2006; Bigo et al., 2008). Numerous authors, drawing on French political and sociological theory, developed more explicit theoretical linkages to the work of Foucault and Bourdieu in order to contribute to the growing literature on securitization (Bigo, 2002; Huysmans, 2004; Berling, 2012). They demonstrated that the allocation of power and the trajectory of cooperation have been influenced not only by authoritative speech acts but also by the constitutive nature of security practice and lower-level ('less-than-existential') security discourses (Balzacq, 2008). The sociological notion of a contested 'field' of internal security, populated by various institutional and professionally defined actors, has also been fleshed out in empirical research (Bigo, 2008; Berenskoetter, 2012). Other, less explicitly critical, analyses of the construction of authority in EU criminal justice cooperation have drawn on related thinking from political sociology (Mégie, 2014).

More mainstream political science studies focused on how the respective EU institutions managed to assert themselves as players in the field of internal security cooperation, using theories drawn from public policy analysis or (new) institutionalism. The main argument in this line of analysis revolved around the policy entrepreneurism of the European Commission or Council Secretariat (Kaunert, 2007; Stetter, 2007; Bossong, 2012), despite their limited formal authority before the Lisbon Treaty. Similarly, path dependence was used to account for policy agendas and the stickiness of decision structures, occasionally punctuated by major events like September 11 (Argomaniz, 2011). Further, analysts traced the emergence and role of epistemic communities and professional networks, or the socializing effects of working parties and administrative forums, in various policy fields of EU internal security (Aus, 2006; Cross, 2011), which in turn had the potential to help construct a shared threat discourse. Another connection between political science and the critical research agenda was made through the analysis of the EU's governance capacity in internal security, focused on networks and 'soft' coordination methods. Here it was shown that negative integration dynamics on the basis of mutual recognition fostered a repressive policy bias and accentuated accountability problems (Lavenex and Wagner, 2007).

With the adoption of the Lisbon Treaty and the abolition of the Third Pillar, the analysis of the political dynamics of EU internal security cooperation has taken another turn and critically explored a possible 'normalization' of politics (Kostakopoulou, 2010). Again, institutionalist approaches have constituted the main theoretical backbone of this agenda (Monar, 2010). The European Parliament has moved from external overseer (and oft-critic) of internal security cooperation to a co-decider (Ripoll Servent and MacKenzie, 2011), while the Commission has extended its powers of agenda-setting and external representation. The Court of Justice, which already adjudicated on financial sanctions against terrorist suspects and various aspects of EU migration law during the 2000s (Martinsen, 2011), is bound to become fully competent in overseeing EU internal security legislation (Hinarejos, 2011). These formal changes generate questions concerning the changing political role or informal strategies of influence of EU institutions as well as new lines of contestation between the EU and national policymaking actors. Indeed, as evident in recent public debates on the Schengen regime, mandatory data retention, and the influx of migrants from North Africa, the traditional assumption of EU internal security cooperation as an area characterized by a lack of politicization, a lack of public interest and the dominance of professional actors (Herschinger et al., 2013) no longer seems valid.

In a related vein, the thesis of executive empowerment—which can apply not only to EU institutions, but also to national executives and ministerial officials—has been more systematically tested in recent years and has triggered more sceptical assessments (Bendel et al., 2011). For instance, recent advances in migration and asylum policy opened cooperation up to a wider number of non-executive actors (Kaunert and Léonard, 2012).[5] Other studies have sought to provide a more fine-grained analysis of the construction of political interests of various security officials and bureaucratic actors in EU internal security (de Maillard and Smith, 2011), whereby sociological and country-specific dynamics may override the assumed coherent preference for more transnational cooperation.

One of the more recent trends in the field is to analyse the development and role of the growing number of agencies in the area of EU internal security (Kaunert et al., 2013), most notably Europol, Eurojust, and Frontex. Most explanations of these agencies (and others) focus on their origins, constitution, and functions, and have long been a part of historically oriented analyses of EU internal security cooperation (including critical variants that foreground securitization dynamics). Distinctive to this more recent agenda, however, is the increasing use of formal theories, such as principal-agent analyses, and a focus on the details of administrative and political accountability structures (Busuioc et al., 2011), while still being motivated by the core normative debates about the legitimacy of security cooperation.

In contrast, theoretically focused analyses of the politics of intergovernmental bargaining in EU internal security remained surprisingly isolated (Lorenz, 2011). This is surprising if we compare internal security research to the literature on the EU's Common Foreign and Security Policy (in which the congruence and divergence of the 'big three' is a common theme), but chimes with the fact that many analysts foreground the diversity of institutional and professional actors in the field of EU internal security. Some studies do look closely at the 'opt out' countries (Wiener, 1999) while studies on migration governance occasionally examine conflicts between countries at the (poorer) outer borders and the North/West countries within the Schengen zone (Zaiotti, 2013). Those conflicts give rise to debates on 'burden-sharing', which have also been analysed from quantitative perspectives in EU studies (Thielemann and Dewan, 2006; Toshkov and de Haan, 2012). The main debate has been on whether burden-sharing in general takes place or not, based on the assumptions of rational bargaining and package deals between countries. However, the specific strategies and power-political influence of individual states have attracted little theoretical attention.

1.3.3 *Focus on Polity*

One important reason scholars have been drawn to the analysis of EU internal security cooperation is the constitutional implications of the field for the nature and direction of the EU as a polity. Cooperation generates fundamental questions regarding the normative and conceptual elements of what the EU 'is' as a political construction, and what it means for European society more broadly. Three strands of research stand out in this regard, loosely associated with the disciplines of EU studies, international relations, and EU law.

The first strand of research is highly normative and identifies internal security cooperation as a decisive factor in transforming what the EU means to its citizens. On the level of official discourse, one could argue that the EU's original mission to generate peace and prosperity within Europe has morphed into a new promise of internal security and stability in a globalizing world (Waever, 1995; Waever, 1996). Critical analysts have seen this as a conservative, neoliberal, and fundamental shift to the EU's original integrative and 'liberating' mission. The erosion of borders internally has resulted in the reestablishment of borders externally, on the EU's frontier, and with new control mechanisms inside Europe and a reconstitution of the neighbourhood as the 'other' outside Europe (Neumann, 1999). Thus, moves towards internal security cooperation have resulted in a new and normatively disconcerting *raison d'être* for the EU, one that may contribute to the building of a common 'us versus them' identity (Bigo, 2001; Huysmans, Dobson et al., 2006; Manners, 2013). This explains the growing use of the term 'Fortress Europe' (Geddes, 2000) along with the less explicitly normative conceptualization of an EU 'protection space' focused on managing extreme events like disasters and emergencies (Rhinard, Boin, and Ekengren, 2006).

Various researchers from constructivist IR perspectives have taken this further and asked whether the EU has become an 'actor' of its own in the area of internal security. This question directs attention to the international repercussions of EU internal security cooperation (discussed further below) and the EU's normative power after the events of September 11 (Manners, 2006; Wade, 2013). And in so far as the EU emerges as a significant police actor or crisis manager (Rozée, 2011; Boin, Ekengren, and Rhinard, 2013), this can be related to IR macro-theories that discern a transition towards a post-Westphalian security governance system with less clarity over the centre and 'monopoly on the legitimate use of violence' (Sperling, Wagnsson et al., 2009).

A second strand of polity-focused research, largely from the field of political science, focuses on the variable 'geometry' of internal security cooperation in Europe. The phenomenon of 'flexible' or 'differentiated' integration includes the partial opt-outs of some EU countries (Rittberger et al., 2014), the participation of some non-EU countries, and the overlapping internal security regimes of the EU, Council of Europe, and informal groups of EU states (G6)—all of which gives rise to complex legal and political dynamics that highlight the shifting nature of the EU's polity. The main theoretical tool to explore these dynamics has been rationalist public choice, or 'club' theory, complemented by more contingent dynamics of political decision-making (Balzacq and Hadfield, 2012; Tekin, 2012; Gaisbauer, 2013) or political practices

(Adler-Nissen, 2009). Scholars of EU law have also been attracted to exploring the exact influence and status of this complex, or fragmented, state of EU internal security law (Fletcher, 2009; McCartney, 2013).

Indeed, legal scholarship constitutes a third stand-alone strand of research, focusing on the treaty-based goal of an AFSJ and the requisite effects on the emerging constitutional nature of the EU. Scholars have noted that internal security cooperation contributes to a new but piecemeal transnational 'public order' or 'architecture' (Guild, 2004; Mitsilegas, 2006a; Schöndorf-Haubold, 2010; Eckes and Konstadinides, 2011). Such an order is not based (as on domestic levels) on a full corpus of criminal law and security policy (Peers, 2011), with accompanying executive competences in a centralized form. Instead, the EU reflects a changing and experimental patchwork of shared competences between the member states and the EU (which also leads to implementation problems, discussed later) (Herlin-Karnell, 2013). A large number of EU and national law scholars have questioned the viability of this state of affairs. They frequently doubt that the EU's AFSJ ambitions are consistent with deeply enshrined principles of constitutional law and of fair criminal justice systems (e.g. rights of the accused and right to a fair trial, *ne bis in idem*, division of powers between different security services and data types) (Bockel, 2010; Hodgson, 2011; Valentini, 2011; Mitsilegas, 2012; Peers, 2013), which has also been reflected in various disputes with national constitutional courts (Aden, 2013).

Conversely, analysts have debated the advantages and dangers of applying established principles and mechanisms of 'regular' Community law, mainly the concept of 'mutual recognition' and the oversight functions of the European Court of Justice, to the area of criminal law and security (Peers, 2004; Mitsilegas, 2006b; Nilsson, 2006; Erbenik, 2012; Murphy, Arcarazo et al., 2014). Another controversial issue is whether criminal law should be used in the service of protecting EU regulatory law and 'Community interests'. This applies, for instance, to the case of environmental crimes as well as to the legal or the constitutional significance of a future European Public Prosecutor (Monar, 2013a).

One last vein of polity-oriented research relates the emerging EU legal system encompassing the AFSJ and its link to international law (e.g. ECHR, UN Security Council resolutions, and financial sanction), where counter-terrorist sanctions have led to a continued debate on the relation between different legal orders (Guild, 2008; Eckes, 2009; Kornezov, 2013). These studies all share the same concern for studying the problematic link between legal rights (as laid out in the treaty provision on Union citizenship) and uneven, shifting, and even contradictory legal frameworks at national, supranational, and international levels—and their impact on the EU's evolving polity.

1.3.4 *Focus on Policy*

Perhaps the highest number of studies on EU internal security cooperation focuses on policymaking within various sub-fields of EU internal security. Considering the variety of those fields, it may be misleading to place such studies in a single category. We could more accurately discuss studies in the relatively distinct areas of operational police (Block, 2008) and criminal justice cooperation (Fichera, 2011), the fight against terrorism (Bureš, 2011), border security (Léonard, 2010; Geddes and Taylor, 2013), cybersecurity (Calderoni, 2010), disaster and crisis management (Rhinard, Hollis et al., 2013) and so on. But what studies in this category share is a focus on policymaking dynamics and policy effects, even if the tools used are not drawn solely from the fields of public policy studies or public administration. In fact, the fields of sociology, political science, ethnography, and law are well represented here, as are perspectives which prioritize race, post-colonialism, and human rights.

Within this category, migration, border, and asylum policy in the EU stands out as the central and most frequent object of study (as further evidenced by the several contributions in this book). While EU asylum and migration law has developed considerably, and in some respects become more nuanced and subject to competing considerations, the tenor of most studies remains critical. Studies have moved from discussing the legal and institutional (re)creation of 'hard' Schengen borders to the increasing 'executive' role of the EU via agency building (e.g. Frontex) or technology support (e.g. SISII, VIS, Eurodac, Eurosur), mostly through a critical lens of understanding (Guild and Bigo, 2010; Basaran, 2011; Broeders and Hampshire, 2013; Ekelund, 2013; Wolff and Schout, 2013). Related theoretical approaches are wide-ranging, including sociological and institutionalist analyses discussed earlier, in-depth ethnological investigations (Feldman, 2011; Zaiotti, 2011) and post-modern approaches that highlight changing forms of 'biopolitics' and governmentality in the management of populations (Huysmans, 2006; Van Houtum and Pijpers, 2007).

In this context, legal studies often illuminate the intersection of EU policy-making with other actors and contexts at all levels of analysis. For instance, the EU has been repeatedly criticized for its inconsistent application or under-standing of the principle of *non-refoulement*, which is not only enshrined in international law but also promoted by the UNHCR (Mink, 2012). Yet much of the operational treatment of migrants and refugees remains in the hands of national governments—despite the relatively high level of communitarization in the area of EU migration law and border security—and different national or even local contexts play a role in how law is implemented (Guild, 2014).

Such research also reflects the wider and complex 'Europeanization' agenda, which may include not only policy, but also political and polity shifts in EU member states as a result of integration processes (Olsen, 2002).

In EU internal security, Europeanization has explicitly been used by legal scholars in respect of criminal and migration law (Guild, 2006; Rackow, 2007), but has also inspired political-science-based analyses of structures and policies (Aden, 1998; Lange, 1999; Lavenex, 2001; Lorenz and Glaessner, 2005; Tholen, 2005).

Other analysts emphasize the question of whether specific EU policies are carried through in practice. The dominant view is one of uneven, tendentious, or even non-existent implementation (Argomaniz, 2010), especially with regard to the former 'third pillar' instruments (framework decisions with no direct effect or compliance mechanisms) (Fortescue, 1995). Decision-makers regularly turn to softer policy instruments such as recommendations and loose guidelines to overcome the constraints of unanimity voting, to limit adaptation pressure, and to preserve informal cooperation networks. Few analysts formally base the analysis of implementation dynamics on theoretical models from public policy analysis or organization theory (Bossong, 2008; Block, 2011), however. The 'normalization' of internal security decision-making since the Lisbon Treaty (approximating the Community Method, with its legal instruments) may prompt scholars to apply the extensive EU studies literature on compliance and transposition more frequently and rigorously.

Yet one should also recall that EU competences remain limited in various areas of internal security cooperation, especially in regards to operational matters. This continues to stimulate other soft forms of governance, such as EU-sponsored networks of crime prevention or civil protection. Scholars of 'security governance' explore such networks and other forms of soft coordination in a growing number of issue areas (Hollis, 2010; Bossong, 2011; Schröder, 2011; Monar, 2013b). The notion of security governance can also highlight the role of private actors (e.g. in the fight against terrorist financing) and opens further avenues to critique the transparency and effectiveness of EU security measures (Ehrhart et al., 2014).

Finally, one should take note of agendas focused on wider trends that interact with, and are sometimes exacerbated by, the EU's internal security policymaking. Studies in this vein explore, and sometimes derive normatively driven hypotheses about, the EU's relationship to broader scale security trends. Rather than explaining the politics, polity, or policy of EU internal security cooperation per se the focus here is assessing the EU as a contributor to such trends as the 'punitive' turn in European criminal justice systems (Baker, 2010; Vaughan and Kilcommins, 2010), changing notions of 'urban security' (Edwards, Hughes et al., 2013), or the growth of surveillance technologies and preventive policing over the last decade (De Goede, 2011; den Boer, 2011). These kinds of studies differ from the critical studies variants mentioned previously, in that EU policy is mostly treated as an independent variable; questions can be asked whether EU security policy accentuates, promotes, or partially counterbalances (e.g. in the area of data protection) such hypothesized macro-trends.

1.3.5 *External Dimension*

Cutting across all of these debates is the simultaneous growth in research on the 'external dimension' of EU internal security cooperation, both in terms of empirical developments and academic analyses (Balzacq, 2009; Wolff et al., 2009; Cremona et al., 2011; Kaunert, 2012; Monar, 2014). The conceptual foundations of this debate can again be found in the dual strands of EU integration theory as well as (critical) security studies, so that one might also speak of a natural co-development of analysis on EU internal security cooperation and its external dimension.

These analyses highlight how migration and visa policy in particular, and internal security/JHA matters in general, have become a growing component of the EU's external governance. This can be seen in a variety of issue areas, including EU enlargement, the European Neighbourhood Policy, or global trade relations (Lavenex, 2004; Jurje and Lavenex, 2013). In principle, externalization could be regarded as another functionalist necessity of the abolition of borders within the EU. This line of argument has been linked to the parallel paradigm shift in (European) security studies and international relations since the end of the Cold War, namely the growing merger between internal and external security issues under conditions of globalization and in response to 'unconventional' or 'asymmetric' threats such as terrorism and organized crime (Rees, 2008; Eriksson and Rhinard, 2009).

However, many critical analyses attest to a restrictive drift of EU migration policies and to related external EU agreements with third countries—as well as the normative problems of the putative merger between internal and external security threats. EU migration policy conducted a parallel debate, whereby the initial 'shift up' for executive empowerment at the EU level may have been replaced by a 'shift out' to EU neighbouring countries (Lavenex, 2006). In a similar vein, legal scholars have taken note of the 'extra-territorialization' of EU migration and border security regimes (Ryan and Mitsilegas, 2010), which creates severe problems for core EU law principles, such as the right to effective remedy.

Last but not least, the fight against terrorism stimulated an extensive critical debate on the EU's involvement in global regimes of 'homeland security' (Pawlak, 2010; Kaunert, Léonard, and Pawlak, 2012; Zaiotti, 2012)—especially in the area of financial controls and sanctions in which it holds most competences (Rees, 2006; Bures, 2010; De Goede, 2012; Kaunert, Léonard, and McKenzie, 2012). The growing field of cybersecurity and cybercrime will extend this into the future, as here global regimes and the involvement of the US are essential to any meaningful security regime. One may analyse such connections under the heading of transnational governance or networks, opening up further interdisciplinary avenues for research areas, such as international political economy or macro-level takes on policy diffusion.

1.4 Chapter Contents

The chapters in this book reflect the main thrusts of theorizing in this growing field. Each is structured in a way that introduces the approach, outlines its main tenets, demonstrates how the approach can be applied, and discusses opportunities for further development. To set the stage, the present introduction is paired with an analysis by Jörg Monar of how the empirical field has developed into the shape that it has. Monar, with decades of experience of writing on JHA cooperation, outlines the key developments that shaped this field and proposes five key drivers that best explain it. These drivers, although not framed in theoretical terms, reappear in various chapters in this volume in terms of state interests, functional spillover, shared perceptions amongst like-minded communities, and institutional entrepreneurs.

In the subsequent part of the book, specific theoretical approaches take centre-stage. Thierry Balzacq summarizes and explains the value of approaches focused on securitization dynamics. He confirms that securitization has become a widely employed perspective used to study EU security cooperation, and argues for a more reflexive and practice-centred perspective that can help to resolve a number of analytical challenges to securitization theory. Didier Bigo then introduces one of the fastest growing—and most critical—approaches to studying EU internal security cooperation that draws from the field of international political sociology. He demonstrates the importance of examining the intersection and practices of transnational, professional groups of actors and their instinctive tendencies to control.

Next, Raphael Bossong and Sandra Lavenex take up the mantel of governance as a concept used to explore the various formats of cooperation in EU internal security, which rarely match standard, formal patterns of integration. The notion of security governance underlines the increasing diversity of actors as well as complexity of objectives that inform the definition of internal security in transnational settings. In slight contrast, Valsamis Mitsilegas presents the utility of deductive legal reasoning, revealing not only the rule-of-law implications generated by EU cooperation in internal security cooperation but also the role of the Court of Justice of the European Union (CJEU) in shaping policy outcomes in both *ex ante* and *ex post* ways.

Arne Niemann applies a classic approach to studying European integration—neofunctionalism—to the field of internal security cooperation. Specifying the mechanisms underlying various forms of neofunctional 'spillover', Niemann shows the approach has great value in explaining the wide variety of non-state actors involved in pushing cooperation forward—even in a highly political issue area. Another widely used approach to studying European integration more generally is institutionalism, a mid-range analytical approach emphasizing the institutional factors that shape and drive policy outcomes. Ripoll Servent and Kostakopoulou provide an incisive review of the main variants of new institutionalist theorizing in the context of EU internal security before illustrating the comparative value of rationalist and constructivist variants in accounting for different EU migration policies.

The conclusion of the book, written by the editors, summarizes the main themes of the volume, identifies overlaps, and sets out gaps requiring future research by new and experienced researchers in the field.

1.5 Conclusion

Theoretically driven research on European internal security cooperation has moved beyond the conventional and critical perspectives that once served to structure theorizing in the field. We have witnessed the arrival of a number of new approaches and perspectives, many of which draw inspiration from different disciplines and varying kinds of assumptions. The result is an exciting but fragmented theoretical literature in which approaches rarely account for one another and even fail to link their findings to the bigger picture. We hope to stimulate more debate (or at least individual reflection) about the larger purpose and goals in analysing this growing area of EU cooperation. Scholars need not remain locked into a particular 'school', a familiar set of analytical instruments, or a standard set of research 'puzzles' or 'gaps'. Individual specialization is valuable, but establishing a common discourse and appreciation for different kinds of analyses could further enrich EU studies, European security studies and other disciplines with a growing stake in this field, such as criminology or political sociology.

Dialogue between different perspectives should ideally lead to an improved mutual recognition of the diverse but growing scholarly community that is forming around the complex issue of EU internal security. We do not aim for a canonical definition of what is and what is not a good approach in the study of these matters. However, a more comprehensive view of the field should allow us to identify pressing and promising areas of new research, and gain inspiration from alternative disciplinary perspective. At the same time, we should avoid accumulation of mechanisms and processes by which we explain or understand different aspects of the EU's internal security policy without trying to tease out more fundamental dynamics. This does not have to take the form of formalized competitive theory testing, not least since the purposes of theory are legitimately diverse. Nevertheless, it would be stimulating to see more than one such exercise (as has occurred in the case of executive empowerment) while more mutual references could be made across varied normative positions in the field.

Most importantly, the number of new researchers coming into this significant field should take courage in the vigour and diversity of approaches we outline here. Beyond the study of the EU in internal security policy, the potential wider structural processes in terms of polity formation or cultural and societal shifts in security provide a wealth of enduring and significant research objectives, and it is our hope that this volume should serve as a supportive guide in this endeavour.

Notes

1. TREVI was an intergovernmental network, established outside of the then-European Community legal framework, of national officials from ministries of justice and interior created by the European Council Summit in Rome, Italy in December 1975. It is sometimes noted that TREVI stands for *Terrorisme, Radicalisme, Extrémisme et Violence Internationale*. It was ended when cooperation was integrated into the so-called Justice and Home Affairs (JHA) pillar of the EU when the Treaty of Maastricht came into force in 1992.

2. While Justice and Home Affairs was the phrase once used widely by researchers in this field, the term has fallen into disuse following the adoption of the Amsterdam Treaty and the effort to preserve a 'rights-oriented' perspective in internal security matters (not least since the Commission divided its relevant Directorate-General into DGs focused on home affairs and justice matters, respectively). From a policy perspective, the Area of Freedom, Security and Justice (AFSJ) moniker has its political benefits, while from a research perspective the term allows us to take an inclusive view of constituent issues.

3. Deeper conceptual meanings and normative criticisms need to be considered with regard to internal security. Internal security is not an unambiguous 'good' that can be 'provided' by instrumental mechanisms or policies alone. Indeed, various contributions to this volume underline that formal security policymaking is just part of the picture: perceptions, discourses, practices, cultural shifts, and symbolic gestures are critical for understanding what 'security' is in contemporary Western societies. However, we first require an empirical framing of our object of analysis. The overview of the existing and diverse academic literature on EU internal security presented below thus starts from the heuristic link to EU policies.

4. Compare our approach to that of Ostromho, according to Sabatier (1999: 6), distinguishes amongst a 'conceptual framework' (a set of variables and specified relationships between them that account for a phenomenon, but does not necessarily identify directions amongst relationships), a 'theory' (which specifies a more logically coherent

set of relationships, discusses variations in variables, and specifies relationships amongst variables), and a 'model' (a representation of a specific situation drawn from theory but quite narrow in scope and assumptions). See Ostrom (1999).

5. Yet the growing limits on executive empowerment by shifting 'up' to the EU level may have increasingly been replaced by a shift 'out' to the EU neighbourhood, as is taken up further later.

References

Aden, H. (1998) *Polizeipolitik in Europe. Eine Interdisziplinäre Studie über die Polizeiarbeit in Europa am Beispiel Deutschlands, Frankreichs und der Niederlande.* Wiesbaden: Westdeutscher Verlag.

Aden, H. (2013) 'Die EU-Innen- und Strafjustizpolitik auf dem Prüfstand des Bundesverfassungsgerichts: Grundrechtsschutz, Ausgeblendete Exekutivdominanz und Wettbewerb zwischen Gerichten', in Lhotta, R., et al. (eds) *Das Lissabon-Urteil.* Wiesbaden: Springer Fachmedien, pp. 137–58.

Adler-Nissen, R. (2009) 'Behind the Scenes of Differentiated Integration: Circumventing National Opt-outs in Justice and Home Affairs', *Journal of European Public Policy,* 16(1), pp. 62–80.

Argomaniz, J. (2010) 'Before and after Lisbon: Legal Implementation as the "Achilles Heel" in EU Counter-terrorism?' *European Security,* 19(2), pp. 297–316.

Argomaniz, J. (2011) *The EU and Counter-terrorism: Politics, Polity and Policies after 9/11.* Abingdon and New York: Routledge.

Aus, J. P. (2006) 'Decision-making under Pressure: The Negotiation of the Biometric Passport Regulation in the Council.' ARENA Working Paper 11.

Baker, E. (2010) 'Governing through Crime: The Case of the European Union, *European Journal of Criminology,* 7(3), pp. 187–213.

Balzacq, T. (2008) 'The Policy Tools of Securitization: Information Exchange, EU Foreign and Interior Policies', *Journal of Common Market Studies,* 46(1), pp. 75–100.

Balzacq, T. (2009) *The External Dimension of EU Justice and Home Affairs: Governance, Neighbours, Security.* Basingstoke and New York: Palgrave Macmillan.

Balzacq, T. and Hadfield, A. (2012) 'Differentiation and Trust: Prüm and the Institutional Design of EU Internal Security', *Cooperation and Conflict,* 47(4), pp. 539–61.

Basaran, T. (2011) *Security, Law and Borders: at the Limits of Liberties.* Abingdon: Routledge.

Bendel, P., Ette, A., and Parkes, R. (eds) (2011) *The diversity of European justice and home affairs cooperation: A model-testing exercise on its development and outcomes,* Berlin: LIT Verlag.

Benyon, J. (1996) 'The Politics of Police Co-operation in the European Union', *International Journal of the Sociology of Law,* 24(4), pp. 353–79.

Berenskoetter, F. (2012) 'Mapping the Field of UK–EU Policing', *Journal of Common Market Studies,* 50(1), pp. 37–53.

Berling, T. (2012) 'Bourdieu, International Relations, and European Security', *Theory and Society,* 41(5), pp. 451–78.

Bigo, D. (1992) *L'Europe des Polices et de la Sécurité Intérieure.* Paris: Espace International.

Bigo, D. (1994) 'The European Internal Security Field: Stakes and Rivalries in a Newly Developing Area of Police Intervention', in Anderson, M. and Den Boer, M. (eds) *Policing across National Boundaries*. London: Pinter, pp. 161–73.

Bigo, D. (2001) 'The Möbius Ribbon of Internal and External Security(ies)', in Albert, M., et al. (eds) *Identities, Borders, Orders: Rethinking International Relations Theory*. Minneapolis: University of Minnesota Press, pp. 91–116.

Bigo, D. (2002) 'Security and Immigration: Towards a Critique of the Governmentality of Unease', *Alternatives*, 27 (special issue), pp. 63–92.

Bigo, D., Bonelli, L., and Deltombe, T. (eds) (2008) *Au nom du 11 septembre... Les démocraties à l'épreuve de l'antiterrorisme*. Paris: Decouverte.

Bigo, E. A. (2008) *The Field of EU Internal Security Agencies*. Paris: Harmattan.

Block, L. (2008) 'Combating Organized Crime in Europe: Practicalities of Police Cooperation', *Policing*, 2(1), pp. 74–81.

Block, L. (2011) *From Politics to Policing: The Rationality Gap in EU Council Policy-making*. The Hague: Eleven Publishing.

Bockel, B. V. (2010) *The ne bis in idem principle in EU Law*. Alphen aan den Rijn, NL: Kluwer Law International.

Boin, A., et al. (2013) *The European Union as a Crisis Manager*. Cambridge: Cambridge University Press.

Bossong, R. (2008) 'The Action Plan on Combating Terrorism: A Flawed Instrument of EU Security Governance', *Journal of Common Market Studies*, 46(1), pp. 27–48.

Bossong, R. (2011) 'Peer Reviews on the Fight against Terrorism: A Hidden Success of EU Security Governance?' EUSECON Working Paper 50.

Bossong, R. (2012) *The Evolution of EU Counter-terrorism: European Security Policy after 9/11*. London: Routledge.

Brodeur, J.-P. (1983) 'High Policing and Low Policing: Remarks about the Policing of Political Activities', *Social Problems*, 30(5), pp. 507–20.

Broeders, D. and Hampshire, J. (2013) 'Dreaming of Seamless Borders: ICTs and the Pre-Emptive Governance of Mobility in Europe', *Journal of Ethnic and Migration Studies*, 39(8), pp. 1201–18.

Bunyan, T. (1993) 'Trevi, Europol and the European State', in Bunyan, T. (ed.) *Statewatching the New Europe: A Handbook on the European State*, Nottingham: Russell Press, pp. 15–36.

Bures, O. (2010) 'EU's Fight against Terrorist Finances: Internal Shortcomings and Unsuitable External Models', *Terrorism and Political Violence*, 22(3), pp. 418–37.

Bures, O. (2011) *EU Counterterrorism Policy: A Paper Tiger?*. Farnham and Burlington, VT: Ashgate.

Busuioc, M., Curtin, D., and Groenleer, M. (2011) 'Agency Growth between Autonomy and Accountability: The European Police Office as a "Living Institution"', *Journal of European Public Policy*, 18(6), pp. 848–67.

Calderoni, F. (2010) 'The European Legal Framework on Cybercrime: Striving for an Effective Implementation', *Crime, Law and Social Change*, 54(5), pp. 339–57.

Collective, C. (2006) 'Critical Approaches to Security in Europe: A Networked Manifesto', *Security Dialogue*, 37(4), pp. 443–87.

Cremona, M., Monar, J., and Poli, S. (eds) (2011) *The External Dimension of the European Union's Area of Freedom, Security and Justice*. Brussels: Peter Lang.

Cross, M. K. D. (2011) *Security Integration in Europe: How Knowledge-based Networks Are Transforming the European Union*. Michigan: University of Michigan Press.

Cullen, D. (1996) *Cooperation in Justice and Home Affairs: An Evaluation of the Third Pillar*. Brussels: European Interuniversity Press.

De Goede, M. (2011) *European Security Culture: Preemption and Precaution in European Security*. Amsterdam: Amsterdam University Press.

De Goede, M. (2012) 'The SWIFT Affair and the Global Politics of European Security', *Journal of Common Market Studies*, 50(2), pp. 214–30.

De Maillard, J. and Smith, A. (2011) 'Projecting National Preferences: Police Co-operation, Organizations and Polities', *Journal of European Public Policy*, 19(2), pp. 257–74.

den Boer, M. (1998) 'Crime et immigration dans l'Union européenne', *Cultures & Conflits*, 31–32, pp. 2–14.

den Boer, M. (2011) 'Technology-led Policing in the European Union: An Assessment', *Journal of Police Studies*, 20(3), pp. 41–58.

den Boer, M. and Walker, N. (1993) 'European Policing after 1992', *Journal of Common Market Studies*, 31(1), pp. 3–28.

Eckes, C. (2009) *EU Counter-terrorist Policies and Fundamental Rights: The Case of Individual Sanctions*. Oxford and New York: Oxford University Press.

Eckes, C. and Konstadinides, T. (2011) *Crime within the Area of Freedom, Security and Justice: A European Public Order*. Cambridge: Cambridge University Press.

Edwards, A., et al. (2013) 'Urban Security in Europe: Translating a Concept in Public Criminology', *European Journal of Criminology*, 10(3), pp. 260–83.

Ehrhart, H.-G., et al. (2014) 'Putting Security Governance to the Test: Conceptual, Empirical, and Normative Challenges', *European Security*, 23(2), pp. 119–25.

Ekelund, H. (2013) 'The Establishment of FRONTEX: A New Institutionalist Approach', *Journal of European Integration*, 36(2), pp. 99–116.

Erbenik, A. (2012) 'The Principle of Mutual Recognition as a Utilitarian Solution, and the Way Forward', *European Criminal Law Review*, 2(1), pp. 3–19.

Eriksson, J. and Rhinard, M. (2009) 'The Internal–External Security Nexus: Notes on an Emerging Research Agenda', *Cooperation and Conflict*, 44(3), pp. 243–67.

Feldman, G. (2011) *The Migration Apparatus: Security, Labor, and Policymaking in the European Union*. Stanford, CA: Stanford University Press.

Fichera, M. (2011) *The Implementation of the European Arrest Warrant in the European Union: Law, Policy and Practice*. Singapore: Intersentia.

Fletcher, M. (2009) 'Schengen, the European Court of Justice and Flexibility under the Lisbon Treaty: Balancing the United Kingdom's 'Ins' and 'Outs', *European Constitutional Law Review*, 5(1), pp. 71–98.

Fortescue, J. (1995) 'First Experiences with the Implementation of the Third Pillar Provisions', in Bieber, R. and Monar, J. (eds) *Justice and Home Affairs in the European Union: The Development of the Third Pillar*. Brussels: European Interuniversity Press, pp. 19–28.

Gaisbauer, H. P. (2013) 'Evolving Patterns of Internal Security Cooperation: Lessons from the Schengen and Prüm Laboratories', *European Security*, 22(2), pp. 185–201.

Geddes, A. (2000) *Immigration and European Integration: Towards Fortress Europe?* Manchester: Manchester University Press.

Geddes, A. and Taylor, A. (2013) 'How EU Capacity Bargains Strengthen States: Migration and Border Security in South-East Europe', *West European Politics*, 36(1), pp. 51–70.

Guild, E. (2004) 'Crime and the EU's Constitutional Future in an Area of Freedom, Security, and Justice', *European Law Journal*, 10(2), pp. 218–34.

Guild, E. (2006) 'The Europeanisation of Europe's Asylum Policy', *International Journal of Refugee Law*, 18(3–4), pp. 630–51.

Guild, E. (2008) 'The Uses and Abuses of Counter-terrorism Policies in Europe: The Case of the "Terrorist Lists"', *Journal of Common Market Studies*, 46(1), pp. 173–93.

Guild, E. (2014) 'Immigration Regulation as a Battleground: The European Union's Anxiety over Federalism', in Baglay, S. and Nakache, D. (eds) *Immigration Regulation in Federal States*. Netherlands: Springer, vol. 9, pp. 223–44.

Guild, E. and Bigo, D. (2010) 'The Transformation of European Border Controls', in Ryan, B. and Mitsilegas, V. (eds) *Extraterritorial Immigration Control: Legal Challenge*, Leiden: Brill, pp. 257–80.

Guiraudon, V. (2000) 'European Integration and Migration Policy: Vertical Policy-making as Venue Shopping', *Journal of Common Market Studies*, 38(2), pp. 251–71.

Guyomarch, A. (1995) 'Problems and Prospects for European Police Cooperation after Maastricht', *Policing and Society*, 5(3), pp. 249–61.

Herlin-Karnell, E. (2013) 'European Criminal Law as an Exercise in EU "Experimental" Constitutional Law', *Maastricht Journal of European and Comparative Law*, 20(3), pp. 442–65.

Herschinger, E., et al. (2013) 'Transgouvernementalisierung und die ausbleibende gesellschaftliche politisierung der inneren sicherheit', in Zürn, M. and Ecker-Ehrhardt, M. (eds) *Die Politisierung der Weltpolitik. Umkämpfte internationale Institutionen*. Berlin: Suhrkamp, pp. 190–212.

Hinarejos, A. (2011) 'Integration in Criminal Matters and Role of the Court of Justice', *European Law Review*, 36(2), pp. 420–30.

Hodgson, J. S. (2011) 'Safeguarding Suspects' Rights in Europe: A Comparative Perspective', *New Criminal Law Review*, 14(4), pp. 611–65.

Hollis, S. (2010) 'The Necessity of Protection: Transgovernmental Networks and EU Security Governance', *Cooperation and Conflict*, 45(3), pp. 312–30.

Huysmans, J. (2000) 'The European Union and the Securitization of Migration', *Journal of Common Market Studies*, 38(5), pp. 751–77.

Huysmans, J. (2004) 'A Foucaultian View on Spill-over: Freedom and Security in the EU', *Journal of International Relations and Development*, 7(3), pp. 294–318.

Huysmans, J. (2006) *The Politics of Insecurity: Fear, Migration and Asylum in the EU*. Abingdon: Routledge.

Huysmans, J., et al. (2006) *The Politics of Protection: Sites of Insecurity and Political Agency*. New York: Routledge.

Jurje, F. and Lavenex, S. (2013) 'Trade Agreements as Venues for "Market Power Europe"? The Case of Immigration Policy', *Journal of Common Market Studies*, 52(2), pp. 320–36.

Kaunert, C. (2007) 'Without the Power of Purse or Sword: The European Arrest Warrant and the Role of the Commission', *Journal of European Integration*, 29(4), pp. 387–404.

Kaunert, C. (2012) 'Conclusion: Assessing the External Dimension of EU Counter-terrorism—Ten Years on', *European Security*, 21(4), pp. 578–87.

Kaunert, C. and Léonard, S. (2012) 'The Development of the EU Asylum Policy: Venue-shopping in Perspective', *Journal of European Public Policy*, 19(9), pp. 1396–413.

Kaunert, C., Léonard, S., and Pawlak, P. (eds) (2012) *European Homeland Security: A European Strategy in the Making?* London: Routledge Chapman & Hall.

Kaunert, C., Léonard, S., and McKenzie, A. (2012) 'The Social Construction of an EU Interest in Counter-terrorism: US Influence and Internal Struggles in the Cases of PNR and SWIFT', *European Security*, 21(4), pp. 474–96.

Kaunert, C., et al. (2013) 'Agency Governance in the European Union's Area of Freedom, Security and Justice', *Perspectives on European Politics and Society*, 14(3), pp. 273–84.

Knelangen, W. (2000) 'Die europäische Zusammenarbeit im Politikfeld Innere Sicherheit an der Integrationsschwelle?' in Janssen, M. and Sibom, F. (eds) *Perspektiven der Europäischen integration*. Wiesbaden: VS Verlag für Sozialwissenschaften, vol. 1, pp. 147–69.

Kornezov, A. (2013) 'The Area of Freedom, Security and Justice in the Light of the EU Accession to the ECHR—Is the Break-up Inevitable?' *Cambridge Yearbook of European Legal Studies*, 15(1), pp. 227–54.

Kostakopoulou, D. (2010) 'An Open and Secure Europe? Fixity and Fissures in the Area of Freedom, Security and Justice after Lisbon and Stockholm', *European Security*, 19(2), pp. 151–67.

Lange, H.-J. (1999) *Innere Sicherheit im politischen System der Bundesrepublik Deutschland*. Opladen: Leske + Budrich.

Lavenex, S. (2001) 'The Europeanization of Refugee Policies: Normative Challenges and Institutional Legacies', *Journal of Common Market Studies*, 39(5), pp. 851–74.

Lavenex, S. (2004) 'EU External Governance in "Wider Europe"', *Journal of European Public Policy*, 11(4), pp. 680–700.

Lavenex, S. (2006) 'Shifting up and out: The Foreign Policy of European Immigration Control', *West European Politics*, 29(2), pp. 329–50.

Lavenex, S. and Wagner, W. (2007) 'Which European Public Order? Sources of Imbalance in the European Area of Freedom, Security and Justice', *European Security*, 16 (3–4), pp. 225–43.

Léonard, S. (2010) 'EU Border Security and Migration into the European Union: FRONTEX and Securitisation through Practices', *European Security*, 19(2), pp. 231–54.

Loader, I. and Walker, N. (2007) *Civilizing Security*. Cambridge and New York: Cambridge University Press.

Lobkowicz, W. D. (2001) *L'Europe et la sécurité intérieure. Une élaboration par étapes*. Paris: Documentation française.

Lodge, J. (1992) 'Internal Security and Judicial Cooperation beyond Maastricht', *Terrorism and Political Violence*, 4(3), pp. 1–29.

Lorenz, A. (2011) 'Cooperation, Integration, Europeanisation? National Novernments' Interests in European Justice and Home Affairs', in Bendel, P., Ette, A., and Parkes, R. (eds) *The Europeanization of Control: Venues and Outcomes of EU Justice and Home Affairs*. Berlin: LIT Verlag, pp. 77–115.

Lorenz, A. and Glaessner, G. J. (eds) (2005) *Europäisierung der inneren Sicherheit. Eine vergleichende Untersuchung am Beispiel von organisierter Kriminalität und Terrorismus*. Wiesbaden: Verlag für Sozialwissenschaften.

Manners, I. (2006) 'European Union "Normative Power" and the Security Challenge', *European Security*, 15(4), pp. 405–21.

Manners, I. (2013) 'European [Security] Union: Bordering and Governing a Secure Europe in a Better World?' *Global Society*, 27(3), pp. 398–416.

Martinsen, D. S. (2011) 'Judicial Policy-making and Europeanization: The Proportionality of National Control and Administrative Discretion', *Journal of European Public Policy*, 18(7), pp. 944–61.

McCartney, C. (2013) 'Opting In and Opting Out: Doing the Hokey Cokey with EU Policing and Judicial Cooperation', *The Journal of Criminal Law*, 77(6), pp. 543–61.

Mégie, A. (2014) 'The Origin of EU Authority in Criminal Matters: A Sociology of Legal Experts in European Policy-making', *Journal of European Public Policy*, 21(2), pp. 230–47.

Mink, J. (2012) 'EU Asylum Law and Human Rights Protection: Revisiting the Principle of Non-refoulement and the Prohibition of Torture and Other Forms of Ill-treatment', *European Journal of Migration and Law*, 14(2), pp. 119–49.

Mitsilegas, V. (2006a) 'Constitutional Principles of the European Community and European Criminal Law', *European Journal of Law Reform*, 8(2–3), pp. 301–23.

Mitsilegas, V. (2006b) 'The Constitutional Implications of Mutual Recognition in Criminal Matters in the EU', *Common Market Law Review*, 43(5), pp. 1277–311.

Mitsilegas, V. (2012) 'The Limits of Mutual Trust in Europe's Area of Freedom, Security and Justice: From Automatic Inter-State Cooperation to the Slow Emergence of the Individual', *Yearbook of European Law*, 31(1), pp. 319–72.

Monar, J. (2001) 'The Dynamics of Justice and Home Affairs: Laboratories, Driving Factors and Costs', *Journal of Common Market Studies*, 39(4), pp. 747–64.

Monar, J. (ed.) (2010) *The Institutional Dimension of the European Union's Area of Freedom, Security and Justice*, Brussels: Peter Lang.

Monar, J. (2013a) 'Eurojust and the European Public Prosecutor Perspective: From Cooperation to Integration in EU Criminal Justice?' *Perspectives on European Politics and Society*, 14(3), pp. 339–56.

Monar, J. (2013b) 'EU Internal Security Governance: The Case of Counter-terrorism', *European Security*, 23(2), pp. 195–209.

Monar, J. (2014) 'The EU's Growing External Role in the AFSJ Domain: Factors, Framework and Forms of Action', *Cambridge Review of International Affairs*, 27(1), pp. 147–66.

Murphy, C. C., et al. (2014) 'Rethinking Europe's Freedom, Security and Justice', in Arcarazo, D. A. and Murphy, C. C. (eds) *EU Security and Justice Law: After Lisbon and Stockholm*. Oxford: Hart Publishing, pp. 1–16.

Neumann, I. B. (1999) *Uses of the other: 'The East' in European Identity Formation*. Minneapolis: University of Minnesota Press.

Nilsson, H. (2006) 'From Classical Judicial Cooperation to Mutual Recognition', *Revue internationale de droit penal*, 77(1–2), pp. 53–9.

Olsen, J. P. (2002) 'The Many Faces of Europeanization', *Journal of Common Market Studies*, 40(5), pp. 921–52.

Ostrom, E. (1999) 'Institutional Rational Choice: An Assessment of the Institutional Analysis and Development Framework', in Sabatier, P. (ed.) *Theories of the Policy Process*. Boulder, CO: Westview Press, pp. 21–64.

Pawlak, P. (2010) 'Transatlantic Homeland Security Cooperation: The Promise of New Modes of Governance in Global Affairs', *Journal of Transatlantic Studies*, 8(2), pp. 139–57.

Peers, S. (2004) 'Mutual Recognition and Criminal Law in the European Union: Has the Council Got It Wrong?' *Common Market Law Review*, 41(1), pp. 5–36.

Peers, S. (2011) *EU Justice and Home Affairs Law*. Oxford: Oxford University Press.

Peers, S. (2013) 'The European Arrest Warrant: The Dilemmas of Mutual Recognition, Human Rights and EU Citizenship', in Rosas, A. et al. (eds) *The Court of Justice and the Construction of Europe: Analyses and Perspectives on Sixty Years of Case-Law—La Cour de Justice et la construction de l'Europe: Analyses et perspectives de soixante ans de jurisprudence*. The Hague: T. M. C. Asser Press, pp. 523–38.

Rackow, P. (2007) 'Problems of the Europeanisation of Criminal Law', *Criminal Law Forum*, 18(1), pp. 175–83.

Rees, W. (2006) *Transatlantic Counter-terrorism Cooperation: The New Imperative*. Abingdon and New York, NY: Routledge.

Rees, W. (2008) 'Inside Out: The External Face of EU Internal Security Policy', *Journal of European Integration*, 30(1), pp. 97–111.

Rhinard, M., et al. (2006) 'Protecting the Union: Analysing an Emerging Policy Space', *Journal of European Integration*, 28(5), pp. 405–21.

Rhinard, M., et al. (2013) 'Explaining Civil Protection Cooperation in the EU: The Contribution of Public Goods Theory', *European Security*, 22(2), pp. 248–69.

Ripoll Servent, A. and MacKenzie, A. (2011) 'Is the EP Still a Data Protection Champion? The Case of SWIFT', *Perspectives on European Politics and Society*, 12(4), pp. 390–406.

Rittberger, B., et al. (2014) 'Differentiated Integration of Core State Powers', in Genschel, P. and Jachtenfuchs, M. (eds) *Beyond the Regulatory Polity?: The European Integration of Core State Powers*. Oxford: Oxford University Press, pp. 189–211.

Rozée, S. (2011) 'The European Union as a Comprehensive Police Actor', *Journal of Contemporary European Research*, 7(4), pp. 435–51.

Ryan, B. and Mitsilegas, V. (2010) *Extraterritorial Immigration Control: Legal Challenges*. Leiden: Brill.

Sabatier, P. (1999) 'The Need for Better Theories' in Sabatier, P (ed.) *Theories of the Policy Process*. Boulder, CO: Westview Press, pp. 3–20.

Schöndorf-Haubold, B. (2010) *Europäisches Sicherheitsverwaltungsrecht*. Baden-Baden: Nomos.

Schröder, U. C. (2011) *The Organisation of European Security Governance: Internal and External Security in Transition*. New York: Routledge.

Sperling, J., et al. (2009) *European Security Governance: The European Union in a Westphalian World*. Abingdon and New York: Routledge.

Stetter, S. (2007) *EU Foreign and Interior Policies: Cross-pillar Politics and the Social Construction of Sovereignty*. New York: Routledge.

Tekin, F. (2012) *Differentiated Integration at Work: The Institutionalisation and Implementation of Opt-Outs from European Integration in the Area of Freedom, Security and Justice*. Baden-Baden: Nomos.

Thielemann, E. R. and Dewan, T. (2006) 'The Myth of Free-riding: Refugee Protection and Implicit Burden-sharing', *West European Politics*, 29(2), pp. 351–69.

Tholen, B. (2005) 'The Europeanisation of Migration Policy: The Normative Issues', *European Journal of Migration and Law*, 6(4), pp. 323–35.

Toshkov, D. and de Haan, L. (2012) 'The Europeanization of Asylum Policy: An Assessment of the EU Impact on Asylum Applications and Recognitions Rates', *Journal of European Public Policy*, 20(5), pp. 661–83.

Valentini, V. (2011) 'European Criminal Justice and Continental Criminal Law: A Critical Overview', *European Criminal Law Review*, 1(2), pp. 188–202.

Van Houtum, H. and Pijpers, R. (2007) 'The European Union as a Gated Community: The Two-faced Border and Immigration Regime of the EU', *Antipode*, 39(2), pp. 291–309.

Vaughan, B. and Kilcommins, S. (2010) 'The Governance of Crime and the Negotiation of Justice', *Criminology and Criminal Justice*, 10(1), pp. 59–75.

Wade, M. (2013) 'The European Union as a Counter–terrorism Actor: Right Path, Wrong Direction?' *Crime, Law and Social Change*, 62(3), pp. 355–83.

Waever, O. (1995) 'Identity, Integration and Security: Solving the Sovereignty Puzzle in EU Studies', *Journal of International Affairs*, 48(2), pp. 389–431.

Waever, O. (1996) 'European Security Identities', *Journal of Common Market Studies*, 34(1), pp. 103–32.

Wiener, A. (1999) Forging Flexibility—The British 'No' to Schengen, *European Journal of Migration and Law*, 1(4), pp. 441–63.

Wolff, S. and Schout, A. (2013) 'Frontex as Agency: More of the Same?' *Perspectives on European Politics and Society*, 14(3), pp. 305–24.

Wolff, S., Wichmann, N., and Mounier, G. (2009) 'The External Dimension of Justice and Home Affairs: A Different Security Agenda for the EU?' *Journal of European Integration*, 31(1), pp. 9–23.

Zaiotti, R. (2011) *Cultures of Border Control: Schengen and the Evolution of European Frontiers*. Chicago and London: University of Chicago Press.

Zaiotti, R. (2012) 'Practising Homeland Security across the Atlantic: Practical Learning and Policy Convergence in Europe and North America', *European Security*, 21(3), pp. 328–46.

Zaiotti, R. (2013) 'The Italo-French Row over Schengen, Critical Junctures, and the Future of Europe's Border Regime', *Journal of Borderlands Studies*, 28(3), pp. 337–54.

2

EU Internal Security Cooperation after Four Decades

Observations and Reflections

Jörg Monar

2.1 Introduction: The 'Academic Career' of a Field

The 'four decades' have been put into the title of this essayistic contribution to remind us that internal security cooperation must now be counted among the older fields of the European construction, much older than Economic and Monetary Union and also significantly older than some other by now more or less well-established EU policies, such as energy, climate, and cultural policies. And yet it in terms of academic interest and coverage it is a much younger field: whereas internal security cooperation had a clear starting point already in 1975 with the establishment of the TREVI cooperation, serious and more systematic scholarly attention only emerged in the mid-1990s.[1] With only slight exaggeration one can say that as a field of academic study EU internal security cooperation is only half as old as the field itself and that it came in after a delay of almost two decades. Why this late start of the 'academic career' of our field? Two main reasons can be identified.

The first one is the *initially highly arcane nature of this cooperation*: the ministries of interior and the (few) specialized police forces involved were dominated by a culture of secrecy on all matters of internal security and for a long time did their best to hide cooperation from the public (and academic) gaze. The EC Council was also a far less open institution in terms of access to documents than it is today, the Commission—tolerated initially only as an observer—had no mandate to publicly communicate on TREVI matters, and there was no empowered European Parliament which could draw important aspects of this cooperation into the light of the day. The purely intergovern-mental and non-EC-treaty-based context, first of TREVI and then from 1985 also of the Schengen cooperation, served as a further veil.[2] All this clearly did not help scholars discovering the field and getting sufficient access to it.

While the initial highly arcane nature of the field was clearly not the academic community's fault it must bear some responsibility in relation to the second reason for the two decades of delay, namely the *initial reluctance to move into a field crossing traditional epistemic-area border lines*: the political scientists, lawyers, sociologists, and representatives of other disciplines spe-cializing in internal security issues were—as were the ministries of interior at the time—used to looking at internal security issues mainly within a domestic context, and as far as external issues were concerned, mainly in the context of the UN and other international non-European frameworks such as Interpol.[3] The emerging cooperation structures and mechanisms between the European Community (and later Union) member states fit into neither of these trad-itional frameworks for conceptualizing and analysing state responses to internal security challenges. At the same time internal security also fell largely outside of the perspectives of specialized EU scholars as it was neither a field of 'supranational' European integration nor an integral part of the existing 'intergovernmental' foreign policy cooperation,[4] which made it, in a sense, a field 'outside' of established epistemic-area frameworks as well. The extent of what may be called the long 'quarantine' applied to the study of European internal security cooperation is—with hindsight—quite remarkable: there were still textbooks on the EU after the 1993 Maastricht Treaty (with its codification of Justice and Home Affairs cooperation) came into force, which managed not to even mention the field.[5]

The academic career of our field only really took off after the Treaty of Amsterdam reforms, the major political impulse given by the Tampere Euro-pean Council (both 1999) and the salience generated by the EU's response to the 9/11 attacks and the internal security and border management challenges of 2004 enlargement. In comparison to the pre-Amsterdam 1990s, the multi-plication of research projects, conferences, and publications during the post-Amsterdam period can almost be described as staggering. It also only after the Amsterdam watershed that the 'theorizing' of EU internal security cooper-ation as a specific field started, whether—as Bossong and Rhinard describe in their introduction—to explain why it had emerged and was growing, to assess it from specific normative perspectives or to conceptualize it within the framework of different interpretative theory approaches. This reflected pri-marily the massive expansion of the EU's agenda in this field. However, an additional factor was the 'discovery'—especially by a younger generation of scholars—of an until then relatively under-researched field of EU cooperation which showed a number of distinctive governance features and offered potential for original research outside of the well-trodden paths, for instance, of research on the EU's Common Foreign and Security Policy.

If one would wish to identify main characteristics of the scholarship on EU internal security cooperation since the post-Amsterdam expansion the following two might be regarded as the most important:

The first one—and it cannot really be regarded as surprising—is a *higher degree of differentiation and specialization*: entire networks of researchers have emerged which focus on single issues such as—to give only a few examples— EU counterterrorism, border management, the challenges EU action poses to civil liberties, the role of EU agencies in the field, or the external dimension of EU action on internal security objectives. While many scholars cover more than one of these single issues there is—compared to the pre-Amsterdam period—a smaller share of them covering developments in the EU internal security domain in all of its different dimensions (internal/external as well as all relevant policy fields from asylum and migration-over-border management to judicial and police cooperation). In terms of approaches we can also observe a trend towards further differentiation, with some scholars pursuing primarily policy analysis perspectives, others more critical normative approaches (one may almost speak about a 'civil liberties school' in our field), still others a primarily institutionalist approach, or efforts to fit internal security cooperation into wider theoretical frameworks (this list is, again, non-exhaustive). While the major expansion of EU developments in the internal security domain clearly warrants a greater specialization and in-depth exploration of single issues and approaches, this tendency also comes with a certain risk of fragmentation and of missing out on relevant linkages and synergy potentials, such as, for instance, the dynamic link between internal and external EU action in the field. Moreover, the specialization and differentiation tendency does not help to overcome disciplinary divides amongst which the one between political science and law remains particularly prominent in spite of the obvious relevance of legal issues to the political dimension of the field— and vice versa. This volume takes useful steps towards illuminating these interconnections.

A second characteristic—and this reflects specific persisting research constraints in this field—is the *often relatively thin empirical basis of much of the published research*. While legal, institutional, and procedural aspects of EU internal security cooperation are empirically reasonably well covered by now, there are very few works on the actual impact and effectiveness of this cooperation both at the European and at the member-state level. The way in which and the extent to which the EU instruments and mechanisms have actually changed national internal security governance, the results which they have actually achieved (or not achieved) in responding to the identified common internal security challenges, and the (related) question of the added value of EU cooperation with regard to traditional national internal security governance remains empirically seriously underexplored. This is partially due to the lack of comprehensive impact data, as the EU institutions have been better at putting into place programming documents, institutional structures, and legal instruments than at thoroughly monitoring and assessing their actual impact. Yet it is also due to the difficulty of ascertaining clear patterns of change and impact in a field in which secrecy—to a large extent justifiable both on legal and operational grounds—continues to be a major obstacle for in-depth empirical research and in which national security authorities and decision-makers—keen to assert their primary role in protecting their citizens—often still tend to minimize the role of the EU instruments and mechanisms. The empirical basis for the theorizing of internal security in the EU remains therefore at least partially rather patchy.

A third characteristic—and this is perhaps somewhat more surprising—is the *lower degree of attention given to questions of the fundamental rationale of EU internal security cooperation*. Whereas at the time of the Amsterdam Treaty reforms and the Convention on the Future of Europe quite a number of academic publications were still raising the fundamental 'so what?' question, and trying critically to discuss what EU internal security cooperation as a whole should or should not be about in the context of the European construction, such wider—and in a sense more fundamental considerations—have become quite rare, with many scholars preferring to limit the use of their analytic capacity to their respective specialized issues and approaches. This tendency mirrors to some extent what is happening in the EU policymaking process—where policymakers seem to spend more and more time and energy on working on legislative, financial, and other operational compromises with often little consideration of more long-term strategic EU issues and objectives. Yet the reduced attention paid by academia to the question of whether EU internal security can be considered as a subject with its own rationale and specificities as such and distinct from the 'traditional' national internal security contexts of the member states may still be regarded as somewhat surprising. Academia normally prides itself in its capacity to identify and address the fundamentals of a subject of study rather than the innumerable phenomena, developments, and part-issues it consists of.

2.2 The Specificity of the Field

Most scholars tend to regard their fields of specialization as being at least to some extent rather specific and—because of this specificity—worthy of their special attention. In what sense, then, can one say that the internal security cooperation field of the European construction is indeed quite a specific one, different from other fields of EU action?

What should be admitted to in the first place is that in quite a few respects—contrary to some political and bureaucratic assertions at the national and the European level—our field is not really so special: much has been made of the huge diversity of national cultures, traditions, challenges, interests, legal frameworks and structures in the internal security field—and the resulting enormous difficulties of surmounting those to arrive at common measures.[6] Yet seen in the context of the overall European integration process, these differences between the national settings are neither something new nor qualitatively of an entirely different nature (for more on this point, see Bossong and Rhinard's concluding chapter 9 in this volume). While it is certainly true that diversity in internal security matters is a fundamental reality and a powerful obstacle, we have also seen often enough by now—such as in the case of the negotiations on the Framework Decision on the European Arrest Warrant[7] in 2001/2—that this diversity can be overcome in this field as in others if there is a sufficient political will to do so.

However, quite a good case can be made for the EU internal security field indeed being marked by three major specificities:

(1) *A specificity due to the field's fundamental public good dimension*: Security is clearly a fundamental public good of the first order—and one can indeed ask how much any other public good is worth if it is not at least accompanied by some degree of security for citizens. With the provision of security therefore being one of the primary and essential functions of any state (as affirmed, for instance, by the repeated confirmation of the 'essential state functions' sensitivity of EU border, police and criminal justice cooperation treaty provisions by the French Conseil constitutionnel),[8] the EU's internal security mandate (most explicitly formulated in Article 67(3) TFEU) has introduced an element of qualitative difference into the European construction. This generates a tension with the declared EU aim to safeguard the 'essential state functions' of member states which are explicitly protected, in particular, by Article 4(2) TEU which affirms the member states' primary competence as regards 'maintaining law and order and safeguarding national security'. It is significant that such an explicit and extensive national state function protection clause cannot be found in any other internal EU policymaking field. This tension between common action objectives and national competence affirmation marks every aspect of internal security cooperation, and the progress and limitations of this cooperation can also be taken as an important wider indicator for the potential and limitations of the European integration process as such.

(2) *A specificity due to the implications of the EU internal security domain for the rights of the individual*: It would seem that the European Commission has

occasionally a bit too easily compared the creation of the Union's 'Area of Freedom, Security and Justice' to that of the Internal Market, especially as regards the application of the mutual recognition principle. There is surely a major qualitative difference, for instance, between the mutual recognition of standards of a consumer product and the mutual recognition of a judicial warrant which can lead to the arrest and surrender of an EU citizen or the sensitive question of the rights which EU citizens should be guaranteed in cross-border criminal procedures.[9] While not all EU internal security cooperation instruments and mechanisms are similarly sensitive there can be no doubt that a substantial part of them can—even if executive powers are still exercised only by national authorities—have major implications for the rights of the individual, from data protection rights to the rights of fair trial in criminal proceedings, but including also, for instance, the rights of third-country nationals in an irregular immigration situation. No other EU policymaking domain involves measures which can be as invasive, have such a major direct impact on the rights—and even lives—of individuals.[10] This makes the EU internal security field arguably 'special' in terms of fundamental rights and values, and accounts for its constant (sometimes—given the often much more invasive measures taken at the national level—overly critical) monitoring by numerous fundamental rights organizations.

(3) *A specificity due to the strong internal cross-border operational dimension of this field of cooperation.* Internal security cooperation requires police officers, border guards, prosecutors, and judges—whose operational powers are normally all restricted to their respective national territories—to act across the borders between the member states, this by way of both legal acts having a cross-border reach (freezing orders, evidence warrants, arrest warrants, etc.) and by their physical participation in operations within the territories of other member states (Joint Investigation Teams, Frontex joint operations, European Border Guard Team deployments etc.). This involves a whole range of departures from the traditional principle of territoriality—the territorial affirmation of national sovereignty—which has led to the development of very specific, and often enough also quite original, mechanisms and instruments (such as the aforementioned Joint Investigation Teams). There is no real parallel for that in any other EU policymaking domain. One may think about CSDP operations as the nearest parallel, but these take place outside of the EU's borders and do not raise the aforementioned specific (and often still rather difficult) political and legal issues of internal cross-border reach.

2.3 Major Development Factors

By any standard of growth the development of EU internal security cooperation since the 1990s—be it in terms of new cooperation mechanisms and instruments, institutional development, or even legislative output—has been impressive. Given the particular national sovereignty sensitivity of the field this is all the more remarkable—which raises the question of the development factors which have rendered this possible. It is possible to identify five main factors, not all of which are obviously of equal importance:

(1) Any cooperation on security issues depends on a *sufficient degree of common threat perception* as a major factor—and EU internal security cooperation has certainly not been an exception to that: The proliferation of terrorist threats in Europe in the 1970s was at the origin of the establishment of TREVI. TREVI's expansion in the 1980s was at least partially driven by member states' concerns about the growth of international organized crime and the partial relocation of the international drug trade to Europe, the 'new' terrorist threat perception linked to the terrorist attacks of New York (2001), Madrid (2004), and London (2005) which played a key role in the massive expansion of internal security cooperation during the last decade, and the 'risk' perception of high levels of illegal immigration which is the origin of the unprecedented institutional (Frontex) and financial (the External Borders Fund and other instruments) investment in border management. The less member states feel confident about being able to handle an internal security threat by purely national means, and the more of them are actually or potentially affected by it, the more political will there is to move cooperation to a new level. The post-9/11 terrorist threat perception remains the most telling example: An essentially transnational threat with a global reach—pushed high up on the political agenda by the 9/11 attacks—which could potentially affect any member state and also threatened all of them in their fundamental values led to an expansion of both internal and international EU cooperation (Argomaniz, 2011, and Bossong, 2012) which few observers would have thought possible at the time, even taking into account the impetus given to EU Justice and Home Affairs cooperation by the 1999 Tampere European Council.

(2) Whereas threat perceptions can obviously vary depending on the pressure of events, this is much less the case with the more long-term and in a sense 'systemic' factor of the *perceived need to take compensatory action with regard to internal security risks stemming from the increased permeability of borders within the EU*: The question of the extent to which the abolition of controls on persons at internal borders within the Schengen system and the facilitation of cross-border economic transactions by the completion of the Internal Market (and later the introduction of the euro) has generated enhanced internal security risks (including those related to illegal immigration, as highlighted rightly or wrongly by debates on the 2015 migration crisis) may be open to debate. Yet there can be no doubt that the rationale of necessary

compensatory action on the internal security side for increasingly permeable internal borders has provided a strong rationale and justification for policy-makers and law enforcements authorities at both the national and the European level to invest political capital and resources into the development of EU cooperation mechanism and instruments. It would surely not be far off the mark to regard the whole Schengen cooperation framework—which remains at the core of the EU's internal security area—essentially as a compensatory response of the member states to the 'opening' of the internal borders.[11] The fact that this compensatory rationale reflects persisting fundamental concerns of member states about the EU's 'open borders' generating specific additional national internal security risks relating to transnational crime and illegal immigration also explains much of the original—and to a considerable extent persisting—intergovernmental orientation of internal security cooperation.

(3) In a crucial period of the development of EU internal security cooperation—at the time of the Treaty of Amsterdam negotiations, Tampere, and in the period immediately after—the *EU's 2004 enlargement* became a major development factor. Member states—and among those especially the Schengen countries—sought to strengthen internal security cooperation in time before a range of countries perceived as internal security risk factors (because of high levels of corruption, organized crime, and insufficient border management capabilities) would be joining the EU. From 1997 onwards a major effort was made to define more clearly key elements and best practices of EU internal security cooperation for the purpose of a more precise and more demanding definition of accession conditions. This contributed to both the 'widening' and the 'hardening' of cooperation mechanisms and frameworks (including the role of Europol). The preparations for accession also led to a massive expansion of EU-funded training measures aimed at the propagation of best practices for practitioners in both the prospective new and the old member states as well as the participation of interior and justice ministries in 'twinning-projects' with counterparts in the candidate countries which brought many of their officials more than ever before into the EU cooperation context. There was also a certain eagerness in the Council to finalize a number of legislative acts—such as the 2003 Framework Decision on the execution of orders freezing property or evidence in the framework of criminal proceedings,[12] the 2003 Framework Decision on combating corruption in the private sector,[13] and the 2003 Protocol amending the Europol Convention[14]—before the new member states would be joining the table and might make things more difficult. This 'enlargement factor', however, receded after the 2004 enlargement and no longer plays a significant role today.

(4) *National political challenges and agendas* have also been an important internal factor of development, although in a rather intermittent way. It remains doubtful, for instance, if the old 'third pillar' with its initial provisions

on internal security cooperation would have made it into the Maastricht Treaty (1993) without the major German domestic concerns at the time about asylum and illegal immigration challenges after the opening of borders in Central and Eastern Europe. Furthermore, major national British and Spanish concerns about illegal immigration, resulting in close coordination and cooperation between Prime Ministers Aznar and Blair, clearly played a key role in the massive upgrading of external border management cooperation decided at the June 2002 Seville European Council. The British government became one of the champions of EU counterterrorism cooperation after the 9/11 attacks because of both a relatively high Islamist terrorist threat perception at the national level and an interest in ensuring a maximum of EU cooperation with the US in this field, and the Italian government, faced with the increased migration and refugee pressure from Northern Africa, unsurprisingly emerged in 2014/15 again as a protagonist of more EU solidarity on illegal immigration and border management challenges as did Germany with regard to refugee reallocation solidarity within the EU in response to the unprecedented influx of (mainly) Syrian refugees in 2015. Yet none of the member states has continuously and generally tried to 'Europeanize' domestic internal security issues.[15] This may be explained by the acute awareness of governments—and especially of the traditionally rather conservative ministries of interior—that any effective 'Europeanization' would necessarily also mean an at least partial loss of national control over national-election-relevant and sensitive public law and order issues. Needless to add that in many instances domestic politics have also had a negative rather than positive impact on a member state's contribution to internal security cooperation—for which the British Government's 2014 'block opt-out' decision regarding parts of the pre-Lisbon Treaty EU policing and criminal justice acquis is probably the prime example.

(5) Last but not least, *the roles, interests, and agendas of EU institutions* must also be considered as a factor in their own right: While it is difficult to identify any major impact of the 'supranational' institutions—Commission, Parliament, and Court—during the 1990s, the situation clearly changed after their empowerment by the Treaty of Amsterdam, as regards the Commission immediately, and with respect to the Parliament after the Treaty, enabled passage to co-decision in at least some internal security relevant fields in 2005 (Monar, 2010). During the period in office of JHA Commissioner Antonio Vitorino (1999–2004), the Commission developed into both a major legislative agenda-setter and a critical evaluator of EU action in the internal security field with fewer and fewer initiatives coming from the member states in spite of a shared right of initiative. The build-up of Commission in-house staff resources and expertise over the last fifteen years has been very significant, and there is no question today of the quality of

Commission proposals normally outclassing those of member states, although the Commission's political judgement (as in the case of the controversial 2011 Schengen governance reform proposals, which would have given it significant powers on national border security issues) may sometimes appear questionable. In the post-Amsterdam period the Commission has clearly pursued a more 'integrationist' agenda in the internal security domain. While advancing (mostly) pertinent effectiveness reasons for the Commission's new post-Amsterdam posture, there may also have been a certain institutional self-interest in this approach as more EU legislation, programming, monitoring, and financing would necessarily also strengthen its own position in this traditionally intergovernmental domain. The same can be said about the European Parliament which has constantly favoured more rather than less legislation in the internal security field (for which its role in the negotiation of the 2006 Schengen Borders Code[16] is an example) and has also been very supportive of expanded EU funding in the internal security domain (which inevitably also increases its own influence because of its budgetary powers). The role of the Court of Justice in the internal security field can so far probably be best classified as a 'corrective' rather than a fundamentally shaping one: It is worthy to note that the Court—even when sharply asserting the respect of high fundamental rights protection standards in relation to EU internal security matters[17]—has always recognized the member states' primary competence to provide security to their citizens, thereby avoiding any potential system-changing intervention in the development of our field (see chapter 6 by Mitsilegas in this volume).

Any survey of the 'institutional factor', however brief, would not be complete without a consideration of the role of the EU agencies with internal security relevant tasks, i.e.—in the order of their creation—the police cooperation agency Europol, the judicial cooperation unit Eurojust (in legal terms a 'body' rather than an 'agency' of the EU), the European Police College CEPOL, the external border management agency Frontex, and the agency for the management of large scale IT systems[18] EU-LISA. Although all of those agencies were established with a mandate of only supporting national authorities in their cross-border cooperation by various coordination support and information exchange and analysis functions, and none of them has been vested with executive operational powers, they have gradually acquired more prominent roles and it would be difficult, today, to deny that they exercise a modest but nevertheless distinctive shaping influence on internal security cooperation.[19] To give only a few examples: The serious and organized crime threat assessments of Europol (SOCTAs)[20] are now a central element of the EU's 'Policy Cycle on Serious and Organised Crime' (now running for its first fully fledged 2014 to 2017 four-year period) with a clear influence on priorities and strategy development at the EU policymaking level. Eurojust's monitoring role at the frontline of criminal justice cooperation—for instance as regards problems with the application of the European Arrest Warrant or efforts to improve the common judicial response to the foreign terrorist fighters challenge (Eurojust, 2015)—have started to influence the revision of existing and the design of new legislation as well as best practice identification and training programmes. The external border risk assessments of Frontex,[21] last but not least, play an important role in the allocation of EU financial resources and the deployment of member states' personnel and technical equipment in joint operations. These examples, which are partially due to the agencies' efforts to assert their roles, could be multiplied. The—often more discrete—shaping influence of the agencies on our field remains heavily under-researched. This is surely an institutional dimension to watch as the increasingly likely establishment of a European Public Prosecutor's Office[22]— with the prospect of EU international security cooperation obtaining its first EU authority with executive powers, even if initially limited to crimes affecting the financial interests of the Union—would mark an important step towards a federal-type law enforcement system. Further qualitative change of EU internal security cooperation may well be on the way—and its theoretical understanding and assessment should not lag behind. This volume is a novel and welcome effort to invigorate that endeavour.

Notes

1. Full credit should be given to the annual Schengen conferences and following publications organized at the EIPA from 1992 onwards first by Alexis Pauly (Pauly, 1993) and then by Monica den Boer (den Boer, 1997) for providing the first major academic forum looking regularly at development trends in internal security cooperation.
2. See Bonnefoi (1995) on the early evolution of TREVI and Schengen.
3. A good example is the at-the-time seminal collection of studies in Wilkinson and Stewart (1987).
4. TREVI started as a part of European Political Cooperation (EPC) but the ministries of interior effectively ensured its institutional and procedural separation from the foreign-ministry-dominated EPC context.
5. An example is the—otherwise quite good—'Understanding the New European Community' (Nicoll and Salmon, 1994) which did not approach our subject further than with a section on 'immigration controls'.
6. For an early example of the strong emphasis on diversity in the police cooperation field, see Benyon (1994).
7. Council Framework Decision of 13 June 2002 on the European arrest warrant and the surrender procedures between Member States (2002/584/JHA), *Official Journal of the European Union*, L 190, 18 July 2002.

8. Starting with its Decision on the Treaty of Maastricht (Constitutional Council, 1992) and reconfirmed most recently by its Decision on the Treaty of Lisbon (Constitutional Council, 2007).
9. Henry Labayle has rightly emphasized that the creation of the EU's Area of Freedom, Security and Justice goes fundamentally beyond the rationale of a common market to that of values ('passage du marché aux valeurs'). See Labayle (2014).
10. With regard to EU criminal-law policy EU Commissioner Reding has specifically recognized the 'intrusiveness' and 'harshness' of the measures it involves. See Reding (2011: 12).
11. On the 'compensatory' logic see Peers (2011: 140).
12. 2003/577/JHA, *Official Journal of the European Union*, L 196, 2 August 2003.
13. 2003/568/JHA, *Official Journal of the European Union*, L 192, 31 July 2003.
14. Council Act of 27 November 2003 drawing up, on the basis of Article 43(1) of the Convention on the Establishment of a European Police Office (Europol Convention), a Protocol amending that Convention, *Official Journal of the European Union*, C 2, 6 January 2004.
15. Europeanization efforts of Member States have generally been marked by strong elements of short-term instrumentalism and opportunism: While the German government, for instance, had been rather lukewarm in response to Greek, Italian, and Maltese appeals for more EU solidarity in response to illegal immigration and refugee pressures during 2013/14, its advocacy of EU solidarity solutions could hardly have been stronger after being the primary target of the Syrian refugee crisis in 2015.
16. Regulation (EC) No 562/2006 of the European Parliament and of the Council of 15 March 2006 establishing a Community Code on the rules governing the movement of persons across borders (Schengen Borders Code), *Official Journal of the European Union*, L 105, 13 April 2006.
17. Such as in Joined Cases C-402/05 P and C-415/05 P (European Court of Justice, 2008).
18. Including the SIS II system which arguably counts amongst the most important EU internal security instruments.
19. For a fairly comprehensive assessment of the agency dimension see Kaunert, Léonard, and Occhipinti (2013).
20. The latest Interim SOCTA was submitted by Europol to the Council in March 2015. See Council of the European Union (2015a).
21. Such as the quarterly situational assessments of the illegal immigration situation at EU external borders provided by the Frontex Risk Assessment Network (FRAN) (latest: Frontex, 2016).
22. At the time of writing (June 2015) considerable progress had been made with the (difficult) negotiations on the first five chapters of the Regulation on the establishment of the European Public Prosecutor's Office, see Council of the European Union (2015b).

References

Argomaniz, J. (2011) *The EU and Counter-Terrorism: Politics, Polity and Policies after 9/11*. Abingdon: Routledge.

Benyon, J. (1994) 'Policing the European Union: The Changing Basis of Cooperation on Law Enforcement', *International Affairs*, 70(3), pp. 516–17.

Bonnefoi, S. A. (1995) *Europe et sécurité intérieure: Trevi, Union européenne, Schengen*. Paris: Delmas.

Bossong, R. (2012) *The Evolution of EU Counter-Terrorism: European Security Policy after 9/11*. Abingdon: Routledge.

Constitutional Council (1992) Décision 92-308 DC of 9 April 1992. Treaty on European Union. Available at: http://www.conseil-constitutionnel.fr/conseil-constitutionnel/english/case-law/sample-of-decisions-in-relevant-areas-dc/decision/decision-92-308-dc-of-9-april-1992.135427.html (Accessed: 3 November 2015).

Constitutional Council (2007) Décision n° 2007-560 DC du 20 décembre 2007. Traité de Lisbonne modifiant le traité sur l'Union européenne et le traité instituant la Communauté européenne. Available at: http://www.conseil-constitutionnel.fr/conseil-constitutionnel/francais/les-decisions/acces-par-date/decisions-depuis-1959/2007/2007-560-dc/decision-n-2007-560-dc-du-20-decembre-2007.1166.html (Accessed: 3 November 2015).

Council of the European Union (2015a) Europol: Interim SOCTA 2015: An update on Serious and Organised Crime in the EU. Council Document 7271/15. Available at: http://www.statewatch.org/news/2015/mar/eu-europol-interim-SOCTA-7271-15.pdf (Accessed: 22 January 2016).

Council of the European Union (2015b) Proposal for a Regulation on the Establishment of the European Public Prosecutor's Office—Policy Debate. Council Document 9372/15. Available at: http://db.eurocrim.org/db/en/doc/2318.pdf (Accessed: 3 November 2015).

Den Boer, M. (1997) *The Implementation of Schengen: First the Widening, Now the Deepening*. Maastricht: European Institute of Public Administration.

Eurojust (2015) Towards a Common Judicial Response to Foreign Fighters. Press Release. Available at: http://www.eurojust.europa.eu/press/PressReleases/Pages/2015/2015-06-26.aspx (Accessed: 2 November 2015).

European Court of Justice (2008) Judgment of the Court. Joined Cases C-402/05 P and C-415/05 P. Available at: http://curia.europa.eu/juris/document/document.jsf?text=&docid=67611&pageIndex=0&doclang=EN&mode=lst&dir=&occ=first&part=1&cid=187905 (Accessed: 2 November 2015).

Frontex (2016) FRAN Quarterly. Quarter 3. July-September 2015, Warsaw 2016. Available at: http://frontex.europa.eu/assets/Publications/Risk_Analysis/FRAN_Q3_2015.pdf (Accessed: 22 January 2016).

Kaunert, C., Léonard, S., and Occhipinti, J. (2013) 'Agency Governance in the European Union's Area of Freedom, Security and Justice', Special issue of *Perspectives on European Politics and Society*, 14(3), pp. 273–402.

Labayle, H. (2014) Marché Intérieur et Espace de Liberté, Sécurité, Justice: propos iconoclastes sur leurs Relations Mutuelles, Réseau Universitaire Européen droit de l'Espace de Liberté, de Sécurité et de Justice. Available at: http://www.gdr-elsj.eu/

2014/04/22/elsj/marche-interieur-et-espace-de-liberte-securite-justice-propos-iconoclastes-sur-leurs-relations/(Accessed: 3 November 2015).

Monar, J. (ed.) (2010) *The Institutional Dimension of the European Union's Area of Freedom, Security and Justice*. Brussels: PIE—Peter Lang.

Nicoll, W. and Salmon, T. (1994) *Understanding the New European Community*. Hemel Hempstead: Harvester Wheatsheaf.

Pauly, A. (ed.) (1993) *Les accords de Schengen: abolition des frontières intérieures ou menace pour les libertés publiques?* Maastricht: European Institute of Public Administration.

Peers, S. (2011) *EU Justice and Home Affairs Law*. Oxford: Oxford University Press.

Reding, V. (2011) 'On Substantive Criminal Law of the European Union', in Klip, A. (ed.) *Substantive Criminal Law of the European Union*. Antwerp: Maklu, pp. 11–14.

Wilkinson, P. and Stewart, A. M. (eds) (1987) *Contemporary Research on Terrorism*. Aberdeen: Aberdeen University Press.

Part II
Theoretical Perspectives

3

Securitization

Understanding the Analytics of Government

Thierry Balzacq

3.1 Introduction

Applying the concept of 'securitization' to study internal security cooperation in the European Union (EU) has become widely popular over the past two decades. At its most basic, a securitization approach seeks to explain how certain issues are constructed as security concerns, leading to those issues being handled in particular ways. This approach has been taken up by scholars from different disciplines interested in understanding the mechanisms and rationales underpinning the relatively swift integration of EU internal security, especially when compared to other sectors such as social and fiscal policies. Merging securitization with international political sociology, for instance, Bigo (2002) endeavours to show how governments generate a general sense of (in)security and unease ('the governmentality of unease') owing to the construction of the enemy 'within and without', which has, in turn, led to the development of a distinctive scheme of EU security cooperation that blurs the divide between internal and external securities. On a different topic but within a similar vein, Huysmans (2006) explains the institutionalization of policies against migrants and refugees through national processes of securitization eventually crystallized at the EU level (cf. also van Munster, 2009). Further, Balzacq and Carrera (2006) demonstrate that the securitization of various categories (through the construction of certain categories of 'migrants', 'refugees', etc.) was a powerful driver behind EU multi-annual programmes (including The Hague and the Stockholm programmes) that decisively structured the Area of Freedom, Security and Justice. Finally, Kaunert (2009) examined how securitization became the central process through which different institutions of the EU, in particular the European Commission, developed their view of integration.

Indeed, securitization can help to explain three major features of EU internal security cooperation: first, it enables us to understand how public problems acquire a particular 'security character'; second, securitization allows us to trace the type of policy that is designed in order to cope with the designated security problem and how the use of such policies may transform the way the EU functions; and third, securitization problematizes the relationship between politics and security, emphasizing the extent to which security trumps politics.

This chapter will also show, however, that approaches using the securitization concept differ markedly from one another, with different effects on our understanding of what constitutes a threat to EU security (or not). At issue are the definition and relative importance of discourses, processes, and practices by which securitization takes place—and how we can know whether it has taken place. In this chapter, I argue that securitization typically reflects, and takes place within a context of, certain governmental and societal practices that are accepted at a given moment and that 'possess up to a point their own specific regularities, logic, strategy, self-evidence, and "reason"' (Foucault, 1991: 75). By examining how issues are crafted and handled in relation to a specific 'regime of practices', we can improve our theorizing regarding how securitization plays out within the EU context.

The chapter proceeds in three steps. First, it begins with a review of securitization's origins, key assumptions, and theoretical affinities. Second, the chapter discusses the ill-defined and contested role of the audience as a participant in securitization processes. As a constructive way forward, the chapter proposes the idea of a 'regime of practices' to extend the analytical reach of securitization. Third, the chapter examines questions of method, or rather methodology, showing the extent to which they help us understand the difficulties associated with using securitization theory in the context of EU internal security cooperation. Specifically, I explore empirical works on migration and asylum policy in so far as they relate to the fight against terrorism and societal security.

3.2 Concepts of Securitization

In this section, I first trace the origins of securitization theory, showing the different theoretical lineages and typical research questions.[1] Next, I present two key but controversial components to any process of securitization, namely practices and audiences, in order to clarify their relation to each other. I also propose a way to overcome the debates amongst different types of securitization theories that can be mainly differentiated by their approach to the role of audiences in receiving and responding to security discourses. This can be done by complementing (and not replacing) discursive approaches to securitization with more practice-centred and contextualized analyses. In this light, securitization theory can be understood as part of a wider 'analytics of government' perspective, which traces how regimes of practices emerge, are reformed and are dismantled (Hansen, 2011: 358, 361–3; Huysmans, 2006: 147; van Munster, 2009: 15; Wæver, 2011). The subsequent section illustrates the point through a discussion of existing empirical analyses.

3.2.1 Origins and Meanings

Introductions to securitization theory typically argue that the so-called 'Copenhagen school' (CS)—a term coined by McSweeney (1996: 81–93)— established the approach in the late 1980s before others followed suit. The CS referred to Wæver and some of his collaborators who were based at now defunct Copenhagen Peace Research Institute (COPRI), and who developed the concept 'securitization', in order to capture how security issues are constructed through discourse.

This standard formulation of securitization theory relies on two major assumptions: first, that security is a 'speech act'; and second, that an audience must agree with the claims put forward by a securitizing actor for the securitizing move (i.e. the speech act) to succeed. A security problem exists 'not necessarily because a real existential threat exists but because the issue is presented as such a threat' (Buzan et al., 1998: 24). Thus, according to the CS, securitization is a speech act: 'security is not interesting as a sign that refers to something more real; it is the utterance itself that is the act. By saying the word, something is done' (Buzan et al., 1998: 26). The articulation of security by a given actor has a strong creative or productive dimension, in the sense that it brings about a new social reality, which delineates not only what can be known, but also what can be done. In this respect, security is a 'self-referential' practice; its conditions of possibility are constitutive of the speech act of saying 'security' (Huysmans, 1998: 232). The core characteristic of performative utterances is therefore their ability to make things happen, hence the considerable power bestowed upon the actor who speaks security. As Wæver (1995: 55) argues, 'by uttering "security"', 'a state representative moves a particular development into a specific area, and thereby claims a special right to use whatever means are necessary to block it'. Thus, according to Wæver, securitization has strong decisionist and linguistic dimensions.

Security research has benefitted from securitization in so far as the approach opened up an innovative angle on the relationship between security and politics (Pram and Petersen, 2011: 315–28). Essential questions could be asked in a fresh way: what makes something a matter of security and what consequences follow from this framing? Traditionally, realist perspectives overshadowed security research and the range of possible answers that could be given to such questions. In simplified terms, realist theories—whether of the more 'classical' or formalist kind—assume that there are objective factors that turn certain issues into security threats and that the resulting security policies tend to involve the use or threat of military force, which, in turn, underpins the perennial security dilemma or sense of suspicion between the security policy actors, that is, states (Walt, 1991). In contrast, securitization theory does not assume that objective characteristics determine the definition of security issues. Instead, the interaction and negotiation between a securitizing actor and different audiences (see section 3.2.2) is central for understanding the emergence of security policies and threat perceptions. From this broader perspective, any aspect of intersubjective life and understanding between securitizing actors and wider audiences may be framed as a security issue. So even if military issues and logics that are associated with the use of force still tend to condition security politics (Mutimer, 1997), the actual range of security affairs is much more flexible and expansive. In short, what counts as security is based on variable, even if historically and contextually embedded, intersubjective agreements that something constitutes a vital threat.

Thus, securitization is closely related with social constructivism in so far as it emphasizes the power of language and argument in world politics (see Kratochwil, 1989; Risse, 2000; Crawford, 2002; Pouliot, 2008; Krebs and Jackson, 2007; Debrix, 2003; Weldes et al., 1999; Epstein, 2008). Generally speaking, at least since the 1970s historians, sociologists, and philosophers have closely examined how social issues take on varying salience over time. For instance, this applied to the construction and practical consequences of social categories, such as abnormality, delinquency, and race (Foucault, 2003; 2004) or Jews, Blacks, Muslims, and women (Delumeau, 1989). Propaganda studies pursued many similar questions (Jowett and O'Donnell, 2006), while using different theoretical concepts such as framing (Sellers and Schaffner, 2009; compare Eriksson, 2001; Vultee, 2011; Watson, 2009) and 'symbolic politics' (Edelman, 1964; Edelman, 1977). Finally, Anglo-American sociologists intensively researched the 'construction of social problems' in relation to specific communities (Best, 2001; Best, 2009; Kitsuse and Spector, 2000; Loseke, 2003). None of these different strands of literature used the label of 'securitization', but each looked at very similar processes and social outcomes.

Securitization theory has further connections with speech act theory (Williams, 2003; Huysmans, 2004), but scholars have increasingly drawn on the works of Pierre Bourdieu and Michel Foucault to extend the analytical depth and reach of this approach (Neal, 2009; Huysmans, 2006; Hansen,

2006). In particular, they have argued that the literature on governmentality and 'analytics of government' (Foucault, 2009; Dean, 2010) enriches securitization theory by adding or revealing security practices. This chapter falls within an analytics of government approach, in the sense that it suggests a novel articulation between linguistic and non-linguistic elements of securitization.

However, before I say more about the added value provided by such an approach, I want to discuss the role of audiences. First, audience constitutes a core element of any theory of securitization, but scholars disagree on the extent to which it really matters and whether it is possible to tease out how it operates. Second, the importance that is consequently granted to the audience tends to differentiate one approach to securitization from another (Balzacq, 2011). Third, if audience assent is necessary for securitization to occur, as the CS surmizes, then we are faced with methodological challenges, because it remains difficult to know precisely when an audience has accepted a claim put forward by a securitizing actor. A critical discussion of the audience, therefore, enables me to pave the way for practices and related decisive changes to our notion of securitization.

3.2.2 Questioning the Role of Audiences

There is a considerable ambiguity as to the role of the audience in the CS's formulation of securitization theory. On the one hand, Wæver and his colleagues argue that security utterances produce threat images thanks to their inherent characteristics as powerful speech acts. In that sense, according to the CS, 'to study securitisation is to study the power politics of a concept' (Buzan et al., 1998: 36). This power depends itself on the 'social capital' of the actor who speaks security. However, at the same time, the CS argues that 'successful securitisation is *not* decided by the securitiser *but by the audience* of the security speech act' (Buzan et al., 1998: 31; emphasis added). Stritzel (2007), by the same token, highlights this 'conceptual tension' that pervades securitization theory, as he observes that the CS conceptualizes security simultaneously as a speech act *event* and the result of a negotiated process between an actor and the relevant audience (i.e. an *intersubjective* endeavour). Thus, Léonard and Kaunert (2011: 58) argue that 'it is not entirely clear what the acceptance by the audience means and entails exactly, and therefore how it could be identified in practice'. This is even more so since the application by Buzan, Wæver, and de Wilde (1998: 171–89) of securitization theory to empirical material does not ascribe any noticeable role to the audience (compare Vuori, 2008; McDonald, 2008). Instead, the emphasis is put on the referent object, which is threatened in its survival, the securitizing actor, who speaks 'security', and the functional actors, whose activities have significant effects on making security (Buzan et al., 1998: 36).

Various scholars have sought to address these problems. In particular, I have drawn attention to the fact that the performative dimension of security sits between semantic regularity and contextual circumstances (Balzacq, 2005). So the semantic register of security is a combination of textual meaning—that is, the knowledge of the concept acquired through spoken and written language—and cultural meaning—that is, the knowledge historically gained through previous interactions and situations (Klüfers, 2014; Pisoiu, 2012). Taken together, these two kinds of meanings form a frame of reference through which security utterances can be understood. In turn, frames structure various developments or properties of an entity by virtue of the conventions governing the use of the concept and the conditions under which its invocation is justified (Balzacq, 2005: 183). Moreover, Balzacq proposes to develop an argumentative approach to securitization drawing upon the work of Crawford (2002). This approach highlights that the power involved in communication is relational, rather than being merely substantial or 'self-actional'. Thus, according to such a perspective, the study of securitization would unpack the intersubjective process through which a securitizing actor induces an audience to agree with a given interpretation of an event or set of events (see also McDonald, 2008). After observing that 'how we know when (securitisation) happens (is) radically under-theorised', he emphasizes that there is 'a clear need…to draw the role of the audiences into the framework more coherently, but in doing so the CS will almost certainly need to downplay either the performative effects of the speech act or the inter-subjective nature of security' (McDonald, 2008: 573).

Another important contribution to the debate has been made by Salter (2008). Drawing upon dramaturgical analysis, he suggested that 'the' audience comprises in fact 'different' audiences in practice. Contrary to speech act philosophy that holds that the securitizing actor and the audience remain unchanged, Salter (2008: 329), in line with Goffman, suggests that 'the presentation of the self changes from different social settings, and that an understanding of the setting can illuminate the exigencies of different performances'. Consequently, this perspective insists upon the variability of securitizing moves. In other words, 'securitizing moves in popular, elite, technocratic, and scientific settings are markedly different—they operate according to different constitutions of actor and audience' (Salter, 2008: 329). Furthermore, how securitizing moves are accepted or rejected depends on 'the grand narratives by which truth is authorized, the characters who are empowered to speak, and the relationships between characters and audience' (Salter, 2008: 330).

In sum, analysts converge around the idea that securitization is an intersubjective phenomenon, which requires, at least, two parties: a securitizing actor and an audience. Yet, when reviewing the literature it emerges therefore that audience, let alone audience acceptance, is difficult to pin down. In the

EU setting these analytical problems become even more acute, as taken up further later. Therefore, the initial formulation of securitization has proven difficult to apply, which is not to say that its insights are not useful. To understand how security issues are designed in concrete settings, components of securitization theory rather have to be rearranged or complemented by others (e.g. context, power relations). Seen in this light, audience assent is one element of a 'larger theoretical pattern in securitisation studies, one which draws its importance in relation to others', for instance, context and political agency (Balzacq, 2011: 8). In contrast, if securitization can operate without an explicit mechanism for audience acceptance, it becomes necessary to integrate new ideas about the formation of security problems. To this end, I have suggested a greater emphasis on practices (Balzacq, 2005: 172, 174, 191) and policy instruments (Balzacq, 2008; Balzacq, 2009; Balzacq, 2011). These two elements depart from the CS approach to securitization, as I will discuss in the following.

3.2.3 Practice and Enactments

A basic claim of scholars who draw on practices is that security problems can be designed through different technical or physical modalities. This approach has recently been extended by a number of scholars, whose works have yet to percolate through the literature on EU internal security (Neumann, 2002; Adler and Pouliot, 2011; Hopf, 2010; Bueger, 2014). While these authors also take various positions, a practice-oriented approach addresses some of the gaps and problems that can beset purely linguistic takes on securitization. As elaborated below, it is fruitful to draw on the notion of a sociological 'field of practices' and 'habitus' (Bigo, 1994; Bigo, 2002) while also referring to wider ideas about 'governmentality' and 'dispositif' (Balzacq, 2011). Each of these concepts contributes distinctive ideas to the understanding of securitization processes.

To start with, the sociological concept of field—theorized by Pierre Bourdieu—has substantially advanced practice-centred analyses of securitization (Bigo, 2005; Huysmans, 2006; Basaran, 2010). As also explained in depth by Bigo in this volume, agents in such a field there are defined by professional backgrounds, as well as by their position in relation to one another and their amount of 'capital'; that is, the resources that grant them a certain type of power. Members of the field have shared sets of interests, common ways of generating knowledge (about threats, in the case of security) as well as common problem-solving perspectives (Bigo, 1994; Pouliot and Mérand, 2013). Seen in this light, a field can also be understood as, and give rise to, shared practices. More specifically, securitizing practices can be compared to other shared field practices of knowledge generation and problem solving. As such, securitizing practices are equally shaped by the specific power relations of a given (professional) field. Fields and regimes of practices share also powerful colonizing impetus (Dean, 2010: 21). Most of the works following the practice-based approach to securitization emphasize the tendency of certain domains, such as the field of insecurity, to conquer other fields and subsume them under their practical logic (Guild, 2003).

Regimes of practice can furthermore be related to the concept of *dispositif*. According to Foucault (1980: 194), a *dispositif* is 'a thoroughly heterogeneous ensemble consisting of discourses, institutions, architectural forms, regulatory decisions, laws, administrative measures, scientific statements, philosophical, moral and philanthropic proposition; in short, the said as much as the unsaid. The *dispositif* itself is the system of relations that can be established between these elements'. A challenge faced by the practice approach to securitization has been how to theorize these interactions without relying on discursive premises. This requires tracing what security practices 'express' by themselves, rather than treating practices only as another form or 'representation'. The proponents of the practice approach to securitization therefore tend to focus on the instruments, or tools, that are used as part of securitization processes (see Guild, 2009; Bigo and Guild, 2003; Balzacq et al., 2010). Balzacq argues that instruments express a specific security relation (Balzacq, 2008). They embody the mindset of security agents and organize the interactions among members of the field of insecurity. Instruments can strongly shape or compel a routine set of practices, and thus also create and not merely reflect a larger *dispositif*. In other words, there is a mutually constitutive relationship between the heterogeneous notion of *dispositif* and a sociological field of actors that operate and interact in a routinized way on the basis of policy instruments.

From here it is not difficult to see the connection between *dispositif* and the analytics of government approach. As Mitchell Dean writes, the analytics of government approach considers 'the characteristic techniques, instrumentalities and mechanisms through which (regimes of) practices operate' (Dean, 2010: 21). He further specifies four aspects to be studied, including (a) characteristic forms of visibility, ways of seeing and perceiving; (b) distinctive ways of thinking and questioning, relying on definite vocabularies and procedures for the production of truth (e.g. those derived from the social, human, and behavioural sciences); (c) specific ways of acting, intervening, and directing, made up of particular types of practical rationality ('expertise' and 'know-how'), and relying upon definite mechanisms, techniques and technologies; and (d) distinctive ways of forming subjects, selves, persons, actors, or agents (Dean, 2010: 33).

This rich and nuanced understanding—or 'analytics'—of government can provide the foundation for a theoretical understanding of securitization that accommodates two types of social mechanisms: both spoken words and non-discursive practices. They jointly constitute a regime of practices. In other words, taking the perspective of analytics of government enables researchers 'to identify the emergence of that regime, examine the multiple sources (verbal and non-verbal) of the elements that constitute it, and follow the diverse processes and relations by which these elements are assembled into relatively stable forms of organisation and (policies)' (Dean, 2010: 21).[2]

Adopting such an approach to securitization processes allows us to build bridges between different approaches to securitization. Regardless of different relationships between speech acts and audiences, securitization theory postulates that there is a specific grammar of security or pattern of security politics. This is characterized by a restriction of decision-making options, a centralization of decision-making processes, and related limitations on public debate and participation. Taken together, securitization and the intersubjective acceptance of the definition of a threat leads to so-called 'deontic powers' (Searle, 2009: 19), that is, special rights and duties, as well as derogations and permissions. Thus, authorities are empowered to take exceptional measures, such as the use of force, suspension of civil liberties, or constitutional change. While it is not necessary to equate securitization to a formal state of emergency or exception, it is possible to define any securitizing moves as attempts at transforming existing regimes of social and political practices.

3.3 Methodological Uncertainties and the Case of the EU

However, this enlargement of discursive to practice-centred perspectives still leaves open the question where and whether securitization has occurred. In particular, the various interpretations of securitization theory reviewed earlier have an important impact on the kind of evidence that counts in both regards. Thus, researchers have pursued three different strategies to establish whether securitization has been successful. The first, in line with its theoretical inspiration from Foucault and Bourdieu, demonstrates securitization by inscribing it within 'a multidimensional process of interconnecting diverse policy issues through institutional codifications...the application of certain skills and routines, the use of particular technologies and the dominance of particular policy orientations and methods' (Huysmans, 2006: 150).[3] The second approach followed by scholars to decide whether securitization has occurred emphasizes a binary view: the presence or lack of 'exceptional' measures. The third and final way is to consider whether the audience has accepted the securitizing move. It is less followed than the other two approaches, which is surprising in light of the debate on the role of audiences discussed earlier. Generally, researchers face empirical difficulties in evaluating whether the audience has been convinced by a specific securitizing move and tend to resort to alternative and indirect data (see Roe, 2008; Karyotis and Patrikios, 2010). In the EU context, problems are aggravated by the prevailing institutional complexity. When there is no clear 'public sphere', the relationship between the securitizing actor and the audience is even more difficult to characterize.

Against this background, the following examines studies on the social construction of migration as a security threat in the EU. This issue has been analysed most often through the lenses of securitization theory, generating both a thematically coherent and ample volume of literature. What is noteworthy, however, is that these studies have not spent their time 'applying' a fixed securitization theory. Instead, these empirical works have contributed, in their own distinctive ways, to the ongoing evolution of the theoretical apparatus of securitization. So my aim is to compare whether in broad strokes scholars have applied securitization theory to the same issue and empirical context in order to illustrate how they decide whether securitization has occurred or not. For reasons just discussed, particular attention is given to the issue of the operationalization of audience acceptance.

In addition to strongly contributing to the dissemination of the CS's ideas, Huysmans (2006) developed an original approach in order to make sense of the peculiarities of dealing with migration and asylum within the EU. He argued that although security approaches increasingly influenced migration and asylum policy in the 1980s and 1990s, 'speech acts explicitly defining migration as a major security threat to the EU did not play a central role in the securitisation of the Internal Market' (Huysmans, 2006: 150). In addition to emphasizing the limitations of the original version of securitization theory for analysing the EU, he lays out the central tenets of his approach to the genealogy of insecurities. Furthermore, in the EU context, 'speech acts are less important in securitisation than various social and political processes that govern migration and asylum on the basis of insecurity (i.e. security rationality)' (Huysmans, 2006: 150; Huysmans, 2011: 377). In other words, the study of securitization goes hand in hand with the analysis of politicization, as none subsumes the other; the process is less expressed in terms of substitution, than in—always reversible—evolutionary terms (cf. Balzacq, 2014; Williams, 2014; Bourbeau, 2013).

Consequently, for Huysmans, analysing securitization of EU migration is viewed as a 'messy process' that is better investigated through the concept of 'domains of insecurity', which is sustained, in turn, by a specific 'technocratic politics'. The real challenge facing securitization scholars, then, is to 'connect the dots' between technocratic and technological processes (Huysmans, 2006: 147). In fact, 'the development and implementation of technological artefacts and knowledge, such as diagrams, computer networks, scientific data . . . often precede and pre-structure political framing in significant ways' (Huysmans, 2006: 8). However, it is not merely a question of replacing audience acceptance critiqued above with technocratic and technological processes. Instead, Huysmans's work draws our attention to the question of the extent to which securitization scholars are prepared to integrate 'conditions that . . . produce a previously unobtainable result' (Greenwald et al., 1986: 211) in their analysis.

This issue is conspicuous in Boswell's work (Boswell, 2007). Gleaning insights from neo-institutionalism and systems theory, she primarily seeks to challenge the predominant view that '9/11 has had far-reaching consequences for the framing of debates on immigration in Europe . . . and (has) provided an opportunity for the securitisation of migration' (Boswell, 2007: 589). The article engages with the dominant literature on the securitization of migration, and criticizes the fact that securitization, as an analytical framework, over-emphasizes the discursive understanding of migration at the expense of other potential framings. Moreover, she argues that the literature on the securitization of migration tends to exaggerate the extent to which actors are interested in maximizing their power at the expense of considering other organizational behaviours. In short, Boswell's (2007: 606) main finding is that migration 'control policies in Europe do not appear to have become securitised as a result of 9/11 or the subsequent terrorist attacks in Madrid and London'.

If one works exclusively within a linguistic approach, then, Boswell's argument is difficult to debunk. For Boswell, linguistic signs are the most fundamental clues on which researchers should rely in order to adjudicate whether a case is an instance of securitization or not. And contrary to Huysmans and van Munster, practices apparently do not constitute sufficient grounds for deciding that an issue has been securitized. This enables her to hold two paradoxical views. On the one hand, she argues that, with regard to discourse, the cognitive constraints and conflicting political interests made it impossible to sustain linkages between migration and terrorism in the medium and long term in the EU. On the other hand, she acknowledges that, as far as policy practices are concerned, there have been more linkages between migration controls and security. Yet her conclusion is surprising. It is not that migration control policies are affected by security concerns in the EU, but rather that those involved in security and counterterrorism policies now resort to migration control instruments.

Yet a perspective derived from a regime of practices, as discussed in previous parts of this chapter, can resolve this tension. It allows us to reconceptualize securitizing moves as discursive or non-discursive acts that challenge and, when successful, transform the existing regime of practices. To test whether securitization has occurred one, therefore, needs to look at the evolution of regime of practices. In this way, reworking the theoretical remit of securitization may generate new results, and bring them closer to grasping the complexity of the phenomena under study.

Van Munster's (2009) work fits with such increased nuance and complexity. His work speaks to Huysmans' approach in the sense that it grants a central role to bureaucratic games and technologies of government, which he situates within the paradigm of risk. Van Munster and Huysmans are both concerned with how Foucault's analytics of modern arts of government plays out in the institutionalization of the internal market (Huysmans) and the EU's Area of Freedom, Security and Justice (van Munster). It is, according to van Munster, the very design of the EU Justice and Home Affairs domain that provides the setting within, and the reservoirs of meaning upon which political officers draw their claims in order to advocate the security-minded approach to migration and asylum.

Specifically, however, van Munster's work resonates with a growing literature within security studies, that is, risk analysis (Corry, 2012; Petersen, 2012; Balzacq, 2015). The paradigm of risk enables the liberal doctrine to achieve its security function in a more efficient way. Put otherwise, the liberal security order consists of sorting out individuals into different categories, which are then granted specific rights and privileges. It is no longer the control of all (*panopticon*) but the suspicion of some (*banopticon*) that is at stake (van Munster, 2009: 99). 'Here is', says Bigo, 'the main technique of securitisation, to transform structural difficulties and transformations into elements permitting specific groups to be blamed, even before they have done anything' (Bigo, 2002: 81). Drawing upon Bigo and Guild (2005), van Munster argues therefore that one of the ways in which 'risky categories' are designed is through the visa regime, as it establishes, in a very subtle but effective fashion, the 'limits and modalities of movements' (van Munster, 2009: 104). This is the basis of the governance of security as it unfolds within the EU today, that is, increasingly through the paradigm of risk (van Munster, 2009: 145).

In this light, risk and governance become central features of EU internal security, as Van Munster manages to relate the bureaucratic level of risk management to the political realm of 'security speak'. Again, the relations between the bureaucratic and political spheres shed a distinctive light on the indeterminate nature of the audience in securitization processes, whereby it can vary depending on the functional aspect of a securitizing move (see also Vuori, 2008). At times, the political elite constitutes the audience, whereas it can become a securitizing actor on other occasions: 'the political level often plays an important role in either authorizing, legitimizing, justifying, thwarting, dislocating or upsetting the enunciations of security professionals' (van Munster, 2009: 6). Yet even though he acknowledges that intergovernmental conferences can be seen as moments of securitization in the EU, characterized by the suspension of the 'normal or regular way of doing things', van Munster (2009: 144) argues that, in the EU context, 'processes of securitisation... remain short of the securitising act or decision that defines the threshold between the social order and the state of exception'. Instead, 'the state of exception has become designed into the flow of everyday life as part of the risk governance' (van Munster, 2009: 145). In other words, the governance of migration (compare Lavenex and Bossong in this volume) through risk rationalities is the consequence of effective securitization. Thus, we are provided with further evidence of securitization in which risk constitutes the new paradigm of security policy (but see Patomäki, 2014).

But when does the absence of exceptionalism indicate a failed securitizing move, particularly when dealing with the EU? This relates to the second way of empirically substantiating securitization mentioned above—namely the binary perspective of securitization versus regular politics and is closest to the original CS understanding: 'when a securitizing actor uses a rhetoric of existential threat and thereby takes an issue out of what under those conditions is "normal politics", *we have a case* of securitization' (Buzan et al., 1998: 24–5; emphasis added). In a study that emphasizes the 'structural uniqueness' of the EU in the security domain, Neal (2009: 351) posits, in contrast, that 'practices of government have become too complex, too plural and too diverse to maintain the plausibility of a sovereign, centre, nominalist understanding of security'. A distinctive element of Neal's (2009: 351) argument is that he interprets the absence of exceptional measures in the case studied as 'revealing the limitations of securitisation theory'. Like van Munster, he analyses EU security practices through the lenses of the paradigm of risk. But unlike van Munster, risk is seen here as a *dispositif* in itself, that is 'a series of micro-practices that are plural and heterogeneous' (Neal, 2009: 349). As a consequence, he proceeds to suggest that the construction of links between migration, borders, security, and terrorism in the EU is better understood by using Bigo's (2002) notion of the 'governmentality of unease', which, in his view, does not imply the invocation of existential threats, nor call for the adoption of exceptional measures.

Perhaps, this is exaggerated. One needs to acknowledge that the methodological nature of exceptionalism receives two different treatments in *Security: A New Framework for Analysis*. While they argue that the existence of exceptional measures unequivocally indicates that securitization has happened, Buzan and his colleagues (1998: 25) also note that they 'do not push the demand so high as to say that an emergency measure has to be adopted'. Put otherwise, exceptional politics is a proxy for a successful securitizing move, but the fact that no exceptional measure is adopted does not necessarily prove the existence of a failed securitizing move (Balzacq, 2014; Williams, 2014). This ambiguity has been interpreted by Williams (2003: 521) as reflecting a continuum vision of security practices 'running from risk to threat, or from uncertainty to danger'. In this light, evidence for securitization is again a matter of policy outcome and does not necessarily need to be focused on exceptional moves and moments (Jackson, 2006; Buzan et al., 1998: 25).

3.4 Conclusion

This chapter reviewed the original conceptual apparatus on securitization as developed by the Copenhagen School and further proposed an alternative understanding of securitization as an analytics of government. To make this case, I first demonstrated that the insistence on audience as a requisite of securitization was theoretically useful, but a methodological hindrance. Secondly, I developed a concrete way to study securitization, which integrates discourse and practice in one unique framework that can be summarized under the analytics of government. Thirdly I compared different attempts at studying the securitization of migration and asylum in the EU. The main result was that the various yardsticks provided by the CS, that is, audience acceptance and exceptionalism, did not quite live up to the exigencies of empirical analysis in the EU context. To address these problems, scholars such as Huysmans, Balzacq, and van Munster, have developed original solutions that highlight wider sociological, technocratic, and bureaucratic rationalities. This implies that securitization theory owes some of its most interesting theoretical advances to the study of EU internal security.

My personal view of securitization shares many affinities with those that work on political sociology, Europeanization, public policy, criminology, and governance. This approach speaks to political sociology's dialogue with Bourdieu and Foucault, but comes to a parting of the ways with its empirical focus on professionals of in/security (see Bigo in this volume). I regard linguistic occurrences and practices as complementary and mutually constitutive, while some scholars in political sociology consider practices to be analytically superior to linguistic enactments. The problem is that actors often use words to justify what they do or defend themselves when things go wrong. In other words, they need to speak 'their mind' to explain why they did what they did. Practices are just not enough; moreover, their legitimacy depends upon linguistic moves. How can they be superior then?

Further, public policy and Europeanization bring new insights, respectively, to the way securitization operates and the potential political implications of securitization. Léonard and Kaunert (2010) articulated the links between Kingdon's three-streams model and securitization, insisting that an important factor of the policy stream was argumentation, one of the basic social mechanisms on which securitization focuses (Kingdon, 1984). In addition, the politics stream has some relevance for political sociology as it insists on the formation of coalitions in order to win an argument which, to take the EU setting, can then serve as ground for further Europeanization.

Finally, securitization and governance enter into one another's theoretical realm. Specifically, securitization and governance depend, for their acceptance, on the legitimacy of both their travails and results. But the analytics of govern-ment approach developed in this chapter has something to offer to the study of governance, in particular the 'new governance' school, which emphasizes policy instruments as main conveyors of policy rationalities (Salamon, 2002; see also Bossong and Lavenex in this volume). For securitization, techniques and technologies of government enable security problems to be visible and, then, managed. In other words, in contrast to the governance approach, which tends to treat tools primarily as techniques of government, securitization considers instruments as central elements through which security problems are designed and regimes of government emerge. This means that securitization theory provides other approaches to EU internal security cooperation with different theoretical layers and may open new avenues for research.

Notes

1. This section draws on a previously unpublished, co-authored paper (Balzacq and Léonard, 2012).
2. For a more detailed discussion on the analytics of government, also as proposed by Dean (2010), see Balzacq et al. (2015).
3. Actually, scholars who focus on such practices and technologies or instruments argue that we need to think about performativity in a different way in order to question the *excessive* power given to language to fix the content of the ontology of security (Aradau, 2010). According to Barad (2003: 802) who has inspired Aradau's work on materiality, 'performativity is actually a contestation of the unexamined habits of mind that grant language and other forms of representation more power in determining our ontologies than they deserve'. In this respect, the status of either language or practice vis-à-vis the construction of a security issues is a matter that should not be fixed a priori. It is empirically ascertained.

References

Adler, E. and Pouliot, V. (2011) 'International Practices', *International Theory*, 3(1), pp. 1–36.

Aradau, C. (2010) 'Security that Matters: Critical Infrastructure and Objects of Protec-tion', *Security Dialogue*, 41(5), pp. 491–514.

Balzacq, T. (2005) 'The Three Faces of Securitization: Political Agency, Audience and Context', *European Journal of International Relations*, 11(2), pp. 171–201.

Balzacq, T. (2008) 'The Policy Tools of Securitization: Information Exchange, EU For-eign and Interior Policies', *Journal of Common Market Studies*, 46(1), pp. 75–100.

Balzacq, T. (2009) 'Constructivism and Securitization Studies', in Mauer, V. and Dunn Cavelty, M. (eds) *The Routledge Handbook of Security Studies*. London: Routledge.

Balzacq, T. (2011) 'A Theory of Securitization: Origins, Core Assumptions, and Variants', in Balzacq, T. (ed.) *Securitization Theory: How Security Problems Emerge and Dissolve*. London: Routledge, pp. 1–30.

Balzacq, T. (2014) *Contesting Security: Strategies and Logics*. London: Routledge.

Balzacq, T. (2015) 'The Rise of Precaution and the Global Governance of Risks', *Political Studies Review* 13(4), pp. 546–59.

Balzacq, T., Basaran, T., Bigo, D., Guittet, E-P., and Olsson, C. (2010) 'Security Practices', in Denemark, R. A. (ed.) *International Studies Encyclopedia*. Oxford: Wiley-Blackwell, pp. 1–30.

Balzacq, T. and Carrera, S. (2006) 'The Hague Programme: The Long Road to Freedom, Security and Justice', in Balzacq, T. and Carrera, S. (eds) *Security versus Freedom? A Challenge for Europe's Future*. London: Ashgate, pp. 1–35.

Balzacq, T. and Léonard, S. (2012) 'Theory and Evidence in Securitization Studies'. Unpublished paper.

Balzacq, T., Léonard, S., and Ruzicka, J. (2015) ' "Securitization" Revisited: Theory and Cases', *International Relations*, article first published online August 8, 2015, doi: 10.1177/0047117815596590.

Barad, K. (2003) 'Posthumanist Performativity: Toward an Understanding of How Matter Comes to Matter', *Signs: Journal of Women in Culture and Society*, 28(3), pp. 801–31.

Basaran, T. (2010) *Security, Law and Borders: At the Limits of Liberties*. London: Routledge.

Best, J. (2001) *How Claims Spread: Cross-national Diffusion of Social Problems*. Hawthorne, NY: Aldine de Gruyter.

Best, J. (ed.) (2009) *Images of Issues: Typifying Contemporary Social Problems*. New Brunswick, NJ: Transaction.

Bigo, D. (1994) 'The European Internal Security Field: Stakes and Rivalries in a Newly Developing Area on Police Intervention', in Anderson, M. and den Boer, M. (eds) *Policing across National Boundaries*. London: Pinter, pp. 161–73.

Bigo, D. (2002) 'Security and Immigration: Toward a Critique of the Governmentality of Unease', *Alternatives*, 27(1): pp. 63–92.

Bigo, D. (2005) 'La mondialisation de l'(in)sécurité? Réflexions sur le champ des professionnels de la gestion des inquiétudes et analytique de la transnationalisation des processus d'(in)sécuritisation', *Cultures & Conflits*, 58(2), pp. 53–101.

Bigo, D. and Guild, E. (2003) *La mise à l'écart des étrangers. La logique du visa Schengen*. Paris: L'Harmattan.

Boswell, C. (2007) 'Migration Control in Europe after 9/11: Explaining the Absence of Securitization', *Journal of Common Market Studies*, 45(3), pp. 589–610.

Bourbeau, P. (2013) 'Politicisation et sécuritisation des migrations internationales', *Critique Internationale*, 61(4), pp. 127–45.

Bueger, C. (2014) 'Pathways to Practice: Praxiography and International Politics', *European Political Science Review*, 6(3), pp. 383–406.

Buzan, B., Wæver, O., and de Wilde, J. (1998) *Security: A New Framework for Analysis*. Boulder, CO: Lynne Rienner.

Corry, O. (2012) 'Securitisation and "Riskification": Second-order Security and the Politics of Climate Change', *Millennium: Journal of International Studies*, 40(2), pp. 235–58.

Crawford, N. C. (2002) *Argument and Change in World Politics: Ethics, Decolonization and Humanitarian Intervention*. Cambridge: Cambridge University Press.

Dean, M. (2010) *Governmentality: Power and Rule in Modern Society*. London: Sage.

Debrix, F. (2003) *Language, Agency, and Politics in a Constructed World*. Armonk, NY: M. E. Sharpe.

Delumeau, J. (1989) *Rassurer et protéger: le sentiment de sécurité dans l'Occident d'autrefois*. Paris: Fayard.

Edelman, M. (1964) *The Symbolic Uses of Politics*. Champaign, IL: University of Illinois Press.

Edelman, M. (1977) *Political Language: Words that Succeed and Policies that Fail*. New York, NY: Academic Press.

Epstein, C. (2008) *The Power of Words in International Relations: Birth of an Anti-whaling Discourse*. Cambridge, MA: MIT Press.

Eriksson, J. (ed.) (2001) *Threat Politics: New Perspectives on Security, Risk and Crisis Management*. Aldershot: Ashgate.

Foucault, M. (1980) *Power/Knowledge: Selected Interviews and Other Writings 1972–1977*, ed. C. Gordon. London: Harvester.

Foucault, M. (1991) 'Questions of Method', in Burchell, G., Gordon, C., and Miller, P. (eds) *The Foucault Effect: Studies in Governmentality*. London: Harvester Wheatsheaf, pp. 73–86.

Foucault, M. (2003) *Society Must Be Defended: Lectures at the Collège de France, 1975–1976*, translated by David Macey. New York, NY: Picador.

Foucault, M. (2004) *Abnormals: Lectures at the Collège de France, 1974–1975*, translated by Graham Burchell. New York, NY: Picador.

Foucault, M. (2009) *Security, Territory, Population: Lectures at the Collège de France, 1977–1978*, translated by Graham Burchell. New York, NY: Picador.

Greenwald, A. G., Pratkanis, A. R., Leippe, M. R., and Baumgardner, M. H. (1986) 'Under What Conditions Does Theory Obstruct Research Progress?' *Psychological Review*, 93(2), pp. 216–29.

Guild, E. (2003) 'International Terrorism and EU Immigration, Asylum and Borders Policy: The Unexpected Victims of 11 September 2001', *European Foreign Affairs Review*, 8(3), pp. 331–46.

Guild, E. (2009) *Security and Migration in the 21st Century*. Cambridge: Polity Press.

Guild, E. and Bigo, D. (2005) *Controlling Frontiers: Free Movement into and within Europe*. Aldershot: Ashgate.

Hansen, L. (2006) *Security as Practice: Discourse Analysis and the Bosnian War*. London: Routledge.

Hansen, L. (2011) 'The Politics of Securitization and the Muhammad Cartoon Crisis: A Post-Structuralist Perspective', *Security Dialogue*, 42(4–5), pp. 357–69.

Hopf, T. (2010) 'The Logic of Habit in International Relations', *European Journal of International Relations*, 16(4), pp. 539–61.

Huysmans, J. (1998) 'Security! What Do You Mean? From Concept to Thick Signifier', *European Journal of International Relations*, 4(2), pp. 226–55.

Huysmans, J. (2004) 'Minding Exceptions: Politics of Security in Liberal Democracies', *Contemporary Political Theory*, 3(3), pp. 321–41.

Huysmans, J. (2006) *The Politics of Insecurity: Fear, Migration and Asylum in the EU.* London: Routledge.

Huysmans, J. (2011) 'What's in an Act? On Security Speech Acts and Little Security Nothings', *Security Dialogue*, 42(4–5), pp. 371–83.

Jackson, N. J. (2006) 'International Organizations, Security Dichotomies and the Trafficking of Persons and Narcotics in Post-Soviet Central Asia: A Critique of the Securitization Framework', *Security Dialogue*, 37(3), pp. 299–317.

Jowett, G. S. and O'Donnell, V. (2006) *Propaganda and Persuasion.* London: Sage.

Karyotis, G. and Patrikios, S. (2010) 'Religion, Securitization and Anti-immigration Attitudes: The Case of Greece', *Journal of Peace Research*, 47(1), pp. 43–57.

Kaunert, C. (2009) 'Liberty versus Security? EU Asylum Policy and the European Commission', *Journal of Contemporary European Research*, 5(2), pp. 148–70.

Kingdon, J. W. (1984) *Agendas, Alternatives, and Public Policies.* Boston, MA: Little, Brown & Co.

Kitsuse, J. and Spector, M. (2000) *Constructing Social Problems.* New Brunswick, NJ: Transaction.

Klüfers, P. (2014) 'Security Repertoires: Towards a Sociopragmatist Framing of Securitization Processes', *Critical Studies on Security*, 2(3), pp. 278–92.

Kratochwil, F. V. (1989) *Rules, Norms and Decisions: On the Conditions of Practical Legal Reasoning in International Relations and Domestic Affairs.* Cambridge: Cambridge University Press.

Krebs, R. R. and Jackson, P. T. (2007) 'Twisting Tongues and Twisting Arms: The Power of Political Rhetoric', *European Journal of International Relations*, 13(1), pp. 35–66.

Léonard, S. and Kaunert, C. (2010) 'Reconceptualizing the Audience in Securitization Theory', in Balzacq, T. (ed.) *Securitization Theory: How Security Problems Emerge and Dissolve.* Abingdon: Routledge, pp. 57–76.

Loseke, D. R. (2003) *Thinking about Social Problems: An Introduction to Constructionist Perspectives.* New Brunswick, NJ: Transaction.

McDonald, M. (2008) 'Securitization and the Construction of Security', *European Journal of International Relations*, 14(4), pp. 563–87.

McSweeney, B. (1996) 'Identity and Security: Buzan and the Copenhagen School', *Review of International Studies*, 22(1), pp. 81–93.

Mutimer, D. (1997) 'Beyond Strategy: Critical Thinking and the New Security Studies', in Snyder, C. A. (ed.) *Contemporary Security Studies.* Basingstoke: Macmillan.

Neal, A. W. (2009) 'Securitizing and Risk at the EU Border: The Origins of FRONTEX', *Journal of Common Market Studies*, 47(2), pp. 333–56.

Neumann, I. B. (2002) 'Returning Practice to the Linguistic Turn: The Case of Diplomacy', *Millennium: Journal of International Studies*, 31(3), pp. 627–51.

Patomäki, H. (2014) 'Absenting the Absence of Future Dangers and Structural Transformations in Securitization Theory', *International Relations*, doi: 10.1177/0047117814526606.

Petersen, K. L. (2012) 'Risk Analysis: A Field within Security Studies?' *European Journal of International Relations*, 18(4), pp. 693–717.

Pisoiu, D. (2012) 'Pragmatic Persuasion on Counter-Terrorism', *Critical Studies on Terrorism*, 5(3), pp. 297–317.

Pouliot, V. (2008) 'The Logic of Practicality: A Theory of Practice of Security Communities', *International Organization*, 62(2), pp. 257–88.

Pouliot, V. and Mérand, F. (2013) 'Bourdieu's Concepts: Political Sociology in International Relations', in Adler-Nissen, R. (ed.) *Bourdieu in International Relations: Rethinking Key Concepts in IR*. London: Routledge.

Pram, U. and Petersen, K. L. (2011) 'Concepts of Politics in Securitization Studies', *Security Dialogue*, 42(4–5), pp. 315–28.

Risse, T. (2000) 'Let's Argue! Communicative Action in World Politics', *International Organization*, 54(1), pp. 1–40.

Roe, P. (2008) 'Actor, Audience(s) and Emergency Measures', *Security Dialogue*, 39(6), pp. 615–35.

Salamon, L. M. (2002) *The Tools of Government: A Guide to the New Governance*. Oxford: Oxford University Press.

Salter, M. B. (2008) 'Securitization and Desecuritization: A Dramaturgical Analysis of the Canadian Air Transport Security Authority', *Journal of International Relations and Development*, 11(4), pp. 321–49.

Searle, J. (2009) 'Language and Social Ontology', in Mantzavinos, C. (ed.) *Philosophy of the Social Sciences: Philosophical Theory and Scientific Practice*. Cambridge: Cambridge University Press.

Sellers, P. J. and Schaffner, B. F. (eds) (2009) *Winning with Words: The Origins and Impact of Political Framing*, London: Routledge.

Stritzel, H. (2007) 'Towards a Theory of Securitization: Copenhagen and Beyond', *European Journal of International Relations*, 13(3), pp. 357–83.

Van Munster, R. (2009) *Securitizing Immigration: The Politics of Risk in the EU*. Basingstoke: Palgrave Macmillan.

Vultee, F. (2011) 'Securitization as a Media Frame: What Happens When the Media "Speak Security"', in Balzacq, T. (ed.) *Securitization Theory: How Security Problems Emerge and Dissolve*. London: Routledge.

Vuori, J. A. (2008) 'Illocutionary Logics and Strands of Securitization: Applying the Theory of Securitization to the Study of Non-Democratic Political Orders', *European Journal of International Relations*, 14(1), pp. 65–99.

Wæver, O. (1995) 'Securitization and Desecuritization', in Lipschutz, R. D. (ed.) *On Security*. New York: Columbia University Press.

Wæver, O. (2011) 'Politics, Security, Theory', *Security Dialogue*, 42(4–5), pp. 465–80.

Walt, S. (1991) 'The Renaissance of Security Studies', *International Studies Quarterly*, 35(2), pp. 211–39.

Watson, S. D. (2009) *The Securitization of Humanitarian Migration: Digging Moats and Sinking Boats*. London: Routledge.

Weldes, J., Laffey, M., Gusterson, H., and Duvall, R. (eds) (1999) *Cultures of Insecurity: States, Communities, and the Production of Danger*. Minneapolis, MN: University of Minnesota Press.

Williams, M. C. (2003) 'Words, Images, Enemies: Securitization in International Politics', *International Studies Quarterly*, 47(4), pp. 511–31.

Williams, M. C. (2014) 'Securitization as Political Theory: The Politics of the Extraordinary', *International Relations*, doi: 10.1177/0047117814526606.

4

International Political Sociology

Internal Security as Transnational Power Fields

Didier Bigo

4.1 Introduction

This chapter introduces international political sociology (IPS) as a way to understand the emergence and the evolution of the field of internal security in Europe. The IPS approach as practiced by what can be called the 'Paris problematization' of security studies refuses to abide by traditional dividing lines apparent within other social sciences—and particularly within political science—such as the opposition between on the one side, a theoretically and/ or norm-driven constructivism lacking empirical observations, and on the other side, an empirical and often cynical positivism which lacks reflection and consideration of its underlying conditions of production (Bigo et al., 2010; Bigo and Walker, 2007).

The premise of the present book is to take seriously the theorization of the field of internal security, and that cannot be done, this chapter holds, by theoretical abstraction detached from observation or by sweeping generalizations (essentially, speculation) made through a very limited number of theoretically defined variables artificially linked together. Nevertheless, in political science this is how theory is frequently conceived and used, leading to false understandings of 'theory' as a form of abstraction based on a simplified model of a complex reality and leading to positivism and platonicism. If one hopes to avoid the narrow *episteme* of the hard sciences of the nineteenth century, and instead learn from both the fruitful lessons borne of contemporary science on complexity *and* the useful insights found in anthropology and sociology as sciences of 'observation' and inductive reasoning, theorization should avoid thin, abstract models with minimal variables and should rather include a deep and thoughtful understanding of the wide diversity of human practices. It requires a *reflexive* approach that is aware of the relations between the observed and the observer in the social realm. Such theorizing would look at the practices of the actors, which are the outcome of a practical sense and *habitus*, resulting from the incorporation of the underlying logics of diverse fields into one's everyday action (Bourdieu, 1998).

An IPS approach therefore wishes to transcend the caricature-like opposition in international relations between so-called idealist versus realist theories or between critical versus mainstream 'camps', and instead aims to be both materialist, constructivist, empirical, and reflexive. It suggests we must think about IR 'sociologically', in terms of practices, relations, and processes (trajectories) and conduct a proper sociological analysis of a specific historical development—as an alternative to prevailing research within political science and its tendencies towards essentialism. In the chapter here, the concern is with the emergence of a European internal security domain of activities or field. This field has its own dynamics, its specific stakes, and, in terms of effects, outcomes that reconfigure globally what security is and is not, obliging the observer to rethink the comingling of the state with private actors, as well as the transnational development of security bureaucracies in the world.

IPS, by its ambition, thus differs from research that tries to understand the emergence of EU internal security cooperation simply as a single case of larger cooperation patterns defined by abstract theory. For instance, EU scholars might identify internal security cooperation as a kind of spillover dynamic mediated by concerns about national sovereignty, lawyers would consider it as a legalistic field privileging mutual recognition and quasi law, or IR constructivist scholars may consider it as another example of the exclusions that new borders generate in terms of alternatives, thus losing the specificities which are produced by the EU internal security field as such.

IPS instead requires that we begin with 'practices', which means to begin with the observation of these practices, and that we deploy research strategies that have to be reconfigured for each specific empirical fields of observation. To begin with practices also means to understand the dynamics of interdependence between these practices in the short and longer terms. It reconciles the study of individuals' interrelations with the study of their societies, states, and international context, rather than separate these dimensions as different levels of analysis. In that sense, an IPS approach is fundamentally inspired by the sociology of Norbert Elias, looking at the configuration and transformation of the 'habitus' of different individuals and the chains of interdependence they are engaged in via their actions. By paying specific attention to the practices of power, the IPS approach is also inspired by Bourdieu, focusing on the relations between human practices, strategies of distinction, and field(s) effects at the transnational scale. The objective of the approach outlined in this chapter is to examine the practices and relations of professionals or 'guilds', as I have termed them, of internal security that shape the field of internal security in Europe as a transnational field of power. These professionals constitute more and more transnational networks in Europe and beyond, and thus participate in reconfiguring nothing less than the dynamics of world politics.

Theorizing internal security properly also demands a discussion of what security is about. The terminology of security is not the signifier for an eternal, unchanging value, a norm that transcends all others due to its relations with death or focus on survival. In other words, security is not necessarily a first or primordial value. Security is a terminology that has different configurations in space and time and takes on very different meanings from one society to another, depending on human relations inside a specific historical *episteme* (Foucault, 1970), regarding conceptions of security and freedom, danger, risk, democracy, politics, and so on (Williams, 2008). What security means is therefore dependent on different 'hotbeds of meanings' that are (re)ignited or not in some circumstances and in different social universes (e.g. security as wisdom, as the end of time, as juridical guarantees, as survival and coercion, as protection and prevention, as a grasp on the future) (Gros, 2013). And this is why security must be considered as an essentially contested concept (Balzacq et al., 2010; Gallie, 1956). Actors competing for the monopoly of the definition of security— and the priorities of the struggles against threats and risks—will try to determine the allocation of tasks and budgets between multiple organizations as well as the scale of the concentration of the major means of coercion in the hands of 'public' actors. The process of (in)securitization, which can be understood as the distribution of the use of violence and coercion between insecurity, security, and fate, will make visible some forms of insecurity and conceal others, and will transform some actions of violence into either an inescapable fate where no one is responsible and nothing can be done, or a way to justify exceptional means and emergency measures to control and tackle them (Bigo, 1994; Bigo, 2013). This process has been embodied by the professionalization of the means of violence by state bureaucracies and their own differentiation between specific apparatuses and professional universes, such as between the military forces, the police forces, and the border guards.

Over the centuries, this process has been organized along the lines of territories conquered by war and the hardening of the notion of 'border' to create a difference between a friendly inside and a dangerous, inimical outside. External security has been considered the purview of military and diplomats. Internal security has been the realm of border guards and police forces. Even if this representation has been far from accurate, it has organized the significations given to internal and external forms of security as two different forms. Yet it seems that a reversal of the differentiation and specialization of forces is occurring and that the entanglement of the inside and outside has created complicated relations between the armed forces, the police, the border guards, and all the private actors that today intervene as professionals of security (Bigo, 2001a). This entanglement has become particularly visible in the European Union, since the principle of freedom of movement of persons inside the Union has reorganized the relation between territorial borders and border controls. It created the distinction between national borders, which are simultaneously external borders of the EU, and other national borders that are only internal to the EU and which must privilege freedom over systematic control of foreigners (Bigo, 2013a).

As will be explained below, it is only by taking this overall context and logics of transformation into account that an understanding of internal security in Europe is possible. A detailed analysis of the EU's former third pillar, or of the Area of Freedom, Security and Justice (AFSJ), only makes sense inside this broader picture of the state—and of the transformations of the relations between the main institutions dealing with coercion, intelligence and espionage, and the fight against criminals, as well as those involved with the management of border controls and the propagation of fear in an assemblage of various 'global' insecurities. I have used the notion of an '(in)security' process to show how the institutions in charge of security are not answering to objective insecurities, but take an active part in constructing some violence as a continuum of major insecurities, while in other instances, violence is considered as a fate against which one has only to be resilient. Yet other acts of violence are defined as forms of 'security' and 'protection' when they originate from the institutions themselves (even when these acts are illegal). The purported legitimacy of these actions is supported by a shift to forms of violence that are not physical but instead generate a fear of others, thus creating a continuum of insecurity surrounding issues such as terrorism, organized crime, and human trafficking. Moreover, this continuum is expanded to fear of migrants, even when these migrants are native to Europe, as well as to refugees fleeing their countries, despite the counter-principle that they need protection (Bigo, 2006; Bigo, 2008a). The effects of the field of the professionals of (in)security are not stable and contained inside the EU, but are centrifugal and extend geographically into the European neighbourhood and transatlantic relations. This leads to major transformations of diplomacy, reflected in conflicting aspects of emergent EU foreign affairs institutions and the external dimension of internal security. More recently, this external dimension has sharpened via intelligence that epitomizes the logic of policing at a distance and via surveillance technologies for 'prevention' activities such as tracking and tracing. These logics challenge the traditional monopoly of diplomats and the military over the realm of external security (Bauman et al., 2014; Bigo, 2014).

Against this general background, this chapter first lays out the main precepts and research questions of IPS in security studies, for which the work of Pierre Bourdieu is an important, but not the only, source. It then proposes a revised 'PARIS' problematization of security analysis (section 4.2) and discusses how such an approach—based on empirical reflexivity—might be carried out (section 4.3). Section 4.4 outlines some representative works in this vein before the conclusion, section 4.5, considers future research agendas.

4.2 International Political Sociology: Theorizing 'Practices'

As suggested above, theorizing from an IPS perspective begins with the observation of the practices of all the agents that act and change the world. The challenge then is to elaborate a theory that is both sufficiently precise and complex to be able to interpret the sense of these practices (being respectful of what the actors say they do), and, at the same time, sufficiently distant from these actors and their investments into their own games (so that we can understand that actors seldom know the full extent of what they do). Pierre Bourdieu has insisted on this sense of reflexivity that is necessary for any sociology and anthropological research. For him and other French social scientists, in contrast to the Anglo-Saxon tradition, social constructivism exists only as a form of reflexivity of the sociologist regarding his or her empirical work of analysing. This empirical work revolves around the practices of the actors within a specific social universe, which is structured as a field, or of actors that find themselves at the crossroads between different social universes, but are gravitating together towards certain 'projects' in 'practical moments' (Boltanski, 2009; Bourdieu, 1985; Bourdieu, 2004; Lahire, 2012).

Bruno Latour, Luc Boltanski, and other 'pragmatists' have sometimes criticized the theoretical pretence that the researcher may have a more thorough knowledge than the actors have of their own actions, and have recommended filling in yet more details of all the 'actants' (human beings and objects in their relations) before abstract claims (e.g. on different social universes) can be made. Despite this objection, which is taken up again further later, the shared inspiration remains valid. A political sociology approach remains based on observation and has to focus on the study of 'immanent practices' (Bigo, 2011; Boltanski, 2009). Theorizing without detaching observation from abstraction is thus dependent on a deep and sensitive understanding of the notion of practice.

So despite the tendency of sociological textbooks to juxtapose pragmatist sociology and critical sociology as irreconcilable, I want to insist here (in line with the efforts of Boltanski) on the possibility of drawing them together—in order to have a view of the different social universes that are constituted transnationally by what might be called competitive guilds of professionals of (in)security management. These universes are, at this scale, fragile and always in the making. They are forms of social international fields, if one accepts the change imposed by this relational and processual perspective in terms of ontology and epistemology. These dimensions of reflexivity and acceptance of plurality, and even heterogeneity, of theorizing or conceptualizing the social, suggest the usefulness of a specific political sociology inspired by such diverse authors as Norbert Elias, Pierre Bourdieu, Luc Boltanski, and also Michel Foucault. Despite their differences, these authors all share an analysis of 'the social' as a relational process always in transformation, and which has to be analysed simultaneously as both a 'heritage'—or a patrimony of disposition as argued by Bernard Lahire—and also as a fragile present always in the making and never certain.

IPS thus implies, in ontological and epistemological terms, that human practices cannot be analysed through rational choice theory, or through a dichotomy or a dialectic of rational choice and emotion. The key notion is about 'practice' and 'practical sense', which encapsulates the rejection of dualism between object and subject, and between materiality and ideas (Bourdieu, 1998). The Bourdieusian notion of practical sense rejects both positivism as well as post-modern understandings of the meaning of practice as determined by norms (Adler-Nissen, 2012; Swartz, 2013). Human practices have to be understood via an extended understanding of rationality, or more exactly, via an understanding of plural rationalities or 'reasons', which are always quite 'practical reasons'. The IPS approach is consequently fundamentally reflexive, pluralist, and conscious of historical trajectories in which situated actions do not exist in a pre-defined, legalistic domain but instead are constantly evolving and practically situated in fluid social fields. These fields are made visible by shining a light on the relations between agents, whereas the agents themselves, as individual actors or 'points of origin', are made relatively less visible. Instead of the agency-structure approach so common in political science, a process-relation approach that transcends the agency vs. structure debate is necessary to understand the shaping of institutional trajectories.

This processual perspective, sometime called a socio-genetic perspective, implies that processes rather than things best represent the phenomena that we encounter in the natural world around us. Process has primacy over things, or, put another way, process has priority over substance. Nicholas Rescher (1996) insisted on this tradition, which first Leibniz illustrated and John Dewey later developed. It requires seeing the world as a sea of flux, comprising a manifold of changes that are not a clear-cut replacement of one hard-edged state by another, but a melting and fusing of boundary-less processes. It suggests that we must think in terms of movement, of trajectories, of becoming, instead of favouring, the fixed and static, the separate and self-contained (see Lapid in Albert et al., 2001). Most institutionalist and neo-institutionalist perspectives, while interested in analysing interaction processes or games, often ignore this point and take institutions for what matters (see chapter 8, for instance). A relational perspective also insists on the fact that the real is relational, and not interactionist: it is made of discrete institutions. The relations between agents are what permits us to understand their practices and what constitutes their identities. The invisible relations between the agents lead the immanent practices that they visibly undertake as actors.

Different versions of this relational perspective exist. Pierre Bourdieu has been one of the most interesting authors by virtue of his transdisciplinary approach founded on his knowledge of anthropology, sociology, and philosophy. He approached this relational perspective via *genetic* structuralism, destabilizing the ahistoricism of structuralism and considering time and trajectories as the key elements of process. As he explains, a relational, reflexive, and processual approach will begin with the moment of making and will consider agents only when they act in relation to each other. Next, drawing a graph of the field is a way to visualize the 'distinctive deviations' (relative distances) between the positions of these agents. This is also to visualize the invisible relations between them by finding what are the best representations of their proximities and distances. It permits us to correlate the positions of actors, which are characterized by their different forms of capital, with their position-takings or authoritative statements, and to see if a homology between the two (positions and position-takings) exist or not. If a structural homology appears, a social universe of actors becomes a field, which is defined by its capacity to stabilize boundaries and generate cost of entry. Often institutions play the role of gatekeeper and provide various levels of legitimacy depending on their duration and history in the field. This is why struggles often confront inheritors that try to reproduce their dominant position in a specific field, with challengers that aim to shake up the boundaries, priorities, or stakes of a field—for which the actors enter into competition.

Tracing the historical trajectories of these actions, struggles, and moment of cooperation allows us to understand the limited repertoires that each social universe constitutes, and also permits us to unpack the strategies of legitimization of any durable institution. Norms neither follow rational interests nor do they emerge from shared beliefs and attitudes. Norms are even less the result of their dialectical relations. Norms (in this context meaning deeply set shapers of action) are the product of the strength of the historical trajectories of an imminent set of actions incorporated into ethos and habitus, which makes sense in regard to specific social universes. Consequently, a proper reflexive analysis has to avoid the trap of being driven either by (a) an 'idealist' view of the world where ideas, norms, discourses, subjectivity, human freedom, and individuals are at the core of the examination of social sciences, or (b) an objectivist, 'structuralist' paradigm, one that simplifies history, trying to discover the law of history and reducing agents to the status of receptacles.

Bernard Lahire and Luc Boltanski have extended and critically reformulated the process-relational approach of Pierre Bourdieu, which, in their view, is too holistic and structuralist. Instead, they sought to follow the pragmatist perspective of Dewey and, more recently, of Bruno Latour and John Law (Latour, 2007; Law, 1992). Lahire insisted on the necessity of a 'pluralization' of both the world and the individual in this relational approach, so as to avoid homogenizing the subject once again (Lahire, 1998; Lahire, 2012). Boltanski warned against the 'science claims' with which some sociologists want to position themselves, or against easily translating an analytically distinct position of reflexivity into a truth claim of superiority (Boltanski and Thévenot, 2000). This has certainly to be taken into account, but does not take away from the core idea that 'social facts are objects, which are also the object of knowledge within reality itself, because human beings make meaningful the world which makes them' (Wacquant quoted in Bourdieu and Wacquant, 1992b: 22). We therefore insist that it is the relation of distinction that constitutes the self by imposing a relative distance to some and proximity with others. This shared positioning applies, even though the will to differentiate is very strong. Relational moves of mimesis (meaning, imitation) are far from providing solidarity or representing a will to identify; instead they create exacerbated rivalry—a dimension that René Girard developed as a mirror image to the one of distinction by Bourdieu (Girard, 1977).[1] And even if new materialism (Bennett el al., 2010) has enriched sociology, the kind of reflexivity that allows us to understand the social as a strong heritage and not only a fragile present is absolutely central.

To summarize, an IPS approach pursues knowledge concerning the 'doing' of actors (and 'actants' as described in that literature), along with the relations of mimesis and distinction which position them in regard to others and which create relative distances. These relations and relative distances help us to understand what actors do and what they say they do. They guide the investigation and analysis of the habitus or dispositions that agents have incorporated and, by their relations of translation, forged with the world of objects surrounding them. This approach searches for 'field effects' generated by relations, effects which crystallize at certain moments. These moments also imply that the boundaries of fields are always changing, but are based on a powerful heritage of previous processes and trajectories of institutions that populate the social universes under investigation (Bigo and Madsen, 2011; Dezalay and Madsen, 2006; Madsen, 2011; Swartz, 2013).

4.3 The 'PARIS' Approach to Studying the Guilds of (In)security Information Management in Europe

Scholars undertaking research along this line must strive to understand the specific configuration of a social space whose boundaries seems to be set up formally by an institutional collaboration (in the EU, the so-called AFSJ area)— but also by the actual practices of actors and their chains of interdependence, including between them and between the institutions with which they interrelate. These chains help to map a sprawling, centripetal, and dynamic field that goes beyond the formal demarcations of institutional relations, and which links the behaviours of multiple actors (public and private). These actors (i) are strongly devoted to the question of (in)security at the European scale, (ii) strive to prioritize their importance vis-à-vis other actors by differently categorizing and prioritizing the lists of threats, risk, and even acts of fate with which they consider the world is confronted, and (iii) work routinely as professionals with different crafts in order to use techniques that they present as the best solutions to violence.

An analysis of security in this kind of relational approach deconstructs the meaning of (in)security in order to trace its origins, while at the same time avoiding the tendency to adopt a trans-historical meaning of security. Each historical case in which the label of 'security' is used can reveal, through careful analysis, the interests of the actors using it and the authority that these actors claim in order to draw their own limits between security and insecurity. But this reflexivity also needs to apply to the terminologies characterizing the 'method' of analysis. In this regard Pierre Bourdieu sometimes has not been so clear. Methodological thinking tools are neither neutral nor ahistorical. Field and habitus are flexible and orientable.

This is why, in a nutshell, this particular approach, which others have called the Paris school of critical security studies[2] should be properly named the PARIS (Political Anthropological Research of International Sociology) problematization. Adopting this version permits rethinking security and insecurity differently, namely as an (in)securitization process that generates a series of fields of practices of power both transnationally and nationally. The PARIS problematization examines, therefore, how multiple fields relate to security, and are configured by the confluence of broader historical trajectories linked to the development and definition of the state.

The international dimension of this political sociology also allows us to challenge the idea of the state as the sole container 'of the society and its rules' related to security. Even the sociology of Bourdieu has a tendency to reproduce this assumption. Instead we need to focus on the existence of transnational solidarities and struggles between groups and specific social universes that cross frontiers, be they state borders or identity borders. So, instead of focusing on norms, values, and/or interest to define security, or to embark on a purely linguistic and/or discursive approach of the symbolic power as some works inspired by Michel Foucault are doing, the PARIS approach requires a multi-faceted study of the practices of the professionals of (in)security in Europe. This broadly consists of investigating (a) who are the actors that participate routinely in practices of (in)securitization, (b) where they come from, especially in a context of intense privatization of some spheres of public activities, and (c) centrally, what do they do, how they are congregating around specific stakes, and what kind of use do they have regarding new technologies.

In short, the PARIS perspective obliges us to reconsider most of the premises of existing theories used to study internal security in the EU. It understands European internal security as a social space that can be mapped through an analysis of the 'sociogenesis', or social evolution and dynamics, of the competitions that have stabilized for a while as a specific social universe, or as a set of institutions under the juridical and political labels of the 'Area of Freedom, Security, and Justice'. One should remain mindful, however, that the competition and the interaction that occurred between different social universes at a national and/or transnational scale are always going beyond the visible institutional field of practices.

It is may be useful to consider the interconnections of the international political sociology perspective discussed herein with approaches based on securitization (see Balzacq in this volume). While both approaches analyse the practices of 'insecuritization', there are distinct differences. One main difference is that a political sociology approach emphasizes practices and a relational perspective. Accordingly, even if the process of securitization is of interest, it is certainly not a speech act, but the result of the struggles of a configuration of professionals in competition for the categorization of threats against the priorities and forms of the struggles against them. It is never one enunciator making a successful speech act in front of an audience, which can move a question outside normal politics by labelling it a security problem. The protagonist is never in a monopolistic position (as 'the' author), even when he is considered to be a 'leader' and to have the right to have the last word. Turning to the audience does not solve the problem of the priority given to the discourse over the non-discursive practices. Focusing on the speech act and its reception tends to bend the analysis not only towards speeches, but also towards important moments and to limited decision situations. It does not break with the idea of exceptionalism. On the contrary, speaking of security as exception is reproducing once again IR and political science discourses that suggest a radical difference between the inside as normal and the outside as exception. For the Copenhagen school, the speech act is in addition very often associated with a sovereign speech act by the professionals of politics. This approach neglects the ones who do not speak so much, but frame the questions by their routine works, that is, the different bureaucracies, industry, and security consumers. For a political sociology approach, namely the PARIS problematization described in this chapter, these agents frame, by their day-to-day work, what the boundaries between security, insecurity and fate are, and are therefore *the* central agents of a social space characterized by a discourse on collaboration between services involved in generating global (in)securities.

4.4 Representative Applications of an IPS Approach

By now one can point to a rich research literature using an IPS perspective, including works concerned with the place of clandestine antiterrorist practices in the making of European security collaboration and the role of Spanish security services therein (Guittet, 2004; Guittet, 2006); the actions of the G8 in defining the norms for collaboration in matters of terrorism and organized crime (Scherrer, 2009); the genealogy of the notion of terrorism and its actual practices with the Department of Homeland Security in the US and transatlantic collaboration (Bonditti, 2008; Bonditti, 2004; Bonditti, 2001); the resistance in everyday practices against the exceptionalism of George W. Bush's policies (Blanc, 2010); the involvement of military doctrines in antiterrorism and their involvement in internal security issues (Bigo et al., 2003; Olsson, 2009; Olsson, 2006); the discourse of freedom of movement and the governmentality of the EU's neighbours (Jeandesboz, 2011; Jeandesboz, 2007; Jeandesboz and Pallister-Wilkins, 2014); the practices of extending EU policies towards Central Asia and the reactions of these different universes (Martin-Mazé, 2013); the practices of visa policies and their technologies (Bigo and Guild, 2005; Infantino et al., 2013); the diplomatic practices of the EU and their relations with the professionals of internal security (Davidshofer, 2009); the development of private security industries (Hanon, 2004); the place of the gendarmeries in Europe and their activities abroad (Arcuddi, 2008); the role of bankers in the framing of global dangers (Amicelle, 2011; de Goede, 2012; Wesseling et al., 2012); the effects of the security services' practices in relation to youth radicalization (Bonelli and Ragazzi, 2014); the emergence of the terminology of societal security and the development of the practices that claim the necessity of resilient human beings (SOURCE, 2014).

More generally speaking, a series of key developments and major research projects gave rise to these rich and diverse insights. The scholar journal *Cultures et Conflits* that appeared at the beginning of 1989 (as a successor to *Etudes Polémologiques*) has been the bedrock of the creation of the Paris School–IPS research agenda after the Cold War. Contrary to the strategic narratives focusing mainly on NATO or traditional foreign affairs and defence, *Cultures et Conflits* insisted on the coherent logics of violence in the Middle East, Asia, Eastern Europe, and especially former Yugoslavia. Ethnographic dimensions and a focus on the practicing actors replaced theoretical IR debates typical in so many journals, leading to the insight that new enmities, especially from the South and under the label of 'terrorism', were constructed and used as a new system of justification for the actions of police and military actors post-Cold War. The police preoccupied itself with transnational political violence of different clandestine organizations, while the military argued that war is changing and became involved in a kind of 'detective work' against small and interconnected adversaries. The journal developed a critique of this functionalist view of security and instead advanced the research hypothesis of a continuum of insecurity merging national state security and individual safety in the name of a so-called confusion of war and crime (Bigo, 2001b; Bigo, 2008b; Bigo and Leveau, 1991; Favarel-Garri Gues, 2001; Friman, 2001; Galy, 2004; Gascon, 1990; Guittet et al., 2005; Mueller, 1995; Peries, 2001; Ravenel, 1991; Tsoukala, 2004). Some authors looked at the restructuration of military doctrines, others on the emergence of migrants as a security threat for different sectors, or on the role of police liaison officers exchanging information abroad, especially on the European level. Although including studies on different issues, the journal consistently showcased the social practices performed by practitioners and the role of intellectuals coming from different academic fields and their own roles, interests, and 'illusions' in contributing to the development of new narratives on new threats.

A series of research projects on the creation of compensatory measures linked to the freedom of movement inside the EU—including the then little-known Schengen agreements—as well as on the development of a discourse surrounding 'European internal security', revolving around terrorism and migration, also helped to generate fascinating, inductively derived insights. The change of configuration of the objective distance between the different players, such as police and military, and the blurring of the previously stark boundaries between an inside and an outside, a national and an international, created opportunities for regional organizations to enter the sphere of security matters and provided a space for the use and proliferation of policing techniques and counter-insurrection tactics.

In my own work, I analyse the socio-genesis of the formation of this (in)security process by analysing how, during the 1980s, cross-border groupings of self-declared 'antiterrorist experts' emerged to challenge the role of traditional police officers (e.g. criminal justice detectives, police in uniforms) for budgets, missions, crime-fighting technologies, and information technologies. The mapping of confidential meetings in the 1970s as well as the discovery of a series of 'clubs' set up between English-speaking countries, and then enlarged to continental Europe, was the first scholarly task required to understand the relations of all these 'policemen going abroad'—along with the intensity of their relations both at the personal level and at the institutional levels. The research investigated this group's success in establishing themselves at the core of public discourses, in gaining budgets, in promoting their agenda (an agenda which was increasingly detached from the so-called threat of euroterrorism, already in decline). The research approach asked: what were the conditions of their success? What about their truth claim concerning terrorist danger? On the surface they appeared rather marginal, and numbered very few. They were not especially good at mobilizing political entrepreneurs beyond a very narrow circle. They just had some connection with the anti-drug squads (as most of them were coming from these squads) or from serious crime investigation units. But they were interconnected and they had contacts abroad (Anderson et al., 1994; Bigo and Hermant, 1990).

In the 1990s, my research agenda continued to focus on the cohering narratives within these different clubs and groups of antiterrorism officials in their purported struggle against organized crime. In focus was the willingness of these groups to compensate for the freedom of movement of people in Europe by pushing 'internal security' as a rising concept, thus forging a semantic 'continuum' going beyond the antiterrorist connections with drugs, and even beyond the control of crime, to connect control of crime with control of borders and surveillance of populations who wanted to migrate or who had arrived recently. By looking at the missions of the 'European police liaison officers' and their central role in the creation of the Schengen agreements and specific instruments like the Schengen Information System, as well as the creation of the so-called third pillar of Justice and Home Affairs (JHA) and the creation of Europol, it became clear that more and more individuals and groups were attracted by this dimension of 'European internal security', even in countries where the local was stronger than the national (Netherlands, UK). A vision of these events in terms of epistemic communities or expertise is certainly interesting, but too narrow to understand what is at stake, because the politics of struggle are often ignored in such studies. Moreover, those approaches analyse the EU through its normative and juridical constitution instead of following a sociological, in-depth inquiry that charts relations and practices.

A central element in this orientation has been to see how the different agencies which did not initially play the Europeanization game were obliged domestically to enter into it, in order to stay 'competitive'. The research goal has been to understand how these agencies reframed their language concerning threats, and how they entered into and exploited the exchange of data and computer technologies in order not to be 'distantiated' by the other players. They feared the comparative advantage gained by those who first entered into this specific issue of internal security in the EU as well as at home. The question was to identify some core groups of agents whose interests seemed to favour 'collaboration against new threats that endanger the common internal security of the EU' as it was said at the time. What was the circulation between these specialized groups? Did they have hegemonic positions or were they marginal among the police in Europe (and in the US)? Did they share a common discourse for ideological reasons or for other reasons, thus blurring and making more complex the notion of 'right' versus 'left', or 'police' versus 'society'? To answer these questions we forged collectively the hypothesis of a making of a 'European reason of state' (Bigo et al., 2015) as the extension of the circuit of legitimization beyond the national state by this group of agents, or 'guilds' of professionals, who profit from transnationalization.

This approach also considered how a full reconfiguration of the status of citizens' security took place, whereby the deterrence argument was downgraded and prediction, preventive, and preparation arguments were upgraded—reinforced by the post-2001 logic that the question is not 'if' an attack will happen, but 'when'. The preventive argument united the proactive policing approach and some military strategists, the two blocks needing an increase of technologies of surveillance, and led further by new possibilities provided by computer technologies and the exchange of information. Further discussion emerged about the connections between this 'discourse formation' and the 'enunciators of these discourses'. Do we have to analyse them as a form of governmentality and/or as a field of (in)security managers in constitution? Was it an effect of intertextuality, or a global logic of surveillance and trace-ability with heterogeneous assemblages, or was it more related to a specific group of transnational actors, a transnational power elite emerging?

New research projects in this vein also allowed us to gain a better understanding of private actors—especially private security companies—and their connections with liaison officers of police and migration in Europe and in the US. This allows us to examine the relation between the EU and transatlantic field, for instance, not as two 'entities' but as one transnational field of power with overlapping boundaries of almost the same actors playing at different games and hybridizing them.[3] This approach examines the practices and relations of these groups or guilds led by a certain idea of 'craft' that links and divides simultaneously the professionals of (in)security according to rules of imitation and distinction (Bigo, 2013b). They are always multinational and sometimes multi-professional. Their scope varies depending on the degree of formalization they have and the operational powers they have in addition to the exchange of information. In most of the cases, their narrative is full of pride concerning their own nationalism and statehood. They insist, through their discourse, on the importance of sovereignty and on the necessity of strong decisions by the professionals of politics while complaining about the present politicians. They are not only public agents and bureaucrats. Private actors from security and surveillance industries, profiling software providers, insurance agents, and banking compliance officers intervene more and more in the construction of priorities and solutions in response to the threats and risks constructed as the most dangerous ones. They form a 'dual core'. To belong to these groups, and to play a role at the European scale, seems to require that one plays a part in the computerized network of information exchange and in the provision of arguments and instruments concerning the categorization of populations as risky or at risk.

To make sense in a synthetic way of all these different developments, our research has tried to present interactive maps of the internal security 'games' taking place across the EU, by highlighting the informal clubs of policing and intelligence (and their transatlantic networks), the more legal and formal agreements of the EU process of juridification of police practices, and the key role of information exchange between databases which generates lists of suspects (of terrorism, of serious crime, of potential migrants, of potential victims of disasters). This mapping technique provides a better sense of the socio-genesis of the internal security field and its transformations in terms of actors, of consistency, and moments of fluidity.[4]

4.5 Conclusions and Future Research Agendas

By way of summing up three decades of research regarding internal security in Europe, our findings provide solid ground upon which to contend that European internal security is too narrowly analysed if one begins with a legal or institutional approach. Such approaches typically take as a point of departure the Maastricht Treaty and then discuss how developments in the following years resembled a pendulum swinging between national sovereignty and a general move towards more community instruments. Yet police forces have cooperated across borders from their very creation (Deflem, 2002). In some ways, global policing existed before regional policing, so European collaboration is not a story of progress due to a lack of collaboration between national polices, but represents a change to it.

The core of this social universe—which in the late 1990s I called the 'field of professionals of internal security', and which now I now prefer to call the 'transnational field of computerized exchange of information in police matters and its European guilds'—is mainly composed of public bureaucracies related to policing and border management. Yet through its internal dynamics and a series of external events (the end of bipolarity, especially), other actors have entered the field to discuss and compete for the formation of an (in) security assemblage composed of the practices involved in antiterrorism and the fight against organized crime (as well as migration management). Coming from what was previously called 'external security', military intelligence specialists and foreign affairs/diplomatic personnel became involved in the internal security field and broadened the scope of the EU's JHA by embedding into it an 'external dimension' (cf. Bossong and Rhinard, Introduction in this volume). Private firms, to which activities became delegated or who are involved in the development of technologies and management of specific tasks, added to the mix. These centrifugal dynamics created an extension of the different professions and crafts involved in the competition for the symbolic power to determine what is (in)security in Europe. The networks of relations that built these chains of interdependence between the actors and institutions were deployed at a European scale, but also at the transatlantic and sometimes global level via international organizations (Interpol, UNODC, etc.), especially through exchange of information in databases and informal networks.

The competitors within this internal security universe are therefore closely connected transnationally: horizontally, beyond the EU, and vertically, by imposing their solutions locally. The relations between some of these key actors, such as internal security agencies, have a wide impact and change the boundaries of what is recognized as (in)security. So even if these networks may be considered very thin in terms of numbers of people, they are powerful in terms of framing what is security and insecurity. They exert this effect via the categories used for exchanging information, and they change previous national configurations by considering some local autonomous events as an example of a bigger picture, which forges a necessary link to the 'globalization of crime and terror'. The configuration of interdependence thus becomes more stable and durable, and, as a result, it is possible to speak about a field in a Bourdieusian sense: the effects of relations have impacts (or 'fields effects' in the terminology of Bourdieu) all along the chains of interdependence, beyond the direct relations of a single network of actors. So, even if the visibility of the field is sometimes limited (and although some observers have been keen to reduce it to a couple of EU agencies that are not clearly related to national activities, thus playing a specific politics of denial), the study of these actors' relations (formal, informal, and via exchange of information) for over thirty years shows that the scope of this field of practices strongly shapes our daily lives and extends beyond European discussions of security and the boundaries of the actors identified as Europeans.

But the creation of a new orthodoxy, which replaced the Cold War conception of security with a global scenario of uneven threats and catastrophes demanding societal resilience, is never consensual in its adoption, for there is a fierce competition between actors and over the change of boundaries of who can intervene in matters of security. The struggles between these actors are intense, but they share the idea that security is necessary and that security solutions can be implemented in order to eliminate insecurity—and without involving a political dialogue with the target designated as the origin of violence. This shared view has overcome the classic view of the Cold War distinction between war and crime, police and military. Others may try to combat these dynamics, mainly actors who come from other fields of practice (welfare, judges, doctors, churches) and who vigorously try to restrain any possibility of a dynamic extension of security (see Mitsilegas in this volume for a rule-of-law perspective). Nevertheless, this seemingly unbound and contested security reverts back to the core of the traditional institutions of security that are obliged to justify secrecy, use of force, and detention much more than before. So the struggles over which threats, risks, or vulnerabilities are to be prioritized has resulted in a more central role for both military (sig-int) and police (hum-int) intelligence as well as the development of massive technologies of surveillance and control involving exchange of information between security agencies and private contractors. In particular, these technologies (including biometrics, DNA, RFID) allow officials to trace and identify physical bodies together with the traces they leave in the numerical world.

In sum, an international political sociology approach, or more specifically the PARIS perspective introduced in this chapter, to studying EU internal security cooperation reveals essential insights into who, how, why, and to what affect a transnational field of experts in pursuing (in)security has emerged across political boundaries. This field has expanded over all the Western societies through its informal and institutional networking, and it is both public and private. Over time, the approach has turned to the study of the computerized exchange of information concerning police and intelligence, border management, and surveillance of minorities, and is connected with the technologies of everyday surveillance that target citizens in city areas and in banking activities, and sometimes are connected with remote military capacity of surveillance of large areas. They are the result and the driver of 'platforms' integrating systems within a system: information gathering, information retention, information filtering, data mining, elaboration of algorithms, profiling by software and expert groups, intelligence evaluation, and the identification of population patterns reduced to very small groups through multi-criteria refined searches. These practices allow for the identification of human behaviour patterns considered 'dangerous' or simply unwanted in the future, for the simulation and anticipation of worst-case scenarios to avoid, for the elaboration of watch lists and the exchange of categories of unwanted population to put under in-depth surveillance, and for the construction of categories of normalized 'personas' under light surveillance (not to mention for the assessment of 'truth' concerning threats, catastrophes, and risks and priorities of struggles). This rich vein of inquiry deserves further mining to reveal the full extent of relational security dynamics and (in)securitization flowing from European security practices.

Notes

1. As René Girard (1977) pointed out, mimesis is founded on a game of reciprocal accusation where everyone thinks of themselves as the victim of the other, and therefore justified in their combat. The law of retaliation is the motor of vengeance-violence, which can end only with the resolution of the crisis through the creation of scapegoats, i.e. victims different from those who perpetrated the violence but who are—or spend time—in their proximity.
2. The idea of a Paris school of thought, opposed to Copenhagen and Aberystwyth, has been popularized, but makes no sense and induces culturalism. The journal *Cultures et Conflits* has been nevertheless one of the major place of debates around the sociology of conflicts and security and had gathered people around the francophone world, living in Paris, but also London, Amsterdam, Brussels, or Canada and the US because they were sharing a political and anthropological approach.
3. A very detailed bibliography and a series of documents as the visualization results coming from EU-funded projects which were obtained during the last ten years on this topic: ELISE- CHALLENGE-INEX- SAPIENT-SOURCE are available via the website http://libertysecurity.org (Accessed: 27 April 2016) on archive at the CERI or in my own website www.didierbigo.com (Accessed: 27 April 2016).
4. Médéric Martin Maze is organizing a new visualization of the different results obtained until now. This will be available at the SOURCE website: http://www.societalsecurity.net/ (Accessed: 27 April 2016).

References

Adler-Nissen, R. (2012) *Bourdieu in International Relations: Rethinking Key Concepts in IR*. Routledge.

Albert, M., Jacobson, D. and Lapid, Y. (2001) *Identities, Borders, Orders: Rethinking International Relations Theory*. Borderlines, V. 18. Minneapolis, MN and London: University of Minnesota Press.

Amicelle, A. (2011) 'The Great (Data) Bank Robbery: Terrorist Finance Tracking Program and the "Swift Affair"'. *CERI Research Questions*.

Anderson, M., den Boer, M., and European Consortium for Political Research (1994) *Policing across National Boundaries*. London and New York: Pinter Publishers.

Arcuddi, G. (2008) 'Sécurité et défense, forces de police et forces armées: où sont les frontières?' PhD dissertation, IHEI Geneva.

Balzacq, T., Basaran, T., Bigo, D., Guittet, E.-P., and Olsson, C. (2010) 'Security Practices', in Denemark, R. A. (ed.) *The International Studies Encyclopedia*, available at: http://www.isacompendium.com/subscriber/tocnode?id=g9781444336597_chunk_ g978144443659718_ss1-2 (Accessed: 3 May 2016).

Bauman, Z., Bigo, D., Esteves, P., Guild, E., Jabri, V., Lyon, D., and Walker, R. B. J. (2014) 'After Snowden: Rethinking the Impact of Surveillance', *International Political Sociology*, 8, pp. 121–44.

Bennett, J., et al. (2010) *New Materialisms: Ontology, Agency, and Politics*. Durham, NC: Duke University Press.

Bigo, D. (1994) 'The European Internal Security Field: Stakes and Rivalries in a Newly Developing Area of Police Intervention', in Anderson, M. and den Boer, M. (eds) *Policing across National Boundaries*. London: Pinter, pp. 161–73.

Bigo, D. (2001a) 'Internal and External Security(ies): The Möbius Ribbon', in Albert, M., Jacobson, D., and Lapid, Y. (eds) *Identities, Borders, Orders*. Minneapolis: University of Minnesota Press, pp. 91–116.

Bigo, D. (2001b) 'La voie militaire de la "guerre au terrorisme" et ses enjeux', *Cultures & Conflits*, 44, pp. 5–18.

Bigo, D. (2006) *Global (in)Security: The Field of the Professionals of Unease Management and the Ban-Opticon*. Traces: A Multilingual Series of Cultural Theory: Translation, Philosophy and Colonial Difference. Hong Kong: University of Hong Kong Press.

Bigo, D. (2008a) 'Globalized (In)Security: The Field and the Banopticon', in Bigo, D. and Tsoukala, A. (eds) *Terror, Insecurity and Liberty: Illiberal Practices of Liberal Regimes after 9/11*. London: Routledge, pp. 10–48.

Bigo, D. (2008b) 'The Emergence of a Consensus: Global Terrorism, Global Insecurity, and Global Security', in d'Appollonia, A. C. and Reich, S. (eds) *Immigration, Integration, and Security: America and Europe in Comparative Perspective*. Pittsburgh, PA: University of Pittsburgh Press, pp. 67–94.

Bigo, D. (2011) 'Pierre Bourdieu and International Relations: Power of Practices, Practices of Power', *International Political Sociology* 5, pp. 225–58.

Bigo, D. (2013a) 'Borders, Mobility and Security', in Kauppi, N. (ed.) *A Political Sociology of Transnational Europe*. Colchester: ECPR studies, p. 282.

Bigo, D. (2013b) 'The Transnational Field of Computerised Exchange of Information in Police Matters and Its European Guilds', in Kauppi, N. and Madsen, M. (eds) *Transnational Power Elites: The New Professionals of Governance, Law and Security*. Abindon: Routledge, pp. 155–82.

Bigo, D. (2014) 'War and Crime, Military and Police', in Bell, C., Bachmann, J., and Holmqvist, C. (eds) *War, Police and Assemblages of Intervention*. London: Routledge.

Bigo, D., Carrera, S., Guild, E., and Walker, R. (2010) *Europe's 21st Century Challenge: Delivering Liberty and Security*. Farnham: Ashgate.

Bigo, D., Carrera, S., Hernanz, N., and Scherrer, A. (2015) 'National Security and Secret Evidence in Legislation and before the Courts: Exploring the Challenges', in *CEPS Studies in Liberty and Security*, No. 78/January.

Bigo, D. and Guild, E. (2005) 'Policing at a Distance: Shengen Visas Policies', in Bigo, D. and Guild, E. (eds) *Controlling Frontiers: Free Movement into and within Europe.* Farnham: Ashgate, pp. 233–64.

Bigo, D., and Hermant, D. (1990) 'Terrorisme et antiterrorisme en France', *Les cahiers de la sécurité intérieure*, 1, pp. 113–48.

Bigo, D. and Leveau, R. (1991) *L'europe de la Sécurité Intérieure.* Paris: Institut des Hautes Etudes de Sécurité Intérieure.

Bigo, D. and Madsen, M. R. (2011) 'Bourdieu and International Relations', *International Political Sociology*, 5(special issue), pp. 219–347.

Bigo, D., Olsson, C., Chapleau, P., et al. (2003) 'Les entreprises de coercition para-privées, de nouveaux mercenaires?' *Cultures & Conflits*, 52, pp. 5–10.

Bigo, D. and Walker, R. B. J. (2007) 'International, Political, Sociology', *International Political Sociology*, 1(1), pp. 1–5.

Blanc, F. (2010) *Dissent after 9/11: The Mobilization of Librarians, the Aclu, City Councils and Lawyers.* Evanston, IL: Sciences-Po Paris and Northwestern University.

Boltanski, L. (2009) *De la critique: Précis de sociologie de l'émancipation.* Paris: Éditions Gallimard.

Boltanski, L. and Thévenot, L. (2000) 'The Reality of Moral Expectations: A Sociology of Situated Judgement', *Philosophical Explorations*, 3, pp. 208–31.

Bonditti, P. (2008) 'Homeland Security through Traceability', in Cavelty, M. D. and Kristensen, K. S. (eds) *Securing the Homeland: Critical Infrastructure, Risk and (In)Security.* Abingdon: Routledge, pp. 130–40.

Bonditti, P. (2001) 'The Organization of the Anti-Terrorist Fight in the United States', *Cultures et Conflits*, 44, pp. 65–76.

Bonditti, P. (2004) 'From Territorial Space to Networks: A Foucaldian Approach to the Implementation of Biometry', *Alternatives*, 29(4), pp. 465–82.

Bonelli, L. and Ragazzi, F. (2014) 'Low-Tech Security: Files, Notes, and Memos as Technologies of Anticipation', *Security Dialogue*, 45, 476–93.

Bourdieu, P. (1985) 'The Genesis of the Concepts of Habitus and Field', *Sociocriticism*, 2, pp. 11–24.

Bourdieu, P. (1998) *Practical Reason: On the Theory of Action.* Stanford, CA: Stanford University Press.

Bourdieu, P. (2004) 'From the King's House to the Reason of State: A Model of the Genesis of the Bureaucratic Field', *Constellations*, 11, pp. 16–36.

Bourdieu, P. and Wacquant, L. (1992b) *An Invitation to Reflexive Sociology.* London: University of Chicago Press.

Davidshofer, S. (2009) 'La gestion de crise européenne ou quand l'Europe rencontre la sécurité: modalités pratiques et symboliques d'une autonomisation', PhD dissertation, Paris, Institut d'études politiques.

de Goede, M. (2012) 'The Swift Affair and the Global Politics of European Security', *Journal of Common Market Studies*, 50, pp. 214–30.

Deflem, M. (2002) *Policing World Society: Historical Foundations of International Police Cooperation.* Oxford: Oxford University Press.

Dezalay, Y. and Madsen, M. R. (2006) 'La construction européenne au carrefour du national et de l'international', in Cohen, A., Lacroix, B., and Riutort, P. (eds) *Les formes de l'activité politique: Élements d'analyse sociologique XVIIIe–XXe siècle*. Paris: Presses Universitaires de France.

Favarel-Garrigues, G. (2001) 'Concurrence et confusion des discours sur le crime organisé en Russie', *Cultures & Conflits*, 42, pp. 9–46.

Foucault, M. (1970) *The Order of Things: An Archaeology of the Human Sciences*. London: Tavistock Publications.

Friman, R. (2001) 'Prise au piège de la folie? Le pouvoir étatique et le crime organisé transnational dans l'œuvre de Susan Strange', *Cultures & Conflits*, 42, pp. 139–60.

Gallie, W. B. (1956) 'Essentially Contested Concepts', *Proceedings of the Aristotelian Society*, 56, pp. 167–98.

Galy, M. (2004) 'De la guerre nomade: Sept approches du conflit autour de la Côte d'Ivoire. *Cultures & Conflits*, 55, pp. 163–96.

Gascon, A. (1990) 'La guerre comme rite géographique', *Cultures & Conflits*, 1, pp. 69–84.

Girard, R. (1977) *Violence and the Sacred*. Baltimore: Johns Hopkins University Press.

Gros, F. (2013) *Le principe sécurité*. Paris: Gallimard.

Guittet, E. (2006) ' "Ne pas leur faire confiance serait leur faire offense": Antiterrorisme, solidarité démocratique et identité politique', *Cultures & Conflits*, 61, pp. 51–76.

Guittet, E. P. (2004) 'European Political Identity and Democratic Solidarity after 9/11: The Spanish Case', *Alternatives: Global, Local, Political*, 29, pp. 441–65.

Guittet, E.-P., Perier, M., Bigo, D., Bonelli, L., and Collectif (2005) *Suspicion et Exception*. Paris: Éditions L'Harmattan.

Hanon, J.-P. (2004) 'Militaires et lutte antiterroriste', *Cultures & Conflits*, 56, pp. 121–40.

Infantino, F. (2013) 'Bordering at the Window: The Allocation of Schengen Visas at the Italian Embassy and Consulate in Morocco', in Carrera, S., Guild, E., and Bigo, D. (eds) *Foreigners, Refugees or Minorities? Rethinking People in the Context of Border Controls and Visas*. Abingdon: Routledge, pp. 227–40.

Jeandesboz, J. (2007) 'Labelling the "Neighbourhood": Towards a Genesis of the European Neighbourhood Policy', *Journal of International Relations and Development*, 10, pp. 387–416.

Jeandesboz, J. (2011) 'Beyond the Tartar Steppe: Eurosur and the Ethics of European Border Control Practices', in Burgess, J. P. and Gutwirth, S. (eds) *Europe under Threat? Security, Migration and Integration*. Brussels: VUB Press, pp. 111–31.

Jeandesboz, J. and Pallister-Wilkins, P. (2014) 'Crisis, Enforcement and Control at the EU Borders', in Lindley, A. (ed.) *Crisis and Migration: Critical Perspectives*. Abingdon: Routledge, pp. 115–35.

Lahire, B. (1998) *L'homme pluriel*. Paris: Nathan.

Lahire, B. (2012) *Monde pluriel: Penser l'unité des sciences sociales*. Paris: Seuil.

Latour, B. (2007) *Reassembling the Social: An Introduction to Actor-Network-Theory*. Oxford: Oxford University Press.

Law, J. (1992) 'Notes on the Theory of the Actor-Network: Ordering, Strategy, and Heterogeneity', *Systems Practice*, 5, pp. 379–93.

Madsen, M. R. (2011) 'Reflexivity and the Construction of the International Object: The Case of Human Rights', *International Political Sociology*, 5, pp. 259–75.

Martin-Mazé, M. (2013) *The International Government of Central Asian Borders*. Paris: Sciences-Po.

Mueller, J. (1995) 'Le scénario catastrophe: Désordre après la guerre froide', *Cultures & Conflits*, 20, pp. 49–72.

Olsson, C. (2006) 'Military Intervention and the Concept of the Political', in Bigo, D. and Tsoukala, A. (eds) *Illiberal Practices in Liberal Regimes*. Paris: Éditions L'Harmattan, pp. 167–203.

Olsson, C. (2009) 'Conquérir "les coeurs et les esprits"? Usages et enjeux de légitimation locale de la force dans les missions de pacification extérieures (Bosnie, Kosovo, Afghanistan, Irak: 1996–2006)', PhD dissertation, Paris, Institut d'études politiques.

Peries, G. (2001) 'Du corps au cancer: La construction métaphorique de l'énnemi intérieu dans le discours militaire pendant la guerre froide', *Cultures & Conflits*, 43, pp. 91–125.

Ravenel, B. (1991) 'Guerres du tiers monde, guerre au tiers monde', *Cultures & Conflits*, 2, pp. 19–31.

Rescher, N. (1996) *Process Metaphysics: An Introduction to Process Philosophy*. New York: SUNY Press.

Scherrer, A. (2009) *G8 against Transnational Organized Crime*. Farnham: Ashgate.

SOURCE (2014) 'D3.1 Methodology Workshop and Review of Available Empirical Sources', http://societalsecurity.net/publication/methodology-workshop-and-review-available-empirical-sources (Accessed: 24 May 2016).

Swartz, D. (1997) *Culture and Power: The Sociology of Pierre Bourdieu*. Chicago: University of Chicago Press.

Swartz, D. L. (2013) *Symbolic Power, Politics, and Intellectuals: The Political Sociology of Pierre Bourdieu*. Chicago, IL: University of Chicago Press.

Tsoukala, A. (2004) 'La lutte contre le crime organisé en Sicile: L'opération militaire vespri siciliani', *Cultures & Conflits*, 56, pp. 51–61.

Wesseling, M., de Goede, M., and Amoore, L. (2012) 'Data Wars beyond Surveillance: Opening the Black Box of Swift', *Journal of Cultural Economy*, 5, pp. 49–66.

Williams, P. D. (2008) *Security Studies: An Introduction*. Abingdon: Routledge.

5

Governance and EU Internal Security Cooperation

Raphael Bossong and Sandra Lavenex

5.1 Introduction

Governance perspectives centre on two core questions. Firstly, they study the increasingly complex settings within which a growing range of political actors interact and shape resulting policies. Secondly, the governance approach addresses the transformation of governing or exercise of public authority itself and its implications for our understanding of statehood. From a disciplinary perspective, governance analyses in European studies and International Relations (IR) trace policy networks and coordination processes in multilevel political systems with flexible boundaries, all of which raise important questions concerning policy effectiveness and legitimacy. A further specialized literature on security governance which spans the literature on IR, security or police studies, risk sociology, and criminology sharpens the question of the role of public actors and normative criteria in the area of security. One of the most famous definitions by Max Weber defines the modern state as the 'human community that successfully claims the *monopoly of the legitimate use of physical force* within a given territory' (Weber, 1910/ 1994). Even though EU member states formally retain the competence for the provision of operational internal security, security governance can thus be read as a crucial factor in the transformation of 'core state powers' (Genschel and Jachtenfuchs, 2013) under conditions of globalization and European integration.

Accordingly, this chapter seeks to tease out some foundational implications of a governance approach to EU internal security cooperation, while also recognizing that much governance research is primarily interested in empirical analyses. We therefore first outline different theoretical origins and perspectives on governance, which need to be born in mind before approaching any field of study. Against that backdrop, the second part of the chapter reviews studies on EU internal security cooperation which focus on the first core question of governance approaches: the interplay between institutional governance structures and resulting policies. These studies frequently take their point of departure in the notion of 'intensive transgovernmentalism' as a particular type of governance (Wallace, 2000). Borrowed from International Relations, this concept highlights the role of cross-border networks composed of lower-level officials in transnational cooperation, and has since been applied across a range of EU policy fields to capture governance dynamics that fall between the classic contrast between intergovernmental and supranational decision-making. In the case of EU internal security governance, intensive transgovernmentalism further helps to conceptualize the geographically and operationally varied patterns of cooperation as well as observed imbalances in policy outcomes. Finally, transgovernmental governance is pertinent for the EU's external relations with third countries that increasingly revolve around internal security concerns. Therefore, the governance mode of intensive transgovernmentalism remains a fruitful perspective even after the Lisbon Treaty, which, formally speaking, shifted EU decision-making on internal security to a more supranational regime.

We then turn to studies of EU internal security which exemplify the second core concern of a governance approach: the links between the security governance constellation in EU internal security and its effect on the exercise of authority. This literature accentuates the polycentric and increasingly complex nature of many contemporary security policies at all levels of governance, which severely challenges the privileged role of public authorities in security affairs. In the case of EU internal security, this trend is particularly evident in technical fields such as critical infrastructure protection or cybersecurity, but also corresponds to the widely espoused preference for 'comprehensive' and preventive approaches across the EU's expanding security agenda. In conclusion, we explore connections with other approaches to studying EU internal security cooperation discussed in this book, and underline how governance helps to expand our view on the range of topics and geographical scope that need to be studied.

5.2 Origins and Orientations

The concept of governance has seen a remarkable rise in use over the last two decades and has generated a vast literature across the social sciences (Benz et al., 2008; Bevir, 2011; Chhotray and Stoker, 2009).[1] From the perspective of political science and EU studies, which are most pertinent to this chapter, its main origins lie in the fields of IR and comparative politics. In IR, the term governance was introduced to conceptualize the emergence of political order at the international level in the absence of a coherent global regime or world government (Rosenau and Czempiel, 1992). In comparative politics the term governance is defined by its opposition to the notion of 'government' and denotes a transformation from interventionist to cooperative state–society relations (Jachtenfuchs, 2001). The following sketches out alternative conceptualizations of governance that stem from these transformations in the exercise of public authority within and beyond states.

5.2.1 *Wide or Narrow Conceptions of Governance*

At its most fundamental, the concept of governance is typically introduced in contrast to two classic ideal types of social coordination, namely hierarchies and markets (Scharpf, 1997a). *Hierarchy* can be understood as a regularized relationship of domination and which corresponds to a form of steering through formal and precise rules that are legally binding and enforceable upon actors. In the EU, the traditional Community Method approximates this ideal type (Börzel, 2010). Here supranational institutions are involved in the generation of law by majority decision-making, while the EU's lack of a monopoly on the legitimate use of force is compensated for by the legal review and sanctioning power of the European Court of Justice.

In an ideal-typical *market*, in contrast, outcomes are the result of competition between formally autonomous actors. In the EU, the principle of mutual recognition can be associated with such coordination by competition, as it revolves around the deconstruction of legal and regulatory barriers to decentralized exchanges across national borders. As is well known, this principle has been crucial to the formation of the single market and the desired free movement of goods, people, services, and capital across the EU. But as will be returned to below, mutual recognition also came to underpin many aspects of Justice and Home Affairs cooperation (Lavenex, 2007; Schmidt and Sievers, 2015) and represents a deliberate political choice for negative integration through liberalization, rather than an acceptance of the automatic spillover effects wrought by personal mobility opportunities in the Schengen zone.

Finally, a governance or *network* constellation delineates an intermediate position that, in contrast to hierarchy, is characterized by more egalitarian or voluntary relations and, in contrast to markets, by more rule-bound or structured coordination (Lavenex, 2004: 682). Networks do not preclude the possibility of power asymmetries as well as internal competition, but imply that participating actors have more equal rights and are interdependent in the pursuit of their aims (Börzel, 2008: 64). Thus, networks usually produce less constraining policy instruments which are based on mutual agreement, and often prescribe procedural modes of interaction rather than final policy solutions. In EU policymaking, this is typically associated with so-called new modes of governance, such as the Open Method of Coordination. These modes of governance are particularly prominent in areas where there is a lack of formal EU competences, but where actors perceive the need for cooperative coordination, such as social or educational policy.[2]

One may assume that governance studies exclusively focus on such network interactions that fall between market-based competition and hierarchical policymaking, since these opposite poles are associated with contrasting models of social coordination. However, when turning to more empirical analyses, scholars are divided between a wide and a narrow operationalization of governance (Mayntz, 2004; Treib et al., 2007). A wide approach would cover almost all forms of purposeful social and political coordination, including hierarchical governing processes. In particular, governance analyses often refer to the shadow of hierarchy (Héritier and Lehmkuhl, 2008; Börzel, 2010), which denotes the idea that seemingly voluntary coordination relies on the potential of hierarchical interventions as a background threat to actors. Moreover, applied research tends to show that important public goods—i.e. goods that are unlikely to be provided by decentralized markets alone—such as environmental protection, monetary stability, and even public security— are generated in complex governance processes that mix hierarchical, coordinating, and competitive elements (Barrett, 2007; Bossong and Rhinard, 2014; Holzinger, 2008; Jakobi, 2013).

Consequently, 'governance' can be framed as the *totality* of efforts for the production of public goods at various levels of social and political organization, spanning from local to European and global governance—as encapsulated in the notion of multilevel governance (Stephenson, 2013)—and which includes private market or civil society actors to varying degrees (Risse, 2013). It thus denotes any institutionalized or rule-bound forms of coordinated action that aim at the production of collectively binding agreements (Mayntz, 2004; Scharpf, 2000). This comprehensive perspective, which includes hierarchy and market mechanisms, explains why scholars have become concerned with classifying a broad range of governances styles (Christiansen and Neuhold, 2012; Torfing and Sørensen, 2014; Treib et al., 2007), which may even be compared at a further abstract level of 'metagoverance' (Jessop, 2011).

This wide understanding of governance is, however, not undisputed. Other scholars have advised a return to a narrow definition of governance in order to preserve the analytical essence of the term. Accordingly, this would exclude hierarchical (even if shadowy) oversight or belief in self-stabilizing market dynamics (Grande, 2012). In this understanding, governance presents a more radical alternative to coordination that underlines the complexity of contemporary policymaking and the uncontrollable results of interdependence.[3] Even if such an understanding of governance processes can include governmental actors, they lose their privileged status or ability to exercise control (or steering).

5.2.2 Critical or Problem-solving Conceptions of Governance

Another distinction present within governance approaches is between problem-solving and critical perspectives. As a problem-solving instrument, governance can be seen to mirror the advantages of the market—namely rich information processing, flexibility, resistance to power concentration, and high productivity—while simultaneously managing negative externalities and stimulating horizontal negotiations between all affected stakeholders. Even if not all advantages may be realized, governance is, thus, seen as the best available approach to address problems that transcend boundaries between policy areas or polities. From a critical perspective, however, the increased complexity of governance processes threatens to undercut social and political public values, such as the allocation of responsibility for collective outcomes or general accountability of policymakers (Curtin et al., 2010; Mayntz, 2010; Steffek, 2010). In this vein, the discursive use of the term governance has been identified as neoliberal practice (van Apeldoorn et al., 2009). Governance may create the image of more democratic, non-hierarchical interactions based on argumentation, while, in practice, it shows little capacity to resist or subvert existing power structures and inequalities (Fawcett and Marsh, 2014; Heinelt, 2010). Finally, governance processes often fall short of the required degree of regulation and have very limited redistributive capacity as typically expected in traditional European welfare states (Scharpf, 1997a).

When considering all options, i.e. narrow and wide, and problem-solving versus critical understandings of governance, it becomes clear why governance research repeatedly faces the charge that it lacks a theoretical core (van Kersbergen and van Waarden, 2004; Grande, 2012). This critique seems unfair when one considers the overall importance of governance research to contemporary conceptions of statehood and coordination under conditions of trans-nationalization and social or political differentiation. However, it is true that many governance studies launch into empirical analyses without positioning themselves on a solid theoretical plane. This is not to say that every contribution has to rehearse the same fundamental questions before tackling any particular topic of interest. Yet analysts should be aware of how their empirical research may fall under different governance perspectives, and what alternative angles may be possible. Reflexivity is even more necessary, since the legitimate breadth and diversity of governance research loosely interacts with an equally broad menu of methodologies or social science paradigms. For instance, while rational choice analyses may be associated with a problem-solving approach, some of the most acerbic critics of the legitimacy and effectiveness of contemporary European governance have emerged from this line of thinking (Scharpf, 1999). Conversely, post-structuralists or constructivists have not only linked governance to critiques of contemporary neo-liberalism—or 'governmentality'—(van Apeldoorn et al., 2009), but also have sought the potential for deliberation and more radical forms of democratic participation in governance networks (Erman, 2013).

In sum, governance represents a truly broad church within the social and political sciences. This requires a more reflective stance than may be readily evident in any particular applied field of research. The fact that policymakers and international organizations have also come to use governance as a legitimating concept, as encapsulated in the label of good governance, underlines this need. In the area of (internal) security, it is of particular importance to be clear about the scope and normative implications of different takes on governance.

5.3 Governance of EU Internal Security

The wider wave of governance research in EU studies (Kohler-Koch and Rittberger, 2006) brought a particular angle to the study of internal security cooperation, namely the categorization and exploration of different policy-making processes in the EU's multilevel system which do not correspond to the traditional Community Method of integration (Héritier, 2002; Tömmel, 2008). This helped to overcome long-standing theoretical debates on EU integration, eternally torn as they are between supranational drivers and countervailing national political control. A governance focus stimulated more comparative research on varying forms of hierarchical and voluntary cooperation across different political levels.

Thus, the EU's nascent internal security policy—which, in the early years, was generally labelled as Justice and Home Affairs (JHA) cooperation or the 'third pillar' of the EU—came to stand for the governance mode of intensive transgovernmentalism. This term captured policymaking that rests 'mainly on interaction between the relevant national policy-makers, and with relatively little involvement by the EU institutions' (Wallace, 2000: 33). On the one hand, the limited role of supranational institutions is a natural assumption in security cooperation due to the sovereignty concerns of states. On the other hand, *transgovernmentalism*—as opposed to classic intergovernmentalism and its purported dominance in areas of high politics—underlines the activities of governmental actors below the level of heads of state and government. Wallace thus fruitfully reconnected EU studies with IR debates on the rise of complex interdependence (Keohane and Nye, 1974; Slaughter, 2004). In this perspective, lower officials act with a certain degree of autonomy from chief executives and develop their own policy agenda. Many impulses for increasing international cooperation therefore stem from transgovernmental networks of professionals and officials, which had already formed in the supposedly state-centric environment of the Cold War, rather than from formal international organizations (supranational institutions in the EU) or governmental leaders.

The added qualifier 'intensive' transgovernmentalism obviously denotes the relative difference of interactions among European states versus the global level.[4] Other characteristics sharpen the difference between intensive transgovernmentalism and other modes of EU governance. The main one is the role of horizontal coordination among national actors based on the mutual recognition of national rules and laws, in contrast to vertical integration based on legal harmonization and the replacement of domestic through common supranational policies (Lavenex, 2009). This goes hand in hand with the low profile of supranational institutions for decision-making and legal oversight. To illustrate, the recent development of European migration policy, as well as the current structure of Council working groups, reflects this transgovernmental approach. Historically, JHA cooperation has emerged from networks composed of national home affairs officials and high-placed security professionals (Benyon, 1994), such as the so-called TREVI group. Notwithstanding gradual communitarization, such transgovernmental networks persist both formally and informally. An example of a formalized transgovernmental forum is the so-called SCIFA committee, composed of senior national officials, that provides an added level of cooperation beyond the diplomatic coordination of COREPER for decision-making level at the Council of Ministers. Informally, transgovernmental networks continue to foster coordination outside EU structures such as the G6, a grouping of home affairs officials from the six biggest EU member states (Lavenex, 2014).

A second characteristic of transgovernmentalism in the EU context is the emphasis on operational and pragmatic modes of cooperation, which often take the form of non-binding agreements and recommendations. Beyond processes of information exchange and mutual learning, as would be the central objective in the so-called Open Method of Coordination, transgovernmental networks can also take on more direct tasks and responsibilities (Slaughter, 2004) that support the implementation of seemingly soft governance instruments. An example in the field of EU Internal Security would be the range of national contact points or liaison officers that are tasked to support transnational crime-fighting or crisis management, even in the absence of an explicit EU legal mandate (Block, 2010). A final point where intensive transgovernmentalism differs from other EU modes of governance, but where it reconnects with its roots in International Relations, is in its openness to geographically and functionally flexible integration. This is evidenced most clearly by the Schengen regime that is characterized by complex national opt-outs as well as the inclusion or association of non-EU members.[5] Moreover, the externalization of EU migration and border security to the European neighbourhood is driven by transgovernmental networks (Lavenex, 2006), as discussed further in section 5.4.2.

While knowledge of the legacies of intensive transgovernmentalism still constitutes the entry point for many students interested in EU internal security cooperation, contemporary studies of this field need to address two questions: What are the normative and practical effects of this mode of governance, both within and beyond the EU? And how far does the policy mode of intensive transgovernmentalism remain relevant when contrasted with the more mature and legally formalized framework for EU internal security policymaking after Lisbon?

5.4 Assessing the Effects of Intensive Transgovernmentalism

Governance approaches assume that the modes of governance and the substance of ensuing policies are interrelated. This section examines studies focused on the main effects of intensive transgovernmentalism, including its negative integration bias and its tendency to expand beyond EU borders.

5.4.1 Negative Integration

In general, EU studies have argued that softer governance modes tend towards a negative integration bias. This mainly manifests itself in liberalizing policies and the aforementioned principle of mutual recognition that seeks to ensure the compatibility, but not harmonization, of national standards. The contrasting notion of positive integration denotes the replacement of domestic policies by common European positions (Scharpf, 1997b). This is clearly a more demanding form of EU policymaking that requires member states to relinquish domestic rules in favour of a common European one. At the same time, positive integration, or harmonization on the basis of a common European rule, can also be seen as a check against downward pressures on regulatory standards.

Wagner and Lavenex (2007) applied this argument to EU JHA cooperation and showed how the decision-making and oversight powers of the EU before the adoption of the Lisbon Treaty privileged a form of deregulation and mutual recognition for enhancing cross-border cooperation between security actors that weakened the applicability of domestic legal and human rights safeguards to the benefit of security considerations. A salient example is the Dublin system for the allocation of the responsibility for examining asylum claims. While generating a need for the development of common minimum standards in asylum procedures, the system allowed traditional asylum-receiving countries in the EU to deflect part of their legal responsibilities for asylum seekers towards other member states which may not provide for the same level of legal (yet alone social and economic) protection (Lavenex, 2001). Another critical area is the introduction of the principle of mutual recognition in criminal law, as exemplified by the European Arrest Warrant, which limited the reach of domestic legal safeguards regarding procedural or substantive rights of the accused (Lavenex and Wagner, 2007; Lavenex, 2008; Schmidt and Sievers, 2015). While this bias against positive integration and common standard setting also reflected the lack of political will on the part of the member states to defer more authority to EU institutions in these sensitive fields, they have been facilitated by the privileged role and priorities of national home affairs officials, border guards, and police forces that constitute most transgovernmental networks. These actors are traditionally more concerned with the safeguarding of internal security than with human or civil rights.

The Treaty of Lisbon strengthened supranational actors and has, at the time of writing, led to more legal harmonization based on the ordinary legislative procedure. For instance, one could point to the adoption of several EU direct-ives that started to redress the previous imbalance with regards to procedural rights in criminal justice proceedings (Anagnostopoulos, 2014)—even though the practical implementation of provisions across all member states is likely to be a long, drawn-out process (Wade, 2015). Similar cautious progress on positive standard-setting can be found in the area of EU migration and asylum policy (Kaunert and Léonard, 2012). Nevertheless, a wider systematic and comparative analysis of policy changes from 2010 to 2014 revealed that the core substance of EU policies has hitherto remained very much the same (Trauner and Ripoll Servent, 2015). In the field of asylum, the persist-ence of negative integration over positive standard-setting is evidenced by obvious political resistance to deeply reform or abolish the Dublin system, even if its practical operation has been largely suspended during the current migration crisis.

A further contemporary driver for transgovernmental forms of cooperation lies in the operational aspect of EU internal security. The Lisbon Treaty did not extend executive responsibility for internal security to the EU (Art. 4(2) TEU), but rather added the clarification that member states are in fact free to define any form of cooperation between themselves for 'safeguarding national secur-ity' (Art. 73 TFEU). This provides a legal basis for the preservation, and even further stimulation, of transgovernmental networks in operational and sensitive fields of internal security, such as in the fight against terrorism (Bures, 2012). It also chimes with the creation of the—essentially transgovernmental—Internal Security Committee (COSI, Art. 71 TFEU) that unites high-level national representatives to improve the operational internal security cooperation in Europe, rather than to support EU law-making in this field.

The persistence of transgovernmental approaches to executive-level cooperation is reflected in the growth of EU agencies dealing with internal security and immigration such as Europol, Frontex, Eurojust or the EU asylum office EASO. For instance, in the field of police cooperation, Europol is both an EU agency and a platform for national administrative networks via the so-called national liaison bureaus (Hillebrand, 2012). In the field of asylum, EASO promotes the exchange of information and best practices in asylum determination procedures, thereby providing an alternative route for domestic policy coordination different from EU-level legislation. Moreover, many aspects of European internal security cooperation simply evolve alongside the EU, as it could not claim exclusivity or competence over the multiplicity of networks and initiatives that have arisen among practitioners.

5.4.2 *External Governance of Internal Security*

EU internal security cooperation has developed a dynamic external dimension in which member states' public officials linked in transgovernmental networks reach out to their peers in countries in the neighbourhood and further afield. Focused on operational cooperation with little supranational obligations, EU internal security networks transgressed EU borders early on and now span far beyond EU member states (Lavenex and Wichmann, 2009; Monar, 2014). In the field of migration, the coincidence of the opening up of Eastern borders with the abolition of internal border controls in the EU has given way to fears about uncontrolled influxes of migrants and criminal subjects, prompting networks of EU border officials to extend their ties to the neighbours. By 1993, member-state border officials preoccupied with the realization of the Schengen Agreement's external border regulations had created a pan-European network with their colleagues from what became the EU candidate countries in Central and Eastern Europe. This network, referred to as the Budapest Process, today includes over fifty governments and spans eastwards towards the Silk Road countries. While border management constitutes an early starter, other pan-European transgovernmental networks have also expanded in the fields of asylum cooperation, the fight against the smuggling and trafficking of persons, anti-corruption activities, and cooperation in other areas of criminal law (Cremona et al., 2011; Lavenex and Wichmann, 2009). Overall, the growth of externalized internal security policies supports the critical argument that European security actors see it as an opportunity to enhance their autonomy from both national and supranational oversight systems (Lavenex, 2006).

Such arguments have also linked up with the wider literature on the relation between the EU and its neighbourhood (Lavenex, 2008), including and going beyond Central and Eastern Europe. Transgovernmental networking with Southern Mediterranean neighbours has been hampered by political instability in the region, but nonetheless constitutes a regular and often criticized feature (Wolff, 2012) whereby European actors build networks to control migration (Carrera et al., 2013) and to support counterterrorism (Joffe, 2008; MacKenzie et al., 2013). At the same time, more global governance networks have developed in the fight against terrorism and illicit finance, especially in collaboration with the US (Pawlak, 2009) but also including various other Western or Middle Eastern countries. A concrete example is the EU's support for the actions of the Financial Action Task Force via legislative instruments as well as the transgovernmental 'FIU net' for more operational information exchange (Gutiérrez Zarza, 2015).

In sum, this extension of EU internal security governance to third countries corroborates the tensions between 'freedom', 'security', and 'justice' that has also been identified within the EU with regard to the persistence of negative integration and intensive transgovernmentalism. The tragedies resulting from the lack of an adequate response to the migration crises around the Mediterranean underline and aggravate these long-term structural deficits in terms of governance capacities and bias towards executive empowerment. As argued, this latter trend is especially pronounced as cooperation on internal and external issues merges, as the existing gap between Brussels decision-makers and European citizens is widened and pushed beyond EU borders, and where there are hardly any opportunities for ensuring accountability. One can still debate whether the growth of external governance of internal security represents a deliberate strategy of venue-shopping or rather a structural trend based on the EU's varied decision-making capacities and international presence. This, in turn, may allow for more diverse EU external governance patterns that are not 'coherent' with regard to security interests. However, EU governance studies consistently underline the need to consider alternative governance modes or to critically reflect on governance outcomes beyond the simple criterion of achieving policy coordination amongst EU member states and with external partners.

5.5 Security Governance in the Context of the EU

The second type of governance approach that has gained prominence in the study of EU internal security is rooted in the analysis of security governance itself, its relations to statehood, and even the understanding of security itself. The basic idea is that we are witnessing a general transformation of contemporary security which also reflects on the pursuit of security via EU governance.

The 'rise of security governance' (Bevir, 2014) is discussed in security studies and IR (Kirchner and Sperling, 2007), risk sociology (Rothstein et al., 2013; van Asselt and Renn, 2011), peace research (Ehrhart and Kahl, 2010; Schroeder et al., 2014), and criminology and police studies (Frevel and Schulze, 2012; Gerspacher and Dupont, 2007; Loader and Walker, 2004).[6]

While one needs to consider different analytical and normative approaches (Ehrhart et al., 2014; Sperling, 2014), the literature on security governance generally tends to emphasize decentred interactions among a multiplicity of actors, which also involve increasingly complex or non-traditional (Hameiri and Jones, 2013) notions of security. This corresponds to a 'narrow' understanding of governance, namely as a complex condition of interdependence that eludes the steering efforts of particular actors. Often-analysed cases are modern peace operations that aim for comprehensive 'security sector reform', including the promotion of the 'rule of law' (Bryden and Hänggi, 2005), which requires broad civil security society involvement and civil–military cooperation. Alternatively, security governance can denote attempts to forge integrated and multilevel approaches to homeland security, resilience, and internal security, since modern societies are seen as increasingly vulnerable to technological breakdown or terrorist attacks (Dunn-Cavelty and Suter, 2009; Kavalski, 2008; Roberts, 2008). In either case, there is deep running tension between the ambition to create ever more comprehensive and flexible approaches to address multi-dimensional, novel or asymmetric security threats (Nance and Cottrell, 2014) and the capacity required to steer the desired multi-stakeholder coordination processes (Daase and Friesendorf, 2010). This tensions runs across all levels of analysis, i.e. from local or 'nodal' policing (Shearing, 2005) to the international system where a variety of regional organizations may provide different, and even overlapping or competing, forms of security governance (Gebhard and Galbreath, 2013; Kirchner and Dominguez, 2011; Sperling and Webber, 2014).

It appears natural to regard the EU as an ideal actor or participant in these forms of comprehensive security governance (Zwolski, 2014), at least in so far it extends beyond national borders. On the policy side, the EU frequently underlines the need for embedding its actions into multilevel regimes and international legal frameworks. For instance, European and EU efforts to address human trafficking have developed as ever more complex stakeholder networks with multiple overlapping legal standards (Friesendorf, 2007). The EU also discursively followed the transformation of internal security beyond police and criminal justice cooperation. Thus, the EU's 2010 Internal Security Strategy lists not only the fight against terrorism, organized crime and illegal migration as the conventional core of the security component of the ASFJ, but also highlights the disaster management (resilience), critical infrastructure protection, and cybersecurity as 'strategic challenges' (Bossong and Rhinard, 2013). Analysts have already sought to map and assess such different manifestations of European security governance, whether with regard to less formalized or cross-cutting aspects of counterterrorism (Bossong, 2008; Bossong, 2014a; Den Boer et al., 2008; Monar, 2014; Schröder, 2011), cyber security (Bendiek and Porter, 2013; Eijkman, 2013), critical infrastructure protection (Bossong, 2014b) or civil protection, and disaster management (Hollis, 2010). But just as these studies document an increasing conceptual sophistication in terms of forward planning and prevention, identification of interdependences and potential 'cascading' effects of security threats, or the need to keep up with new technologies, they also underline the gap between ambitions of comprehensive and innovative approaches to internal security and the available governance capacities.

Regarding governance participants, focus is placed on the fact that the broadening field of internal security involves many diverse authorities at multiple levels of governance, where lower levels cannot be considered merely as bureaucratic cogs to execute EU strategic governance ambitions. Instead, European internal security presents itself as an extremely complex playing field that is not characterized by a pyramidal ordering of responsibilities, but rather where initiatives and actor roles emerge from practice and in response to different security crises. For instance, the recent EU policy cycle for improving the coherence of national actions in the fight against serious and organized crime (Paoli, 2014) underlines the related challenges of effective coordination. At the same time, technical systems for data-sharing, such as the Schengen Information System, are accessed at different levels of governance and by different security authorities in different European states. Other overarching architectures for horizontal cooperation, such as a putative European Criminal Intelligence Model remain vague and largely unused. In more recently evolved areas of internal security cooperation, such as disaster management, it is even unclear who would be the appropriate cooperation partners across national borders, as national systems remain highly diverse and often structured from the bottom-up when dealing with day-to-day challenges of local policing and emergency management.

In sum, governance processes for EU internal security do not follow a uniform model or are not exclusively focused on high-level transgovernmental networks. This requires an awareness or sensitivity to different governance processes for internal security that are more polycentric, broken down into regional patterns (esp. neighbouring states) as well as into professional sub-fields. A final, yet highly important, complication in the resulting systemic patterns of internal security governance is the role of private actors. In the wider security governance literature, the engagement of private stakeholders or direct governance providers is typically discussed with regard to security guards or military companies (Krahmann, 2011). However, other aspects and dimensions of internal security have become increasingly relevant, including at the European level. Even if European states and the EU are not experiencing massive transformations of internal security functions—which could, for instance, be compared with the privatization of prisons in the US—there is a new level of engagement in more technical issue areas, such as critical infrastructure protection, cybersecurity, and the growing technological dimension of border and surveillance policies. This raises questions for both legitimacy and effectiveness, since it is not obvious that public actors can maintain control over processes or outcomes. For instance, the EU's efforts to increase the resilience of critical infrastructures followed a comprehensive governance logic, including many non-hierarchical elements for coordination, but failed with regard to its initial ambitions, as voluntary stakeholder cooperation has not been forthcoming (Bossong, 2014). Conversely, in the area of security research and technology one may surmize European policy forums have become increasingly intertwined with private industrial interests (Hoijtink, 2014; Liem et al., 2011). Further complex dynamics can be observed in the rapidly growing area of cybersecurity, where one can simultaneously observe a reluctance of many private actors to bear the costs of public security policies, while some other IT companies are proactively engaged in cooperation with security services. This also increasingly applies to the EU, in particular to Europol, where a recent cybercrime centre (termed EC3) fuses public and private actors and operates flexibly within and far beyond the EU's borders, including in operational joint actions with the US in third countries.

In sum, security governance provides an exploratory tool for highlighting an increasing diversification of actors and objectives for security cooperation. It also places a focus on the geographical reach and association with particular venues of governance networks. As a deeper structural condition, security governance is close to a narrow understanding of governance. This translates into a critical view of the steering capacity by any particular policymaker or public authority. It also resists a single overarching or uncontested trend in contemporary security provision, such as 'privatization'. The security governance literature, therefore, is less helpful to test specific hypotheses, such as executive empowerment in EU internal security cooperation, but remains an essential perspective to sharpen our understanding of the breadth and diversity of our field of study.

5.6 Conclusions

Existing theorizing on EU internal security cooperation from a governance perspective first sought to understand the effects of institutional interactions and decision-making processes in this particular issue area, interactions and processes which neither conform to a balance of power between supranational and national actors (as in many forms of institutionalist analysis) nor to traditional trajectories of integration (as in grand integration theories such as neofunctionalism). Instead, the dominant concern has been the output and wider implications of a policy-field-specific governance process, first in terms of internal effects and then increasingly in terms of external effects on the EU's neighbourhood. As such, governance perspectives that are mainly derived from EU studies continue to revolve around research questions that highlight the puzzle of cooperation beyond sovereignty constraints and the relative merits as well as the limits of governance combinations in the EU context or its neighbourhood.

Secondly, governance approaches are frequently marked by preceding thematic labels—such as security governance, risk governance, environmental governance, etc. These perspectives seek to identify the distinctive features and trends of the subject area—in contrast to general modes of governance and their connection to different polities, such as the EU. For instance, internet governance, where political initiatives to (re)create more binding forms of regulation clash with radically decentralized visions of adaptive self-governance, strongly contrast with conventional understandings of internal security governance, where Europeans expect a near-exclusive role of public authorities and emphasis on formal legal bases for actions.

As apparent in the discussion above, perspectives of EU modes of governance and security governance share a number of core empirical and normative interests (Ehrhart et al., 2014), which could be further developed in the context of internal security cooperation. They encourage us to investigate whether there is a discernible centre of policymaking and coordination in EU internal security, even if it is indirect and networked, or pushed into third states and beyond the view of EU citizens. They furthermore direct our attention to comparing more binding with less binding forms of governance, which is summarized in the mode of intensive transgovernmentalism and implicit in many discussions of the practical relevance of comprehensive models or strategies for internal security. Finally, rather than taking various institutions and actor constellations for granted, as is arguably the case in many variants of institutionalist research, governance analyses remain highly sensitive to the question of the composition and constitution of policymaking actors. Are they located in public institutions, or are they increasingly found in the private sector or society? At which level of governance can they be located, if we depart from a conventional top-down model of steering? And can we consider governance outcomes as genuine public goods, or rather as biased in favour of transgovernmental elites or of private security providers?

Such a broad understanding of governance research obviously also features many common concerns with other theoretical perspectives that are assembled in this book. New institutionalism and networked governance are affiliated in so far as both address wider frames for preference formation and action orientation (Börzel, 2010; Olsen and March, 1989; Scharpf, 1997a) beyond formal institutions. Both perspectives provide analytical space for the study of institutionalized incentives, such as relative opportunities for empowerment in different venues, as well as the impact of shared norms, such as coordination reflexes or Europeanized problem definitions, since both are seen to drive the capacity growth and geographical extension of EU governance. A further, and perhaps more surprising, overlap is with the PARIS school, which posits the importance of evolutionary field dynamics among diverse professional groups in Europe (see Bigo in this volume). This perspective can be compared to critical—not functionalist or experimental problem-solving—interpretations of the notion of security governance. Both underline the importance of unintended outcomes, the extension of the range of participating 'stakeholders' and the problems of ever more comprehensive security objectives. Nevertheless, security governance differs in its reluctance to extrapolate larger sociological dynamics and patterns that can be transferred across cases and issues. For instance, the proliferation of governance initiatives and networks in EU internal security that may not add up to consistent set of norms, beliefs, or 'habitus' among a related field of professionals.

Finally, researchers should pay heed to the deeper links between neofunctionalist reasoning and some basic assumptions of governance studies, namely the transformation of politics towards a more technocratic and territorially flexible form of social coordination. The resulting tensions between the functionalist dictum that form follows function, and the neofunctionalist expectations of a clustering of cooperation around certain regional institutions have then been reproduced in the familiar contrast between 'type 1' of territorially layered and 'type 2' of functionally differentiated forms of multilevel governance. What is specifically relevant for EU internal security cooperation, then, is the old question of whether some forms of governance, such as intensive transgovernmentalism, will not only spillover beyond EU borders (Lavenex, 2014), but also eventually lead to the adoption of more binding forms of governance, which allow for more positive integration. As outlined in this chapter, the record so far is highly mixed, in so far as the Lisbon Treaty marked the last stage of communitarization, but without doing away with the main features of intensive transgovernmentalism in internal security matters. Finally, a radically decentred vision of security governance would rather expect a movement towards more fragmented and privatized, rather than supranationally integrated, governance authorities. These broader historical trends and reflections clearly require more research and theoretical dialogue.

Notes

1. Governance, or the idea of 'good governance', has also crossed between academic analysis and political practice with regard to economic regulation and public administration as well as the provision of justice. It also continues to evolve and interact with these foundational notions, as is evident in debates on the 'transformation of modern statehood' under conditions of 'global governance'. While other theoretical perspectives surveyed in this book equally cover broad strands of thinking—witness the debate on 'new' institutionalism—governance therefore represents a particular broad approach.

2. Sabel and Zeitlin (2012) argued that a much larger part of EU policymaking, including areas where strong Community competences apply, converge in political practice on a similar 'experimentalist' logic that emphasizes learning and voluntary exchanges over hierarchical decision-making.

3. This can also be related to work by Elinor Ostrom (e.g. 2005) who underlines the value of genuinely 'poly-centric' and diverse governance arrangements in contrast to conventional assumptions about the need for central decision-making or private markets to resolve collective action problems (such as the 'tragedy of the commons').

4. In the case of JHA, one could illustrate this by reference to long-standing transgovernmental and global patterns of police cooperation via Interpol in comparison to the denser networks among European police forces, which were reinforced by the growth of Europol.

5. But one can also add other and less prominent areas of EU internal security cooperation, such as civil protection, that are mainly based on transgovernmental networks of variable reach into the European neighbourhood (Hollis, 2010; Bremberg, 2015).

6. As such the governance approach is emblematic of the challenge and interest analysed by this book, namely how to fruitfully and productively use both general theoretical toolkits from political science and EU studies as well as more issue-specific concerns and considerations from security studies. This corresponds to other policy fields too; such as when one examines financial markets, the environment or security, discussions increasingly revolve around the growth of networks, the rising importance of private actors, and greater policy volatility or coordination challenges—all of which tend to elude traditional hierarchical governing instruments.

References

Anagnostopoulos, I. (2014) 'Criminal Justice Cooperation in the European Union after the First Few "Steps": A Defence View', *ERA-Forum*, 15(1), pp. 9–24.

Barrett, S. (2007) *Why Cooperate? The Incentive to Supply Global Public Goods*. Oxford and New York: Oxford University Press.

Bendiek, A. and Porter, A. L. (2013) 'European Cyber Security Policy within a Global Multistakeholder Structure'. *European Foreign Affairs Review*, 18, pp. 155–80.

Benyon, J. (1994) 'Policing the European Union: The Changing Basis of Cooperation on Law Enforcement', *International Affairs*, 70 pp. 497–517.

Benz, A., Lütz, S., Schimank, U., and Simonis, G. (2008) *Handbuch Governance*. Wiesbaden: Springer VS.

Bevir, M. (2011) *The Sage Handbook of Governance*. Los Angeles, CA and London: Sage.

Bevir, M. (2014) 'The Rise of Security Governance', in Bevir, M., Daddow, O., and Hall, I. (eds) *Interpreting Global Security*. London: Routledge, pp. 17–34.

Block, L. (2010) 'Bilateral Police Liaison Officers: Practices and European Policy', *Journal of Contemporary European Research*, 6, pp. 194–210.

Börzel, T. A. (2008) 'European Governance—Verhandlungen und Wettbewerb im Schatten der Hierarchie', in Tömmel, I. (ed.) *Die Europäische Union: Governance und Policy-Making*. Wiesbaden: VS Verlag für Sozialwissenschaften, pp. 61–91.

Börzel, T. (2010) 'European Governance: Negotiation and Competition in the Shadow of Hierarchy', *JCMS: Journal of Common Market Studies*, 48, pp. 191–219.

Bossong, R. (2008) 'The Action Plan on Combating Terrorism: A Flawed Instrument of EU Security Governance', *JCMS: Journal of Common Market Studies*, 46, pp. 27–48.

Bossong, R. (2014a) 'EU Cooperation on Terrorism Prevention and Violent Radicalization: Frustrated Ambitions or New Forms of EU Security Governance?' *Cambridge Review of International Affairs*, 27, pp. 1–17.

Bossong, R. (2014b) 'The European Programme for the Protection of Critical Infrastructures—Meta-Governing a New Security Problem?' *European Security*, 23, pp. 210–26.

Bossong, R. and Rhinard, M. (2013) 'The EU Internal Security Strategy: Towards a More Coherent Approach to EU Security?' *Studia Diplomatica*, LXVI, 2, pp. 45–58.

Bossong, R. and Rhinard, M. (2014) *Explaining EU Internal Security Cooperation: The Problem(s) of Producing Public Goods*. London: Routledge.

Bremberg, N. (2015) 'The European Union as Security Community-Building Institution: Venues, Networks and Co-operative Security Practices', *JCMS: Journal of Common Market Studies*, 53(3), pp. 674–92.

Bryden, A. and Hänggi, H. (2005) *Security Governance in Post-Conflict Peacebuilding*. Piscataway, NJ: Transaction Publishers.

Bures, O. (2012) 'Informal Counterterrorism Arrangements in Europe: Beauty by Variety or Duplicity by Abundance?' *Cooperation and Conflict*, 47, pp. 495–518.

Carrera, S., Parkin, J., and den Hertog, L. (2013) 'EU Migration Policy after the Arab Spring: The Pitfalls of Home Affairs Diplomacy', *Policy Paper No 74*.

Chhotray, V. and Stoker, G. (2009) *Governance Theory and Practice: A Cross-Disciplinary Approach*. Houndsmills: Palgrave Macmillan.

Christiansen, T. and Neuhold, C. (2012) *International Handbook on Informal Governance*. Cheltenham: Edward Elgar.

Cremona, M. and Monar, J. (eds) (2011) *The External Dimension of the European Union's Area of Freedom, Security and Justice*. Brussels: Peter Lang.

Curtin, D., Mair, P., and Papadopoulos, Y. (2010) 'Positioning Accountability in European Governance: An Introduction', *West European Politics*, 33, pp. 929–45.

Daase, C. and Friesendorf, C. (2010) *Rethinking Security Governance: The Problem of Unintended Consequences*. Contemporary Security Studies. London and New York: Routledge.

Den Boer, M., Hillebrand, C., and Nölke, A. (2008) 'Legitimacy under Pressure: The European Web of Counter-Terrorism Networks', *JCMS: Journal of Common Market Studies*, 46, pp. 101–24.

Dunn-Cavelty, M. and Suter, M. (2009) 'Public–Private Partnerships Are No Silver Bullet: An Expanded Governance Model for Critical Infrastructure Protection', *International Journal of Critical Infrastructure Protection*, 2, pp. 179–87.

Ehrhart, H.-G., Hegemann, H., and Kahl, M. (2014) 'Towards Security Governance as a Critical Tool: A Conceptual Outline', *European Security*, 23, pp. 145–62.

Ehrhart, H.-G. and Kahl, M. (2010) *Security Governance in Und Für Europa: Konzepte, Akteure, Missionen*. Baden-Baden: Nomos.

Eijkman, Q. (2013) 'Digital Security Governance and Accountability in Europe: Ethical Dilemmas in Terrorism Risk Management', *Journal of Politics and Law*, 6, p. 35.

Erman, E. (2013) 'In Search of Democratic Agency in Deliberative Governance', *European Journal of International Relations*, 19, pp. 847–68.

Fawcett, P. and Marsh, D. (2014) 'Depoliticisation, Governance and Political Participation', *Policy & Politics*, 42, pp. 171–88.

Frevel, B. and Schulze, V. (2012) 'Kooperative Sicherheitspolitik—Safety and Security Governance in Zeiten Sich Wandelnder Sicherheitskultur', in Daase, C., Offermann P., and Rauer, V. (eds) *Sicherheitskultur*. Frankfurt: Campus, pp. 203–25.

Friesendorf, C. (2007) 'Pathologies of Security Governance: Efforts against Human Trafficking in Europe', *Security Dialogue*, 38, pp. 379–402.

Gebhard, C. and Galbreath, D. J. (2013) *Cooperation or Conflict? Problematizing Organizational Overlap in Europe*. Farnham: Ashgate.

Genschel, P. and Jachtenfuchs, M. (2013) *Beyond the Regulatory Polity? The European Integration of Core State Powers*. Oxford: Oxford University Press.

Gerspacher, N. and Dupont, B. (2007) 'The Nodal Structure of International Police Cooperation: An Exploration of Transnational Security Networks', *Global Governance: A Review of Multilateralism and International Organizations*, 13, pp. 347–64.

Grande, E. (2012) 'Governance Forschung in Der Governance-Falle? Eine Kritische Bestandsaufnahme', *Politische Vierteljahresschrift*, 53, pp. 565–92.

Gutiérrez Zarza, Á. (2015) 'EU Networks for Administrative, Police and Judicial Cooperation in Criminal Matters', in Gutiérrez Zarza, A. (ed.) *Exchange of Information and Data Protection in Cross-Border Criminal Proceedings in Europe*. Berlin and Heidelberg: Springer, pp. 107–13.

Hameiri, S. and Jones, L. E. E. (2013) 'The Politics and Governance of Non-Traditional Security', *International Studies Quarterly*, 57, p. 473.

Heinelt, H. (2010) *Governing Modern Societies: Towards Participatory Governance*. London: Routledge.

Héritier, A. (2002) 'New Modes of Governance in Europe: Policy Making without Legislating?' Reihe Politikwissenschaft Institut für Höhere Studien (IHS).

Héritier, A. and Lehmkuhl, D. (2008) 'Introduction: The Shadow of Hierarchy and New Modes of Governance', *Journal of Public Policy*, 38, pp. 1–17.

Hillebrand, C. (2012) *Counter-Terrorism Networks in the European Union: Maintaining Democratic Legitimacy after 9/11*. Oxford: Oxford University Press.

Hoijtink, M. (2014) 'Capitalizing on Emergence: The 'New' Civil Security Market in Europe', *Security Dialogue*, 45, pp. 458–75.

Hollis, S. (2010) 'The Necessity of Protection: Transgovernmental Networks and EU Security Governance', *Cooperation and Conflict*, 45, pp. 312–30.

Holzinger, K. (2008) *Transnational Common Goods: Strategic Constellations, Collective Action Problems, and Multi-Level Provision*. 1st ed. New York, NY: Palgrave Macmillan.

Jachtenfuchs, M. (2001) 'The Governance Approach to European Integration', *JCMS: Journal of Common Market Studies*, 39, pp. 245–64.

Jakobi, A. P. (2013) *Common Goods and Evils? The Formation of Global Crime Governance*. Oxford: Oxford University Press.

Jessop, B. (2011) 'Metagovernance', in Bevir, M. (ed.) *The Sage Handbook of Governance*. London: Sage, pp. 106–23.

Joffe, G. (2008) 'The European Union, Democracy and Counter-Terrorism in the Maghreb', *JCMS: Journal of Common Market Studies*, 46, pp. 147–71.

Kaunert, C. and Léonard, S. (2012) 'The Development of the EU Asylum Policy: Venue-Shopping in Perspective', *Journal of European Public Policy*, 19, pp. 1396–413.

Kavalski, E. (2008) 'The Complexity of Global Security Governance: An Analytical Overview', *Global Society*, 22, pp. 423–43.

Keohane, R. O. and Nye, J. S. (1974) 'Transgovernmental Relations and International Organizations', *World Politics*, 27, pp. 39–62.

Kirchner, E. J. and Dominguez, R. (2011) *The Security Governance of Regional Organizations*. Routledge Global Institutions Series. London and New York: Routledge.

Kirchner, E. J. and Sperling, J. (2007) *Global Security Governance: Competing Perceptions of Security in the 21st Century*. Abingdon and New York: Routledge.

Kohler-Koch, B. and Rittberger, B. (2006) 'Review Article: The Governance Turn in EU Studies', *Journal of Common Market Studies*, 44, pp. 27–49.

Krahmann, E. (2011) 'Beck and Beyond: Selling Security in the World Risk Society', *Review of International Studies*, 37, pp. 349–72.

Lavenex, S. (2001) 'The Europeanization of Refugee Policies: Normative Challenges and Institutional Legacies', *JCMS: Journal of Common Market Studies*, 39(5), pp. 851–74.

Lavenex, S. (2006) 'Shifting up and out: The Foreign Policy of European Immigration Control', *West European Politics*, 29, pp. 329–50.

Lavenex, S. (2007) 'Mutual Recognition and the Monopoly of Force: Limits of the Single Market Analogy', *Journal of European Public Policy*, 14, pp. 762–79.

Lavenex, S. (2008) 'A Governance Perspective on the European Neighbourhood Policy: Integration beyond Conditionality?' *Journal of European Public Policy*, 15, pp. 938–55.

Lavenex, S. (2009) 'Intensive Transgovernmentalism in the European Area of Freedom, Security and Justice', in Tömmel, I. and Verdun, A. (eds) *Innovative Governance in the European Union: The Politics of Multilevel Policymaking*. Boulder, CO: Lynne Rienner, pp. 255–72.

Lavenex, S. (2014) 'The Power of Functionalist Extension: How EU Rules Travel', *Journal of European Public Policy*, 21, pp. 885–903.

Lavenex, S. and Wagner, W. (2007) 'Which European Public Order? Sources of Imbalance in the European Area of Freedom, Security and Justice 1', *European Security*, 16 (3–4): 225–43.

Lavenex, S. and Wichmann, N. (2009) 'The External Governance of EU Internal Security', *European Integration*, 31, pp. 83–102.

Liem, K., Hiller, D., and Castex, C. (2011) 'A European Perspective on Security Research', in Thoma, K. (ed.) *European Perspectives on Security Research*. Berlin and Heidelberg: Springer, pp. 13–26.

Loader, I. and Walker, N. (2004) 'State of Denial? Rethinking the Governance of Security', *Punishment & Society*, 6, pp. 221–8.

MacKenzie, A., Kaunert, C., and Léonard, S. (2013) 'EU Counterterrorism and the Southern Mediterranean Countries after the Arab Spring: New Potential for Cooperation?' *Democracy and Security*, 9, pp. 137–56.

Mayntz, R. (2004) 'Governance Theory Als Fortentwickelte Steuerungstheorie?' Max-Planck-Institut für Gesellschaftsforschung Working Paper.

Mayntz, R. (2010) 'Legitimacy and Compliance in Transnational Governance', Max-Planck-Institut für Gesellschaftsforschung Working Paper 10.

Monar, J. (2014) 'EU Internal Security Governance: The Case of Counter-Terrorism', *European Security*, 23, pp. 195–209.

Monar, J. (2014) 'The EU's Growing External Role in the AFSJ Domain: Factors, Framework and Forms of Action', *Cambridge Review of International Affairs*, 27, pp. 147–66.

Nance, M. and Cottrell, P. (2014) 'A Turn toward Experimentalism? Rethinking Security and Governance in the Twenty-First Century', *Review of International Studies*, 40, pp. 277–301.

Olsen, J. P. and March, J. G. (1989) *Rediscovering Institutions: The Organizational Basis of Politics*. New York: Free Press.

Ostrom, E. (2005) *Understanding Institutional Diversity*. Princeton, NJ: Princeton University Press.

Paoli, L. (2014) 'How to Tackle (Organized) Crime in Europe? The EU Policy Cycle on Serious and Organized Crime and the New Emphasis on Harm', *European Journal of Crime, Criminal Law and Criminal Justice*, 22, pp. 1–12.

Pawlak, P. (2009) 'Network Politics in Transatlantic Homeland Security Cooperation', *Perspectives on European Politics and Society*, 10, pp. 560–81.

Risse, T. (2013) *Governance without a State? Policies and Politics in Areas of Limited Statehood*. New York: Columbia University Press.

Roberts, P. S. (2008) 'Dispersed Federalism as a New Regional Governance for Homeland Security', *Publius: The Journal of Federalism*, 38, pp. 416–43.

Rosenau, J. N. and Czempiel, E.-O. (1992) *Governance without Government: Order and Change in World Politics*. Cambridge: Cambridge University Press.

Rothstein, H., Borraz, O., and Huber, M. (2013) 'Risk and the Limits of Governance: Exploring Varied Patterns of Risk-Based Governance across Europe', *Regulation & Governance*, 7, pp. 215–35.

Sabel, C. F. and Zeitlin, J. (2012) 'Experimentalism in the EU: Common Ground and Persistent Differences', *Regulation & Governance*, 6(3), pp. 410–26.

Scharpf, F. W. (1997a) 'Introduction: The Problem-Solving Capacity of Multi-Level Governance', *Journal of European Public Policy*, 4, pp. 520–38.

Scharpf, F. W. (1997b) 'Balancing Positive and Negative Integration: The Regulatory Options for Europe', Max-Planck-Institut für Gesellschaftsforschung Working Paper 1997/8.

Scharpf, F. W. (1999) *Governing in Europe: Effective and Democratic?* Oxford: Oxford University Press.

Scharpf, F. W. (2000) *Interaktionsformen: Akteurzentrierter Institutionalismus in der Politikforschung.* Opladen: Leske + Budrich.

Schmidt, S. and Sievers, J. (2015) 'Squaring the Circle with Mutual Recognition? Democratic Governance in Practice', *Journal of European Public Policy*, 22, pp. 1–17.

Schröder, U. C. (2011) *The Organization of European Security Governance: Internal and External Security in Transition.* Security and Governance Series. New York: Routledge.

Schroeder, U. C., Chappuis, F., and Kocak, D. (2014) 'Security Sector Reform and the Emergence of Hybrid Security Governance', *International Peacekeeping*, 21, pp. 214–30.

Shearing, C. (2005) 'Nodal Security', *Police Quarterly*, 8, pp. 57–63.

Slaughter, A.-M. (2004) *A New World Order.* Princeton, NJ and Oxford: Princeton University Press.

Sperling, J. (ed.) (2014) *Handbook of Governance and Security.* Cheltenham: Edward Elgar.

Sperling, J. and Webber, M. (2014) 'Security Governance in Europe: A Return to System', *European Security*, 23, pp. 126–44.

Steffek, J. (2010) 'Public Accountability and the Public Sphere of International Governance', *Ethics & International Affairs*, 24, pp. 45–68.

Stephenson, P. (2013) 'Twenty Years of Multi-Level Governance: "Where Does It Come From? What Is It? Where Is It Going?"' *Journal of European Public Policy*, 20, pp. 817–37.

Tömmel, I. (2008) *Die Europäische Union: Governance Und Policy-Making.* Wiesbaden: Springer.

Torfing, J., and Sørensen, E. (2014) 'The European Debate on Governance Networks: Towards a New and Viable Paradigm?' *Policy and Society*, 33, pp. 329–44.

Trauner, F. and Ripoll Servent, A. (eds) (2015) *Policy change in the Area of Freedom, Security and Justice: How EU Institutions Matter.* London: Routledge.

Treib, O., Bähr, H., and Falkner, G. (2007) 'Modes of Governance: Towards a Conceptual Clarification', *Journal of European Public Policy*, 14, pp. 1–20.

van Apeldoorn, B., Horn, L., and Drahokoupil, J. (2009) *Contradictions and Limits of Neoliberal European Governance: From Lisbon to Lisbon.* London: Palgrave Macmillan

van Asselt, M. B. A. and Renn, O. (2011) 'Risk Governance', *Journal of Risk Research*, 14, pp. 431–49.

van Kersbergen, K. and van Waarden, F. (2004) ' "Governance" as a Bridge between Disciplines: Cross-disciplinary Inspiration Regarding Shifts in Governance and Problems of Governability, Accountability and Legitimacy', *European Journal of Political Research*, 43, pp. 143–71.

Wade, M. L. (2015) 'Securing Defence Rights in Transnational Proceedings', *European Journal of Crime, Criminal Law and Criminal Justice*, 23, pp. 145–69.

Wallace, H. (2000) 'The Institutional Setting: Five Variations on a Theme', in Wallace, H. and Wallace, W. (eds) *Policy-Making in the European Union*, 4th ed. Oxford: Oxford University Press.

Weber, M. (1910/1994) 'The Profession and Vocation of Politics', in Lassman, P. and Speirs, R. (eds) *Weber: Political Writings (Cambridge Texts in the History of Political Thought)*. Cambridge: Cambridge University Press, pp. 306–69.

Wolff, S. (2012) *The Mediterranean Dimension of the European Union's Internal Security*. Basingstoke: Palgrave Macmillan.

Zwolski, K. (2014) 'How to Explain the Transnational Security Governance of the European Union?' *JCMS: Journal of Common Market Studies*, 52, pp. 942–58.

6

Rule of Law

Theorizing EU Internal Security Cooperation from a Legal Perspective

Valsamis Mitsilegas

6.1 Introduction

The emergence of the European Union as an internal security actor has raised a number of critical legal questions and challenges. This chapter thus focuses on theorizing EU internal security from the perspective of the rule of law, which is recognized as a central principle of EU cooperation more broadly (see Article 2, TEU). In particular, the chapter develops a comprehensive conceptualization of the rule of law from an analytical perspective, addressing principles that apply in the negotiation and adoption of legislation (*ex ante*) as well as principles applicable to the stage of implementation of legislation (*ex post*).

As a demonstration of how these perspectives help to illuminate internal security cooperation in practice, this chapter addresses EU internal security law per se and examines for four pertinent cases from the field of counterterrorism. The first two examples focus on the *ex ante* rule of law, when questions such as legal competence and transparency figure prominently in how we analyse legal frameworks. The second set of examples examine *ex post* rule of law, when questions like legal certainty and procedural justice help to direct the researcher's attention. These four examples are based on the case law of the Court of Justice of the EU (CJEU), which has become a key actor in the development of EU internal security cooperation. By focusing on judicial approaches to EU counterterrorism law, this chapter thus demonstrates the growing need for a theorization of EU internal security from the perspective of the rule of law underpinned by a strong emphasis on the protection of human rights.

6.2 The Rule of Law and Internal Security in the EU

A useful starting point for a rule-of-law analysis in EU internal security cooperation is the typology put forward by Tamanaha (2004). Tamanaha distinguishes between formal and substantive versions of the rule of law. Moving from 'thinner' to 'thicker' categories, formal rule-of-law versions start with rule-by-law (law as an instrument of government action), moving to formal legality (law is general, prospective, clear, certain) and then to rule of law as democracy and legality (consent determines content of law). Substantive versions of the rule of law focus on the protection of individual rights, moving to the right of dignity and to justice, and ultimately to social welfare (Tamanaha, 2004: 91). Tamanaha stresses the importance of 'rule of law, not man', as man is arbitrary (Tamanaha, 2004: 122). Key elements in the typology are reflected in the theorization of the rule of law by the late Lord Bingham, former President of the UK Supreme Court (Bingham, 2010). According to Bingham, the core of the rule of law principle is that 'all persons and authorities within the state, whether public or private, should be bound by and entitled to the benefit of laws publicly made, taking effect (generally) in the future and publicly administered in the courts' (Bingham, 2010: 8). Bingham's understanding of the rule of law is based primarily on procedural aspects, including the accessibility of the law, the importance of legal rules and not discretion, limits to the exercise of public power, the provision of means enabling dispute resolution without prohibitive cost or inordinate delay, and compliance by the state with its obligations in international law as in national law. However, rule of law also includes substantive aspects including equality before the law and the protection of human rights, which are both apparent in the principle of the right to a fair trial.

Such a comprehensive understanding of the rule of law is clearly significant to analysing the development of internal security cooperation. The rule of law is important in establishing clear parameters and limits, as well as checks and balances, with regard to the exercise of public power and executive action. Legal limits are even more important in a field like (internal) security, where the framing of issues such as terrorism as emergency threats requiring an imminent and strong response (see Balzacq on securitization in this volume) can lead to an uncritical increase in state power at the expense of the protection of fundamental rights (see inter alia Bigo et al., 2010; Mitsilegas, 2014a; Roach, 2011; Waldron, 2010). Thus, from a normative or prescriptive perspective, theorizing internal security from a legal perspective is essential to understand the implications of legislative and executive action, both at the stage of the adoption and at the stage of the implementation of legislation within clear constitutional parameters. From a critical analytical perspective, theorizing internal security from a legal perspective is important in order to fully comprehend the impact of securitized legislation on the relationship between the individual and the state, as well as on issues related to the separation of powers and the functioning of institutions.

A rule-of-law approach also sheds light on the role of the judiciary in shaping cooperation, new institutions and public policy. Indeed, particularly post-September 11 it has been the judicial branch in most Western democracies that has reminded legislators and the executive of the importance of ensuring full respect of fundamental rights in any polity which wishes to claim that it upholds the rule of law. In the EU, this fact points towards the CJEU and its case law: a central focus of this chapter. One should not forget, however, the role of other EU institutions such as the European Commission in attempting to conceptualize the rule of law in European cooperation. According to the Commission (2014), for instance, the rule of law is based on a non-exhaustive list of principles including legality, which implies a transparent, accountable, democratic, and pluralistic process for enacting laws; legal certainty; prohibition of arbitrariness of the executive powers; independent and impartial courts; effective judicial review including respect for fundamental rights; and equality before the law (European Commission, 2014: 4). The Commission perceives the rule of law as a constitutional principle with both formal and substantive components, meaning that respect for the rule of law is intrinsically linked to respect for democracy and for fundamental rights.

From these various components, a categorization can be developed for academic analyses: *rule of law ex ante*, which relates to principles which are applicable in the lawmaking process, including legality, transparency, and democracy; and *rule of law ex post*, which includes principles which are applicable after the enactment of legislation—including legal certainty, prohibition of arbitrariness, and effective judicial protection including the protection of human rights. This broad conceptualization is also reflected by specific constitutional features of the EU, including the principle of conferral and the evolving inter-institutional balance. However, as a new and contested field of EU powers, EU internal security cooperation initially developed largely under the unique and exceptional constitutional framework of the so-called third pillar (Mitsilegas, Monar, and Rees 2003; Monar, 2010a). Member states' reluctance to cede sovereignty and to move towards supranationalism (or *'Communautarisation'*) in the field has led to a number of rule-of-law challenges.

From the perspective of *ex ante* rule of law, such challenges related to the legality of competences. In other words, to what extent did the EU have powers to legislate on internal security under the third pillar and to what extent should these powers be exercised under not the third but under the first pillar?[1] These critical questions were linked with issues of inter-institutional balance, most notably concerning the limited role of the European Parliament in the development and scrutiny of third-pillar internal security law, which resonated with broader questions of democracy and transparency in the EU. The role of the Court of Justice was limited under the third pillar, with the Court in particular having no jurisdiction to rule on infringement proceedings brought against member states on the grounds of incorrect implementation of EU law, and limited jurisdiction (dependent on the political will of each member state) to receive requests for preliminary rulings by national courts.

From the perspective of *ex post* rule of law, challenges emerged from the plethora and nature of internal security measures adopted under the third-pillar regime and possible violations of safeguards regarding the protection of human rights and the rule of law (for an early overview, see Douglas-Scott, 2004). When looking broadly at how the EU has acted legislatively in the area of internal security cooperation, five characteristics can be discerned: (1) it harmonized national criminal legislation by defining serious criminal offences and related minimal sanctions; (2) it facilitated judicial cooperation in criminal matters via the principle of mutual recognition; (3) it established a series of EU criminal justice agencies whose remit includes the fight against transnational crime; (4) it boosted the collection, exchange, and processing of personal data, including via the establishment of EU-wide databases; (5) and it complemented internal criminal-law measures by a strong external action dimension, including the conclusion of a number of international agreements with the US. Taken together, it is not hard to see how the historical development of EU internal security cooperation raised significant challenges to legal certainty, as well as to effective judicial protection and respect for fundamental rights (Mitsilegas, 2009a).

The entry into force of the Lisbon Treaty in 2010 officially transformed and addressed many of these problems. Most notably, the Treaty abolished the third pillar and introduced, *in principle,* the supranationalization (or 'Lisbonization') of internal security law, including a greater involvement for the European Parliament under the Ordinary Legislative Procedure (OLP). The Treaty also strengthened the protection of human rights by constitutionalizing the EU Charter of Fundamental Rights, which constitutes a benchmark for the EU and national judiciaries when adopting and implementing EU internal security law. However, as will be seen below, both *ex ante* and *ex post* rule-of-law challenges continue to shape the configuration of internal security cooperation in the post-Lisbon EU.

6.3 Counterterrorism, Internal Security, and the Rule of Law in the EU

Counterterrorism measures are helpful illustrations of a how rule-of-law considerations shape EU cooperation in internal security. The fight against terrorism has been emblematic of the emergence of the EU as an internal security actor, while counterterrorism measures pose perhaps the most acute challenges to the rule of law. Around the world, the post-9/11 legal landscape has been characterized by the introduction of a series of 'exceptions' to fundamental legal principles underpinning liberal democracies and by the gradual normalization by legislators of the state of emergency (see inter alia Waldron, 2010). These developments have been mirrored in the EU legal order. On the one hand, the EU has adopted a number of measures directed against terrorism, such as the broad criminalization of terrorism and the introduction of new terrorist offences (Galli and Weyemberg, 2012; Mitsilegas, 2009b); the introduction of legislation criminalizing and regulating responses against terrorist financing (Mitsilegas and Gilmore, 2007); and the introduction of asset-freezing sanctions against suspected terrorists by implementing relevant Security Council Resolutions (Eckes, 2009). On the other hand, the fight against terrorism has been used in order to advance more general EU criminal-law measures, including key and pioneering instruments such as the Framework Decision on the European Arrest Warrant, the Decision establishing Eurojust and the Second Money Laundering Directive (Mitsilegas, 2009a), while it also boosted various mechanisms for generalized collection, processing, exchange, and transfer of everyday personal data (Mitsilegas, 2015). Last but not least, the EU's post-9/11 response raised its international profile as a security actor, leading to a series of transatlantic agreements in criminal matters, including on extradition and mutual legal assistance (Mitsilegas, 2003) as well as on the transfer of passenger and financial (SWIFT) data to US authorities (Mitsilegas, 2014a).

In light of this wide range of counterterrorism and related legal instruments, an *ex ante* rule-of-law approach questions the EU's competence to adopt counterterrorism law, or its choice of legal basis (in line with the 'rule of law as legality/competence' perspective). The main problem here is that counterterrorism measures fall between internal and external security (Anderson et al., 1995). As will be seen in sections 6.3.1 and 6.3.2, the classification of a counterterrorism measure as an external security measure can sidestep the ordinary legislative procedure that should in principle apply to internal security measures after Lisbon. This has substantive implications for the transparency of lawmaking. Furthermore, the dominance of the executive in the adoption of counterterrorism law casts doubt over *ex post* rule of law. In light of the move towards prevention and pre-emption of putative security threats,[2] legal certainty, procedural justice, and the protection of fundamental rights may be undermined.

More concretely, and more central to this chapter, the intervention of the Court of Justice itself on both *ex ante* (concerning legality as competence and transparency) and *ex post* (concerning legal certainty and procedural justice/

human rights) grounds has had a direct influence over how internal security cooperation and policy has taken shape. Sections 6.3.1 and 6.3.2 examine two cases of *ex ante* considerations and two cases of *ex post* considerations.

6.3.1 Rule of Law Ex Ante: The Rule of Law as Competence

The legality of EU actions to freeze the assets of terrorist suspects, mainly in order to implement UN Security Council Resolutions 1267 and 1373, have been persistently questioned by legal scholars. Before the Lisbon Treaty, the treaties did not confer an express legal basis either to the Community or the Union to legislate on sanctions against individuals. The Court of Justice accommodated the legality of the adopted measures in the *Kadi I* case that is discussed more specifically below (Mitsilegas, 2010). The Lisbon Treaty addressed the constitutional gap with not one, but two articles—namely, Article 75 and Article 215(2) TFEU—although this dual legal basis led to a continuation of litigation before the Court of Justice, as the two articles stipulate different legislative procedures for the adoption of sanctions. For instance, when the Council chose to amend Regulation 881/2002, which set out the initial terrorist financing sanction regime, it did so on the basis of the second legal basis, Article 215(2), which falls under the Union's external competences and consequently does not foresee the Ordinary Legislative Procedure (Council Regulation, 2009). This move was contested by the European Parliament, which sought the annulment of the amendment, Regulation 1286/2009, by the Court of Justice.[3]

The Court established in the case that the procedural differences in Articles 75 and 215(2) TFEU render them incompatible—but nevertheless dismissed the action. The argument was based on three steps. First, the Court found that the pre-Lisbon Articles 60 EC, relating to restrictions of capital movements and payments, and 301 EC on the interruption or reduction of economic relations with third countries, were mirrored in Article 215 TFEU. Second, the Court noted that combating terrorism and its financing may well be among the objectives of the Area of Freedom, Security and Justice (AFSJ) (Article 3(2) TEU), but that the fight against international terrorism and its financing in order to preserve international peace and security corresponds to the Treaty provisions on external action by the Union. On the basis of this emphasis on international peace and security, and the establishment of a general link between security and EU foreign and defence policy, the Court asserted that measures taken in order to give effect to the EU's external actions—and, in particular, restrictive measures for the purpose of Article 215(2) TFEU—can be used to combat terrorism. Third, the Court quoted *Kadi I* (discussed below) and stated that the essential purpose of the contested Regulation 1286/2009 is to combat *international terrorism*, and therefore relates to a decision taken by the EU under the Common Foreign and Security Policy (CFSP). The Parliament's argument that it is impossible to distinguish the combating of 'internal' terrorism, on the one hand, from the combating of 'external' terrorism, on the other, was not considered as a refutation for the choice of legal basis. The Court accepted that participation of the Parliament in the legislative process reflects the fundamental democratic principle of popular representation, but asserted that the difference between Article 75 TFEU and Article 215 TFEU is the result of the choice made by the framers of the Treaty of Lisbon conferring a more limited role on the Parliament under the CFSP. The Court added that the duty to respect fundamental rights is imposed, in accordance with Article 51(1) of the Charter of Fundamental Rights of the EU, on all the institutions and bodies of the Union, including measures giving effect to resolutions of the UN Security Council.

This chain of argument, however, is premised on a number of contradictions. The Court accepted the Council's statement that it is the legal basis of a measure that determines the legislative procedures to be followed, yet its reasoning is based essentially on procedural arguments. In the first place, the Court has chosen to exclude the possibility of Articles 75 and 215(2) acting as joint legal bases for the contested Regulation, whereas earlier case law accepted dual legal bases, including Treaty provisions with different legislative procedures. In these cases, the Court opted for the adoption of the procedure which respects the Parliament's prerogatives more fully (De Baere, 2013). Secondly, the Court's emphasis on procedure is evident in its attempt to justify the legality of Article 215(2). It adopted a historical approach to link the post-Lisbon legal bases on terrorist sanctions with the pre-Lisbon legal bases for the Regulation. Yet as mentioned above, before the Lisbon Treaty, the treaties did not include an express legal basis to adopt sanctions against individuals. In *Kadi I*, the Court of Justice went out of its way to uphold the legality of EU action by establishing a bridge between the first-pillar legal bases and the CFSP (Mitsilegas, 2010). To address this situation, the Lisbon Treaty then included an express legal basis for the adoption of terrorist sanctions against individuals, including Article 75 TFEU. To establish a continuum between the pre-Lisbon and the post-Lisbon legal bases, therefore, is to disregard the new constitutional situation.

The Court's approach has profound implications for the conceptualization of security in EU law. The Court rightly did not attach weight to the artificial distinction made by the Council between 'internal' and 'external' terrorists. Yet at the same time the Court treats the imposition of terrorist sanctions on individuals as a matter of 'international terrorism'. By giving security such a broad meaning in order to justify an external-relations legal basis—and at the same time finding that this renders it incompatible with an AFSJ legal basis—the Court strengthened the standing of the CFSP (Eeckhout, 2011: 181–3). Article 40 TEU has been seen as establishing an equal relationship across EU policies,[4] yet the Court's ruling effectively grants primacy to CFSP for any measure which may fall under the very broad scope of security, including internal security and the AFSJ (Neframi, 2013). There is very little room for pure 'internal security' when a large part of counterterrorism law can be interpreted as related to external security.[5]

However, the key issue which the Court's ruling fails is the impact on individuals. As confirmed by the Court of Justice in its case law, including the *Kadi* litigation, terrorist sanctions have profound consequences for the daily lives and fundamental rights of affected individuals. The Court's reference to international peace and security echoes UN law, which has been initially designed to govern inter-state relations. Yet post-9/11 terrorist sanctions reflect a paradigm change, in that international and EU sanctions law targets not states, but individuals. This individual dimension ostensibly belongs within the ambit of the AFSJ, which focuses on law enforcement and contains a specific provision on terrorist sanctions, and whose Treaty title confirm the necessary counterweight of justice, free movement, and fundamental rights. Finally, the Court seems to imply that fundamental rights will be observed by referring to its prior *Kadi* litigation, whereas the impact of terrorist sanctions also necessitates the possibility for continuous scrutiny by the European Parliament.

6.3.2 *Rule of Law Ex Ante: The Rule of Law as Transparency*

Debates on the legality or legal bases of EU counterterrorism law, as discussed above, are inextricably linked to transparency. Transparency is a principle that can underpin democratic legitimation in the EU (Heritier, 2003) as well as respond to criticism over secrecy and civil liberties violations (Curtin, 2009: chapter 8). Both views are of relevance in EU counterterrorism, where calls for transparency have been made to counter hidden practices by the Union executive and to ensure meaningful scrutiny by the European Parliament (Curtin, 2013). The EU–US Terrorist Finance Tracking Programme (TFTP) Agreement exemplifies these arguments and the inter-institutional confrontations that accompanied them.

In 2009 the European Parliament rejected the first EU–US TFTP Agreement and forced its renegotiation under the post-Lisbon regime, under which the Parliament would gain a fuller scrutiny role (Monar, 2010b). In the run-up to the first agreement, efforts by Member of the European Parliament (MEPs) to obtain relevant documents were refuted. In particular, MEP Sophie in 't Veld was refused access to the opinion of the Council's Legal Service concerning a recommendation from the Commission to the Council to authorize the opening of negotiations on the TFTP Agreement. Sophie in 't Veld challenged this decision before the Court of Justice. At first instance, the General Court ruled largely in her favour (in 't Veld v Council, T- 529/09, EU T:2012:15). The Court found that aside from those elements of the requested document which concern the specific content of the envisaged agreement or negotiating directives, disclosing positions on the respective legal basis would not threaten the EU's interest in the field of international relations (see in particular paragraphs 40–60 of the judgment). The Court thus made essentially a distinction between information relating to the content of the agreement and information relating to its legal basis. The Court emphasized in this context the constitutional significance of the choice of the appropriate legal basis, both for internal and international EU activity. The Court found that disclosing a potential disagreement between EU institutions on this issue is not a sufficient basis for concluding that the public interest may be undermined. Rather, any confusion as to the nature or legal basis of EU powers, which could weaken its position in international negotiations, can only be made worse without a prior debate between all the institutions concerned. Those findings were particularly justified at the time when different views concerning the legal basis of the envisaged TFTP were within the public domain. The Court's opinion thus suggests that transparency and public debate on rule-of-law and constitutional issues must factor into the Union's international relations.

A further link made by the Court between transparency and legitimacy in the negotiation of international agreements deserves attention. According to the Court, the mere fact that the legal advice contained in the document in question concerns the field of the international relations of the EU is not in itself sufficient to restrain access, as is specified in Article 4(2) of Regulation 1049/2001 on access to EU documents. On the contrary, the preamble to the open-access regulation highlights the advantages of increased openness or transparency, in so far as it enables citizens to participate more closely in the decision-making process and guarantees that the administration enjoys greater legitimacy and is more effective and more accountable in a democratic system. Such considerations cannot be ruled out in international affairs, especially where a decision authorizing the opening of international negotiations may have an impact on the EU's regular legislative activity. The Court noted in this context that the envisaged US–EU TFTP agreement concerns, in essence, the processing and exchange of information in the context of police cooperation, which may also affect the protection of personal data (see in particular paragraphs 88–102 of the judgment). In sum, having accepted the salience of transparency considerations in the field of EU external action, and recognizing the human-rights implications of EU external action in the present case, the Court agreed with the applicant that there was an overriding public interest in the disclosure of the document in question. It is, in fact, rather a lack of information and debate which is capable of giving rise to doubts in the minds of citizens, not only as regards to the lawfulness of an isolated act, but also as regards to the legitimacy of the decision-making process as a whole.

The ruling of the General Court was upheld on appeal (Case C 350/12 P, *Council v in't Veld*, judgment of 3 July 2014). The Court noted that the institution remains obliged to explain how disclosure of a document could specifically and actually undermine the legally protected interest as defined in Article 4(2) of Regulation 1049/2001, while the risk must not be purely hypothetical. In response to the Council and the Commission's attempts to distinguish the internal EU legislative activity from the decision-making process during the negotiation of an international agreement,[6] the Court stated that non-legislative activity of EU institutions does not fall outside the scope of Regulation No 1049/2001. So even in the case of a security-related international agreement, the Court affirmed the important link between transparency and legality, at least in order to ensure appropriate scrutiny of the chosen legal basis. Combined with a more recent ruling in matters of piracy,[7] this underlines the importance of transparency as a critical competent of *ex ante* rule of law in European transnational and internal security cooperation.

6.3.3 *Rule of Law Ex Post: The Rule of Law as Legal Certainty*

As mentioned above, the aftermath of 9/11 has led to the adoption of a raft of broader EU criminal law measures deemed necessary in the fight against terrorism. These measures include the Framework Decision on the European Arrest Warrant (EAW),[8] which is emblematic of the application of the principle of mutual recognition in the field of criminal law. The application of the principle of mutual recognition aims to regulate the interaction of national legal orders within Europe's AFSJ by ensuring the judicial decisions emanating from one EU member state are recognized and executed with a minimum of formality and with maximum speed by judicial authorities in other member states (Mitsilegas, 2012). Mutual recognition is not necessarily linked with harmonization of substantive criminal law. The executing authority is in principle obliged to execute a decision emanating from a different legal system whose rules must be respected extraterritorially, leading thus to a journey into the unknown (Mitsilegas, 2006). This process has considerable implications for legal certainty, in that affected individuals may potentially face legal consequences which they may not have been able to predict.

In particular, legal certainty has been challenged by the abolition of the requirement for the executing authority to verify dual criminality; that is, whether the conduct in question is a criminal offence in the jurisdictions of both the issuing and executing member state. The executing state may thus be asked to deploy its law enforcement mechanism to pursue an offence that is not recognized or specified under its domestic law. Specifically, the European Arrest Warrant Framework Decision eliminates the dual criminality control for thirty-two categories of offences, including terrorism, which has also been subject to broad criminalization at EU level. The abolition of the requirement to verify dual criminality has been a central element of the application of the principle of mutual recognition in the field of criminal law in the European Union, based on a minimum of formality, automaticity, and speed (Mitsilegas, 2006). The need to facilitate judicial cooperation was deemed to prevail over national differences in terms of criminalization. However, this choice was considered to challenge legal certainty, in particular in the executing State. The implications for legal certainty have been explored by the Court of Justice in *Advocaten voor de Wereld*.[9] The Luxembourg Court was asked to answer whether Article 2(2) of the EAW Framework Decision—in so far as it sets aside the verification of dual criminality—is compatible with the then-Article 6(2) TEU and the principle of legality in criminal proceedings. The Court found that it is compatible with the principle of legality, since legality should be examined in accordance with the law of the issuing member state which determines the definition of the offences and penalties included in Article 2(2) of the Framework Decision. The Court added to this finding that, on the basis of Article 1(3) of the Framework Decision, the issuing state must respect fundamental rights and fundamental legal principles as enshrined in Article 6 TEU and, consequently, the principle of the legality of criminal offences and penalties.

The Court has thus upheld a vision of the rule of law in a system of mutual recognition and interaction of national legal orders by conceptualizing European legality as being grounded on the *national* level, namely the legal system of the member state issuing a judicial decision. The Court has attempted to grant legitimacy to this approach to legality by backing up this choice with a general statement that the rule of law in this context needs to be enforced by the protection of human rights in the executing state. This imperative is even more pressing in light of Article 49 of the Charter of Fundamental Rights, which became binding with the Lisbon Treaty and which establishes the principle of legality and proportionality of criminal offences and penalties (Mitsilegas, 2014b).

6.3.4 *Rule of Law Ex Post: The Rule of Law as Procedural Justice*

At the heart of the legal debate regarding the relationship between internal security, counterterrorism, and the rule of law in the EU has been litigation concerning the legality of EU legislation implementing UN Security Council

Resolutions, and in particular UNSC Resolution 1267 imposing asset-freezing sanctions on suspected terrorists. Observers criticized not only the legality of enacting these sanctions (see section 6.3.1 above), but also the impact of the sanctions on the affected individuals and the relationship between EU and international law. Moreover, it raised fundamental questions on the relationship between the executive and the judiciary and the extent to which Courts were entitled to review sanctions that were adopted as emergency measures with limited transparency.

The Court of Justice has ruled on these issues extensively in what has become known as the *Kadi* litigation. The first set of cases *(Kadi I)* involved rulings by both the Court of First Instance[10] and, on appeal, the Court of Justice.[11] The Court of Justice eventually annulled the initial EU Regulation 881/2002 that enacted the highly publicized terrorist asset-freezing regime. The Court justified this decision by stressing unequivocally that the Community is based on the rule of law, adding that fundamental rights form an integral part of the general principles of law whose observance the Court ensures, that respect for human rights is a condition for the lawfulness of Community acts, and that measures incompatible with respect for human rights are not acceptable in the Community. At the same time, the Court stressed the *autonomy* of the Community legal order and argued that an international agreement, such as UN Security Council Resolutions, could not affect the allocation of powers fixed by the treaties or, consequently, the autonomy of the Community legal system and its constitutional principles.

To be precise, the Court noted that the primacy of international agreements in Community law does not extend to primary law, in particular to the general principles of which fundamental rights form a key part. The Court thus asserted its full power to review, in principle, any Community measure in light of fundamental rights, since this had to be considered as a constitutional guarantee in a community based on the rule of law. The Court then annulled the sanctions Regulation (setting aside the CFI judgment) on the grounds that the rights of the defence, in particular the right to be heard, and the right to effective judicial review of those rights, were patently not respected. By this decision, the Court also upheld the autonomy of the EU legal order in relation to international law, and in particular the framework established by the UN Security Council.[12] The *Kadi I* ruling has been pioneering in this regard, with subsequent Court of Justice rulings, and most notably the Court's Opinion 2/13 on the accession of the European Union to the European Convention on Human Rights, emphasizing further the need to uphold the autonomy of the European Union legal order vis-à-vis other legal orders. While in *Kadi I* the quest for autonomy has resulted in an increased protection of fundamental rights, in Opinio 2/13 the same quest for autonomy has led to a series of limitations in the protection of these rights.

Following a request by Mr Kadi to annul the revised EU asset-freezing Regulation,[13] which continued to list him, the Court revisited the case. During the *Kadi II* litigation a number of new developments had to be taken into account, most notably the improvements to the UN Security Council system of listing individuals whose assets should be frozen under Resolution 1267.[14] Nevertheless, the Court of Justice reiterated the need, in principle, for a full review of the lawfulness of Union acts in the light of fundamental rights and mentioned in particular the respect for the rights of the defence and the right to effective judicial protection as enshrined in Articles 41(2) and 47 of the Charter respectively. As regards the extent of judicial review, the Court found that the EU judiciary must determine whether the competent EU authority has complied with the procedural safeguards and that decisions on listing persons are taken on a sufficiently solid, factual basis. Judicial review cannot be restricted to an abstract assessment of the reasons relied on, but must answer whether those reasons—or, at the very least, one of those reasons—can be deemed sufficient to support that decision. To that end, EU judicial authorities can request the competent EU institution, when necessary, to produce information or evidence, confidential or not, that is relevant to such an examination.

The Court of Justice thus put forward a standard of judicial review *in concreto*, which consists of the substantive review of the listing based on evidence submitted to the European judiciary. In order to strike a balance between the requirements attached to the right to effective judicial protection and those flowing from the security of the EU or its member states (or the conduct of their international relations), the Court considered limiting the necessary information disclosure to summary outlines. Having regard to the preventive nature of the restrictive measures at issue, if at least one of the reasons mentioned in the summary provided by the Sanctions Committee is sufficiently detailed and specific to support the decision, it could be upheld—or annulled if no such reason is provided. However, the principle holds that *it is for the Courts of the European Union* to assess whether and to what the extent the failure to disclose confidential information or evidence to the person concerned affects the probative value of the confidential evidence. The Court then went on to review the substance of the allegations against Mr Kadi and concluded that none of the allegations presented against Mr Kadi in the summary provided by the Sanctions Committee are such as to justify the adoption, at EU level, of restrictive measures against him, either because the statement of reasons is insufficient or because information or evidence which might substantiate the reasons is lacking. Overall, the Court reiterated that such a judicial review is indispensable to ensure a fair balance between the maintenance of international peace and security and the protection of the fundamental rights and freedoms of the person concerned, *those being shared values of the UN and the European Union.* While the emphasis on shared values may have been included to diffuse tensions, the Court reiterated the substantial negative impact of sanctions to the affected individuals and argued that improvements at UN level in the listing process still failed to ensure effective judicial protection to the affected individual. In an example of judicial cross-fertilization, the Court of Justice based this finding on the ruling of the European Court of Human Rights in *Nada*.[15] In *Nada,* the European Court of Human Rights found Switzerland in breach of the Convention in a case involving a travel ban adopted in implementation of UN Resolution 1390 (2002). The Court rejected the automaticity argument posed by Switzerland, namely that the Swiss Government did not have any margin of appreciation in implementing the relevant UN Security Council regime. It stressed the particular individual circumstances and realities regarding the applicant and found that the possibility of deciding how the relevant Security Council resolutions were to be implemented in the domestic legal order should have allowed some alleviation of the sanctions regime applicable to the applicant, having regard to those realities, in order to avoid interference with his private and family life, without however circumventing the binding nature of the relevant resolutions or compliance with the sanctions provided for therein.

The Court of Justice thus confirmed the autonomy of the EU legal order based on the respect for the rule of law and fundamental rights. While the Court's ruling in *Kadi I* had a noticeable impact in improving listing procedures at UN level, the Court of Justice in *Kadi II* reminded the international community that authorities should respect the individual when imposing restrictive sanctions. At the same time, the Court of Justice in *Kadi II* sent a clear message that the executive cannot use secrecy and confidentiality to evade judicial scrutiny, especially when fundamental rights are at stake. However, the Court of Justice seems to accept the preventive nature of sanctions, and did not engage with the argument that procedural defects lead to a disproportionate impact of the affected individuals' right to property. In this light, *Kadi II* should be viewed as a triumph of procedural justice, perhaps at the expense of the protection of substantive fundamental rights including the right to property (Mitsilegas, 2014c). While the Court has upheld the rule of law in terms of emphasizing the need to comply with the principle of effective judicial protection seen to encompass procedural safeguards and remedies for the affected individual, it has left open the question of whether the very system of sanctions—consisting of pre-emptively freezing assets of individuals who have not been convicted of criminal offences but who are merely suspects—is compatible with human-rights law.

6.4 Conclusion: Rule of Law and the Future of Internal Security Cooperation

By focusing on the role of the judiciary in counterterrorism litigation at EU level, the chapter has attempted to provide a conceptualization of internal security from the perspective of the rule of law. More generally, it sought to show how a legal perspective can illuminate our understanding of European internal security cooperation by highlighting the role of the EU courts in shaping not only how common policies are made, and the institutional rights and rivalries therein, but also in terms of the substance and orientation of outcomes.

From the perspective of *ex ante* rule of law, namely principles underpinning the negotiation and adoption of legislation at EU level, serious challenges remain with regard to the translation, in constitutional terms, of the concept of internal security in EU law. Current practice by the Council, affirmed by the Court of Justice, tends to treat a raft of counterterrorism legislation primarily as issues of external security or foreign policy, even when such legislation has clear internal security implications. The Court seems to be affording primacy to external relations and external security at the expense of considerations related to the AFSJ and internal security. This approach disregards the direct and considerable impact that counterterrorism measures (such as terrorist sanctions) have on individuals, and has the effect of shielding the adoption of these measures by effective scrutiny at EU level, especially by marginalizing the European Parliament from the lawmaking process. The Court has, however, attempted to compensate for these deficits by developing another aspect of *ex ante* rule of law, namely the transparency dimension. It has introduced significant steps towards greater transparency expressed via the Parliament's right to be fully informed in the process of EU external action, including external action on counterterrorism.

As regards the rule of law *ex post*, involving the implementation of EU internal security law, the Court has attempted to uphold the construction of EU internal security as a system of judicial cooperation based on mutual recognition by defining legal certainty from a national perspective and underpinning rule-of-law safeguards with calls for the protection of human rights by the *national* judiciary. The Court has followed a similar approach in subsequent cases concerning the European Arrest Warrant (in particular *Melloni* and *Radu*) and in Opinion 2/13 on the accession of the EU to the ECHR. In this line of case law, the Court has placed emphasis on the effectiveness of judicial cooperation and the existence of mutual trust, and placed the protection of fundamental rights within this arguably restrictive framework. The Courts' ruling in *Melloni* has posed significant rule-of-law questions by reaching an outcome which was seen as challenging established provisions of domestic constitutional law, but domestic courts in Spain have since moved to align domestic law with EU law (Torres Pérez, 2014). Rule of law and human-rights considerations appear to be largely subsumed under the need to achieve the effectiveness of judicial and law enforcement cooperation across the EU.

Similar concerns arise specifically with regard to EU counterterrorism action. The Court has admittedly underlined the importance of the rule of law by the protection of human rights in the *Kadi* litigation. However, in *Kadi* upholding the rule of law has taken the form primarily of procedural justice, with the Court's rulings affirming the powers of judicial review vis-à-vis the executive via the affirmation of the individual right to judicial protection. The Court, however, stopped short—in both *Kadi I* and *II*—from criticizing the legality of the sanctions system per se in respect of its impact on the substantive rights of affected individuals, and in particular the right to property. A greater emphasis on the impact of internal security on the individual, and a stronger underpinning of the rule of law by human-rights considerations, can be seen from this perspective as essential for the development of an EU internal security paradigm further in the post-Lisbon, post-Charter of Fundamental Human Rights era.

In this context, the ruling of the Court of Justice in *Digital Rights Ireland* concerning the validity of the data retention Directive is a welcome development. The Court annulled the Directive, which had introduced a system of mass surveillance via the blanket retention of mobile phone data by private companies, as being contrary to the fundamental right to privacy. The protection of human rights here is essential also to uphold the rule of law, as a system of mass surveillance such as the one established in the Directive could lead to a significant erosion of trust between the citizen and the State and create a so-called chilling effect in democratic societies (Mitsilegas, 2015). The Court's ruling in *Digital Rights Ireland* is a good example of how the protection of human rights can strengthen rule-of-law safeguards in the EU security architecture.

In sum, legal analysis and theorizing on EU internal security cooperation is presented with a mixed picture that does not allow for a clear normative reading or historical interpretation. On the one hand, one could witness a rise of judicial oversight and improvements in both *ex ante* and *ex post* rule-of-law controls. In this regard, classic expectations on the inherent logic of law and the need to ensure respect for human rights could be partially confirmed. This provides an important counterpoint to critical analyses from security studies and political sociology that tend to underline the dominance or independence of security professionals and practices. On the other hand, the analysis has also shown how the EU legal system and the Court of Justice remain tied to a particular legal tradition and emphasis on general procedural norms of effectiveness and reliance on national courts. This does not automatically correspond to a systematic protection of human rights and adequate controls in the particularly sensitive field of internal security. Thus, the Court deserves further close analysis from both legal and institutionalist scholars—as has taken place in the field of economic integration and the political role of the Court in emphasizing economic freedoms or labour rights.

Notes

1. Inter-pillar competence disputes in relation to internal security measures have arisen pre-Lisbon in the context of powers to adopt criminal offences and sanctions (Commission v Council, Case C-176/03 ECR [2005] I-7879; Commission v Council Case C-440/05 ECR [2007] I-9097); in the context of a transatlantic agreement on the transfer of PNR data (European Parliament v Council, Case C-317/04 ECR [2007] 278); and in the context of the EU data retention Directive (Ireland v Council and Parliament Case C-301/06). For an analysis see V. Mitsilegas, *EU Criminal Law*, Hart Publishing, 2009 (chapter 2 for the criminal law cases and chapter 6 for the PNR case). On the data retention ruling, see Konstadinides (2010).
2. On prevention and pre-emption see Ashworth and Zedner (2014); de Goede (2012); Bigo and Walker (2008); Murphy (2012); Mitsilegas (2015).
3. Case C-130/10, European Parliament v Council, judgment of 19 July 2012.
4. On different views on the relationship between CFSP and other areas of EU policy post-Lisbon, see Eeckhout (2011); Van Elsuwege (2011: 494).
5. The Court's willingness to prioritize CFSP at the expense of AFSJ objectives in the context of security is confirmed in its recent ruling concerning piracy: Case C-658/11, European Parliament v Council, judgment of 24 June 2014. However, the Court emphasized in this ruling the transparency aspects of the Parliament's scrutiny role and in particular its involvement under Article 218(10) TFEU.
6. See paragraphs 89–91. According to the Council, there is an important distinction between cases where the European Union is acting in its legislative capacity and those where it is acting in its executive capacity in conducting international relations.
7. Case C-658/11, European Parliament v Council, judgment of 24 June 2014, paragraphs 75–87. See also Opinion of Advocate General Kokott in Case C-263/14, European Parliament v Council, delivered on 28 October 2015.
8. Framework Decision on the European Arrest Warrant and the surrender procedures between member states, OJ L190/1, 18.7.2002.
9. Case C-303/05 Advocaten voor de Wereld [2007] ECR I-363.
10. Case T-315/01 Yassin Abdullah Kadi v Council and Commission [2005] ECR II-3649; Case T-306/01 Ahmed Ali Yussuf and Al Barakaat International Foundation v Council and Commission [2005] ECR II-3533.
11. Joined Cases C-402/05 P and C-415/05 P, Yassin Abdullah Kadi and Al Barakaat International Foundation v Council and Commission [2008] ECR I-6351.

12. For two different views with regard to the Court upholding the autonomy of the EU legal order vis-à-vis international law, see de Burca (2009: 36); Tridimas (2009: 103).
13. Regulation EC No 1190/2008 amending for the 101st time Regulation No 881/2001 (OJ 2008 L322, p.25).
14. The analysis of *Kadi II* in this section is based on Mitsilegas (2014c).
15. Judgment of 12 September 2012, *Nada* v. *Switzerland* (No 10593/08), paragraph 195.

References

Anderson, M. et al. (1995) *Policing the European Union*. Oxford: Clarendon Press.

Ashworth, A. and Zedner, L. (2014) *Preventive Justice*. Oxford: Oxford University Press

Bigo, D., Carrera, S., Guild, E., and Walker, R. B. J (2010) *Europe's 21st Century Challenge. Delivering Liberty*. Farnham: Ashgate.

Bigo, D. and Walker, R. B. J. (2008) 'Le Régime de Contre-Terrorisme Global', in Bigo, D., Bonelli L., and Deltombe T. (eds) *Au nom du 11 Septembre . . . les démocraties à l'épreuve de l'antiterrorisme*. Paris: La Découverte, pp. 13–35.

Bingham, T. (2010) *The Rule of Law*. London: Allen Lane.

Council Regulation (2009) No 1286/2009 of 22 December 2009 amending Regulation (EC) No 881/2002 imposing certain specific restrictive measures directed against certain persons and entities associated with Usama bin Laden, the Al-Qaeda network and the Taliban (OJ 2009 L 346, p. 42).

Curtin, D. (2009) *Executive Power of the European Union. Law, Practices, and the Living Constitution*. Oxford: Oxford University Press.

Curtin, D. (2013) 'Official Secrets and the Negotiation of International Agreements: Is the EU Executive Unbound?', *Common Market Law Review*, 50, pp. 423–58.

De Baere, G. (2013) 'From "Don't Mention the *Titanium Dioxide* Judgment" to "I Mentioned it once, but I Think I Got away with it all right": Reflections on the Choice of Legal Basis in EU External Relations after the *Legal Basis for Restrictive Measures* Judgment', *Cambridge Yearbook of European Legal Studies 2012–13*, 15, pp. 537–62.

De Burca, G. (2009) 'The European Court of Justice and the International Legal Order after Kadi', NYU School of Law Jean Monnet Working Paper 01/09.

Douglas-Scott, S. (2004) 'The Rule of Law in the European Union: Putting Security into the EU's Area of Freedom, Security and Justice', *European Law Review*, 2, pp. 219–42.

Eckes, C. (2009) *EU Counter-Terrorist Policies and Fundamental Rights. The Case of Individual Sanctions*. Oxford: Oxford University Press.

Eeckhout, P. (2011) *EU External Relations Law*, 2nd ed. Oxford: Oxford University Press.

European Commission (2014) Communication from the Commission to the European Parliament and the Council, A New EU Framework to Strengthen the Rule of Law, COM (2014) 158 final, Brussels, 11.3.2014.

Galli, F. and Weyembergh, A. (eds) (2012) *EU Counter-Terrorism Offences*. Brussels: Éditions de l'Université de Bruxelles.

de Goede, M. (2012) *Speculative Security*. Minneapolis: University of Minnesota Press.

Héritier, A. (2003) 'Composite Democracy in Europe: the Role of Transparency and Access to Information', *Journal of European Public Policy*, 10, pp. 814–33.

Konstadinides, T. (2010) 'Wavering between Centres of Gravity: Comment on Ireland v. Parliament and Council', *European Law Review*, 35(1), pp. 88–102.

Mitsilegas, V. (2003) 'The New EU–US Co-operation on Extradition, Mutual Legal Assistance and the Exchange of Police Data', *European Foreign Affairs Review*, 8, pp. 515–36.

Mitsilegas, V. (2006) 'The Constitutional Implications of Mutual Recognition in Criminal Matters in the EU', *Common Market Law Review*, 43, pp. 1277–311.

Mitsilegas, V. (2009a) *EU Criminal Law*. Oxford: Hart Publishing.

Mitsilegas, V. (2009b) 'The Third Wave of Third Pillar Law: Which Direction for EU Criminal Justice?' *European Law Review*, 34, pp. 523–60.

Mitsilegas, V. (2010) 'The European Union and the Globalisation of Criminal Law', in Barnard, C. and Odudu, O. (eds) *The Cambridge Yearbook of European Legal Studies, 2009–2010*, vol. 12. Oxford: Hart Publishing, pp. 337–407.

Mitsilegas, V. (2012) 'The Limits of Mutual Trust in Europe's Area of Freedom, Security and Justice: From Automatic Inter-state Cooperation to the Slow Emergence of the Individual' in *Yearbook of European Law*, 31, pp. 319–72.

Mitsilegas, V. (2014a) 'Transatlantic Counter-terrorism Cooperation and European Values: The Elusive Quest for Coherence', in Curtin, D. and Fahey, E. (eds) *A Transatlantic Community of Law*. Cambridge: Cambridge University Press, pp. 289–315.

Mitsilegas, V. (2014b) 'Article 49—Principles of Legality and Proportionality of Criminal Offences and Penalties', in Peers, S., Hervey, T., Kenner, J., and Ward, A. (eds) *The EU Charter of Fundamental Rights: A Commentary*. Oxford: Hart/Beck, pp. 1351–73.

Mitsilegas, V. (2014c) 'The European Union and the Global Governance of Crime', in Mitsilegas, V., Alldridge, P., and Cheliotis, L. (eds) *Globalisation, Criminal Law and Criminal Justice: Theoretical, Comparative and Transnational Perspectives*. Oxford: Hart Publishing.

Mitsilegas, V. (2015) 'The Transformation of Privacy in an Era of Pre-Emptive Surveillance', *Tilburg Law Review*, 20, pp. 35–57.

Mitsilegas, V. and Gilmore, B. (2007) 'The EU Legislative Framework against Money Laundering and Terrorist Finance: A Critical Analysis in the Light of Evolving Global Standards', *International and Comparative Law Quarterly*, 56, pp. 119–41.

Mitsilegas, V., Monar, J., and Rees, W. (2003) *The European Union and Internal Security*. Basingstoke: Palgrave.

Monar, J. (2010a) 'The Institutional Framework of the AFSJ: Specific Challenges and Dynamics for Change', in Monar, J. (ed.) *The Institutional Dimension of the European Union's Area of Freedom, Security and Justice*, Oxford: Peter Lang, pp. 21–52.

Monar, J. (2010b) 'Editorial Comment. The Rejection of the EU–US SWIFT Interim Agreement by the European Parliament: A Historic Vote and Its Implications', *European Foreign Affairs Review*, 15, pp. 143–51.

Murphy, C. (2012) *EU Counter-Terrorism Law*. Oxford: Hart Publishing.

Neframi, E. (2013) 'L'aspect externe de l'espace de liberté, de sécurité et de justice: quel respect des principes et objectifs de l'action extérieure de l'Union?' in Flaesch-Mougin C. and Rossi, L. S. (eds) *La dimension extérieure de l'espace de Liberté, de Sécurité et de Justice de l'Union Européenne après le Traité de Lisbonne.* Brussels: Bruylant, pp. 509–32.

Roach, K. (2011) *The 9/11 Effect.* Cambridge: Cambridge University Press.

Tamanaha, B. Z. (2004) *On the Rule of Law: History, Politics, Theory.* Cambridge: Cambridge University Press.

Torres Pérez A. (2014) '*Melloni* in Three Acts: From Dialogue to Monologue', *European Constitutional Law Review*, 10, pp. 308–31.

Tridimas, T. (2009) 'Terrorism and the ECJ: Empowerment and Democracy in the EC Legal Order', *European Law Review*, 34, 103–26.

Van Elsuwege, P. (2011) 'The Adoption of "Targeted Sanctions" and the Potential for Inter-institutional Litigation after Lisbon', *Journal of Contemporary European Research*, 7, 4, pp. 488–99.

Waldron, J. (2010) *Torture, Terror and Trade-Offs. Philosophy for the White House.* Oxford: Oxford University Press.

7

Neofunctionalism and EU Internal Security Cooperation

Arne Niemann

7.1 Introduction

In an edited volume that takes stock of theorizing internal security cooperation in the EU, neofunctionalism arguably constitutes one of the more obvious choices for analysis. First, since the early developments of cooperation in the field of Justice and Home Affairs (JHA) in the 1980s, observers have pointed to functional interdependencies between the Single European Market and JHA issues. Second, EU JHA have undergone an astonishing ascent from modest and obscure beginnings to an increasingly mature and vibrant field of EU policymaking. At the constitutional level it has shifted, in less than two decades, from an intergovernmental regime—in which only a handful of member states participated outside the Treaty framework—towards an almost fully communitarized EU policy area.[1] Neofunctionalism with its particular focus on *explaining* policymaking outcomes (Wiener and Diez, 2009), and its core competence with regard to the *dynamics* of European integration should be apt to account for these changes. Third, although neofunctionalism is one of the most widely criticized theories of European integration, it has remained relevant in the academic discourse over the years (cf. Niemann and Schmitter, 2009).

Treaty revision in the field of JHA is a particularly interesting and important research issue from a neofunctionalist perspective, as it may constitute a 'decisive battlefield in the struggle between the predominance of the nation-state and supranational integration in Europe' (Monar, 1998: 137). On the one hand, this area has become one of the most dynamic and fastest moving domains of the European integration project. On the other hand, it remains very close to the heart of national sovereignty, i.e. an area of 'high politics', and thus thought of as one of the least suitable fields for the workings of the spillover logic (cf. Hoffmann, 1964; Hoffmann, 1966).

The chapter proceeds as follows: section 7.2 specifies the neofunctionalist tenets and the concept of spillover, before discussing current trends in neofunctionalist theorizing. Section 7.3 focuses on ontological and methodological issues, including typical research questions to which neofunctionalism is likely to contribute. Section 7.4 provides a case study on EU migration policy Treaty revision from a neofunctionalist perspective. This section—which focuses empirically on the last Treaty revision leading to the Lisbon Treaty—makes use of the sub-concepts of functional, political, and cultivated spillover in order to analyse the extent to which neofunctionalism contributes to understanding and explaining the development of JHA at the constitutional level. Finally, I draw some conclusions and also assess the limitations of the neofunctionalist approach (with regard to analysing EU internal security).

7.2 Neofunctionalism

Neofunctionalist theory was built on the intellectual foundations provided by functionalist, federalist, and communications theories, combined with the indirect contribution of the 'group theorists' of American politics. Its earliest advocates, most notably Ernst Haas (1958) and Leon Lindberg (1963), combined functionalist mechanisms with federalist goals to explain and analyse the establishment and functioning of the European Coal and Steel Community (ECSC) and the European Economic Community (EEC).

7.2.1 *Main Tenets and Dynamics*

Neofunctionalism's fundamental assumptions can be summarized as follows: (1) integration is understood as a process. Implicit in the notion of process is the assumption that integration processes are subject to evolution over time and develop their own dynamic. (2) The actors participating in and shaping regional integration are assumed to be multiple, diverse, and changing, forming and reforming transnational coalitions (Haas, 1964: 68ff.). (3) Decisions are taken by rational actors, who are nonetheless able to learn from their experiences in cooperative decision-making (Haas, 1958: 291). (4) Incremental decision-making is given primacy over grand designs, as seemingly marginal adjustments are often prompted by the unintended consequences of previous decisions. (5) Neofunctionalists argued that positive sum-games and a supranational style of decision-making were typical forms of interaction in the Community setting, where participants seek to attain agreement by means of compromises upgrading common interests (Haas, 1964: 66). The neofunctionalist conception of change is succinctly encapsulated in the notion of 'spillover'. This notion has generally been subdivided into three subtypes: functional, political, and cultivated spillover (Tranholm-Mikkelsen, 1991).

Functional spillover pressures arise when an established objective can be assured only by taking further integrative actions (Lindberg, 1963: 10). Individual policy sectors and issue areas tend to be so interdependent in modern polities and economies that it is difficult to isolate them from one another. This interdependence causes further integrative pressures to arise and permeate other policy/issue areas (Haas, 1958: 297, 383). Functional pressures thus stem from the various endogenous interdependencies, i.e. the tensions and contradictions arising from within, or which are closely related to, the European integration project, which encourage or require policymakers to pursue related integrative action in order to secure their original objectives.

Political spillover describes the process through which (national) elites come to recognize that problems of substantial interest cannot be effectively addressed at the domestic level. This should lead to a gradual learning process whereby elites transfer their political expectations, efforts and—according to Haas— even loyalties to a new European centre. These national elites thus come to push for further integration, adding a political impetus to the process. Haas (1958: chapters 8–9) devoted particular attention to the pressures exerted by non-governmental elites, whilst Lindberg (1963: chapters 1, 4) as well as Lindberg and Scheingold (1970: 119ff.) attributed great significance to the effect of socialization processes on governmental elites bringing about consensus formation among member governments (and thus more integrative outcomes).[2] Neofunctionalists have pointed out that the proliferation of working groups and committees at the European level has led to a complex system of bureaucratic interpenetration that brings thousands of national and EU civil servants into frequent and recurrent contact. This provides an environment conducive to the development of mutual trust and a certain esprit de corps among officials in Community forums, and thus facilitates socialization processes. The underlying assumption is that the duration and intensity of interaction positively reinforces socialization and learning processes (Lindberg, 1963; cf. Lewis, 1998).

Cultivated spillover describes the role of supranational institutions[3] that, seeking to expand their own powers, become agents of integration, because they are likely to benefit from the progression of this process. Once established, they tend to take on a life of their own and are difficult to control by those who created them. Supranational institutions may foster the integration process, for example, by acting as policy entrepreneurs, and through promotional brokerage, lifting agreements beyond the lowest common denominator (e.g. Haas, 1964: 75ff.; Lindberg, 1963: chapter 3). Moreover, through leveraging their positions of centrality or authority in the Community's political system, institutions may be capable of directing the dynamics of relations with various types of actors (Nye, 1970: 809; Lindberg and Scheingold, 1970: chapter 3).

7.2.2 Current Trends in Neofunctionalist Theorizing

The heyday of neofunctionlist theory was between the late 1950s and the mid-1960s, when the momentum of European integration seemed to clearly corroborate its assumptions. Thereafter, however, a series of adverse empirical developments exposed the theory to growing criticism (cf. Niemann, 2006: 20–3). In response, several neofunctionalists worked to reformulate their theory in the 1960s and early 1970s, with mixed results—some consequent modifications proving insightful, others less so. The theory's detractors argued that neofunctionalism became increasingly reactive to spontaneous occurrences and, therefore, so indeterminate in its conclusions as to provide no clear direction for research (Moravcsik, 1993: 476). The upshot was that by the mid-1970s, most academic observers had dismissed neofunctionalism as either out-of-date or out-of-touch and Haas himself (1976) declared the theory to be 'obsolete'. Nonetheless, the revitalization of the European integration process in the mid-1980s was mirrored by a revival of neofunctionalism. Some authors suggested that the approach still contains a number of useful building blocks for contemporary theorizing (Keohane and Hoffmann, 1991; Marks et al., 1996; Pierson, 1996). Others went further, arguing that the Community's resurgence in the mid-1980s warrants the (wholesale) resurrection of the theory (Taylor, 1989; Tranholm-Mikkelsen, 1991).

It is worth noting that a number of more recent approaches owe something of an intellectual debt to neofunctionalism, and that neofunctionalist insights have also informed other theoretical approaches, such as multilevel governance and institutionalist scholarship on the EU (Niemann, 2006: chapter 5), though few authors give the theory explicit credit. The 'supranational governance' approach espoused by Stone Sweet and Sandholtz (1997) draws heavily on neofunctionalism (as the authors acknowledge, though without any apparent intent to revise the theory), emphasizing the role and importance of transnational exchange, EU rules, and supranational institutions. They argue that cross-border transactions generate a demand for Community rules, which EC institutions seek to supply. Once Community legislation develops, supranational society emerges as (business) actors realize that one set of rules is preferable to numerous sets of (national) rules. Actors working within the new Community framework would then test the limits of EC rules. This would in turn lead to more precise rules (due to clarifications from EC adjudicators) that develop ever further away from member governments' original intentions. Stone Sweet and Sandholtz argue that the transfer of competence to the Community is uneven and depends on the intensity of demands for EC regulation in a given issue area. They most significantly depart from (early) neofunctionalism by leaving open whether actors' loyalties and identities eventually shift to the European level and by laying greater emphasis on the relevance of intergovernmental bargaining in EC politics.

Very few scholars currently self-identify as 'neo-neofunctionalists' who continue to rework the original theory. Philippe Schmitter is one of them. He first turned to the task of reformulating neofunctionalism in the early 1970s and returned to the subject thirty years later. Schmitter's analysis (2004a; 2004b) stresses the importance of external/exogenous factors alongside endogenous tensions and contradictions related to the regional integration project—not just as impediments but as a potentially facilitating factor in the integration process. As for the role of supranational institutions in fostering integration, he belatedly emphasized the role of the European Court of Justice in making major contributions to the assertion of EU supra-nationality. Schmitter illustrates the dynamic of his revised approach through a model of decision cycles. 'Initiating cycles', which the present EU has passed through long ago, are followed by 'priming cycles' that account for the changing dynamics of member states in between decision cycles. 'With each successive crisis resolved... regional-level rules...gain in significance to the point that they begin to overshadow the opinions and actions of national governments, associations and individuals' (Schmitter, 2004b: 61). As the effects of regional processes become more pronounced, national actors may become more amenable to changing the competences and authority of regional institutions.

Nonetheless, in his revised theory, Schmitter rejects the assumed 'automaticity of spillover', positing alternative strategic responses such as (a) 'spill-around', the proliferation of functionally specialized, independent, but strictly intergovernmental, institutions; (b) 'build-up', the concession by member states of greater authority to the supranational organization without expanding the scope of its mandate; (c) and 'spill-back', to describe instances where member states pull back from previous commitments. He points out that so far each of the EC/EU decision cycles has generated further imbalances and contradictions thus preventing 'encapsulation', a state of stable self-maintenance. He further implies that the EU has yet to enter the 'transforming cycle', where the potentialities for functionally integrating national economies (would) have been exhausted and attention would turn to the integration of polities.

Another revised neofunctionalist framework was developed by the present author (Niemann1998; 2004; 2006). Taking early neofunctionalism as a starting point, I make a number of modifications to the original theory. First, the ontological scope is expanded to a degree—beyond what Haas (2001) *post hoc* described as 'soft rational choice' for the original neofunctionalist account (cf. section 7.3). Second, my revised approach should be understood as a wide-ranging, but partial, theory wherein integration is no longer seen as an automatic and exclusively dynamic process, but rather as a conditional, context-dependent, and dialectic process (cf. Tranholm-Mikkelsen, 1991: 18–19), i.e. the product of both dynamics and countervailing forces that may either be stagnating or opposing in nature. This revised neofunctionalist framework accommodates two such countervailing forces: the first being 'sovereignty-consciousness', where actors oppose delegating competences to the supranational level on the basis of national traditions, identities, and ideologies; and the second, 'domestic constraints and diversities', accounting for the circumscription of national governments' autonomy to act due to constraints by actors (e.g. lobby groups or coalition partners) or structural limitations (such as a country's economy, demography, or legal tradition) in the domestic political system. These countervailing pressures may be exacerbated by diversities between member states, which may entail considerable adjustment costs for some and thus obstruct integrative endeavours.

I also further elaborate and specify the dynamics of integration. The scope of functional spillover, for example, is expanded beyond mere economic linkages and the concept is freed from its deterministic ontology. I argue that the degree of interdependence between policy areas is not the sole determinant of the strength of functional spillover logics and that functional structures do not determine actors' behaviour in a mechanical or predictable manner. Rather, for functional logics to gain traction they must be *perceived* as plausible or compelling (Niemann, 2006: 30–1). In addition to other spillover pressures, I also refined the concept of political spillover (in terms of non-governmental elites). I argue that not only the quantity, but also the *quality* of interaction impacts on cooperative norm socialization and learning processes. Learning and socialization are no longer regarded as constant (as implied by early neofunctionalists) but contingent on conditions such as 'a commonly shared lifeworld', 'uncertainty and insufficient knowledge', 'the possibility for lengthy discussion', and 'low levels of politicization'. Under such conditions, actors are predisposed to deliberate, reason, argue, and persuade, rather than bargain, and may consequently undergo more deeply rooted (reflexive) learning: rather than simply adapting the means to achieve essentially unchanged goals, actors in such more deliberative/communicative mode tend to redefine their very priorities and preferences in processes aimed at reaching a (more) reasoned consensus (in contrast to what happens in purely strategic negotiations).[4]

In the introduction to the 2004 edition of the *Uniting of Europe*, Haas made a final contribution to European integration theory. While this piece does not constitute an outright attempt to revise his neofunctionalist theory, Haas makes some astute observations on how new developments in IR and political science theory relate to, challenge, and (potentially) stimulate neofunctionalism. In particular, Haas makes it his task to see how neofunctionalism 'can become part of a respectable constructivism' (Haas, 2004: xvii). He suggests that neofunctionalism may be considered a forerunner, and part of, constructivism. Haas also considers the utility of (old and new) institutionalist approaches. He concludes that revised neofunctionalist approaches benefited from institutionalist thinking, as a result of which the neofunctionalist tradition, in his view, 'has a new lease on life' and should be considered 'no longer obsolescent' (Haas, 2004: liii).

7.3 How to Apply it: Ontological and Methodological Considerations

7.3.1 *Ontology*

Early neofunctionalists made little effort to spell out any systematic ontology to underpin their theorizing, but it can to an extent be inferred from their writings, where it is emphasized that decisions are taken by rational actors, who are nonetheless able to learn from their experiences in EC decision-making (Haas, 1958: 291). A more coherent theoretical understanding and a more meaningful application of neofunctionalist theory, however, requires a more specific elaboration of neofunctionalist ontology. Haas (2001: 22–4) provides something of a retrospective ontological framework for his original neofunctionalist theory, describing the neofunctionalist ontology as a 'soft' rational choice, thus assuming that societal actors 'calculate' their interests, 'nationalism [is] trumped by the utilitarian-instrumental human desire to better oneself', but 'ideas and values [define] actor preferences'.

My revised neofunctionalist framework broadly affirms this stance, but slightly broadens the ontological scope by drawing on constructivism to a larger extent (Niemann 2004; 2006). This extension was deemed necessary because (a) early neofunctionalism was pervaded by interests in cognitions, perception, and the sociological dimension of institutionalist interaction (cf. Rosamond, 2005), and (b) his account places more explicit emphasis on socialization and learning than Haas's early neofunctionalism. My ontological position acknowledges 'that there is a real (material) world out there, which offers resistance when we act upon it, [but actors] frame or construct the [material] world according to their knowledge, norms, experience, and understandings. Hence, actors' interests and identities are moulded and constituted by both cognitive and material structures' (Niemann, 2004: 20). Given the significance of functional structures, my revised neofunctionalist framework accords an approximately equal significance to structure and agency (which mutually constitute each other), unlike early neofunctionalism, which favoured the latter (cf. Haas, 2001: 28–9).

In his final contribution Haas (2004) seems to have become more sympathetic to the view of neofunctionalism as embedded within a (pragmatic) constructivist ontology, while still putting greater emphasis on agency.

7.3.2 *Areas of Typical Application/Typical Research Questions*

It has been rightly argued in the literature—and also been taken to heart by those revising the theory—that neofunctionalism does not and cannot provide a general theory of integration. The theory possesses certain analytical tools to deal with certain kinds of questions, i.e. those related to (describing and) explaining integration. Hence, (typical) research questions, to which neofunctionalism can provide insights include: How can EU decision outcomes be explained? Why does European integration take place (e.g. in a particular policy area)?[5]

While scholars have shifted their attention to questions such as the nature of the EU political system, the social and political consequences of the integration process and the normative dimension of European integration since the 1990s (cf. Diez and Wiener, 2004), the issue of explaining outcomes of EU decision-making, which has occupied scholars since the 1950s, is still a very important one. The ongoing salience of this question partly stems from the continuing disagreement among analysts regarding the most relevant factors accounting for the dynamics and standstills of the European integration process and certain segments of it.

As for the area of typical application, neofunctionalism operates at the nexus of explaining all dimensions of the triad of *polity*, *politics*, and *policy*. While most applications of neofunctionalism focus on the interface of *politics* (process/style) and *polity* (form/institutional design) (e.g. Haas, 1958; 1970; Lindberg, 1966; Schmitter, 2004a; Niemann, 2006; 2008; 2011), the *policy* (content) dimension is also relevant in the latter works and features more prominently (Lindberg; 1963: chapters XI, XII; Mutimer, 1989; Jensen, 2000).

7.3.3 *Application to JHA*

There is very little scholarship that analyses JHA issues from a decidedly neofunctionalist perspective (Niemann, 2006; 2008). However, many authors and studies have (implicitly) echoed neofunctionalist assumptions or insights. Sassen (2008) for example has argued that the internationalization of the economy, the growth of transnational exchanges, and the increased judicialization of European politics has diminished state sovereignty and reinforced supranational cooperation. In addition, the role of supranational institutions, and especially the European Commission, as promoters of integration in this policy area has also been highlighted, both in terms of Treaty revision (Niemann, 2008; 2012; see section 7.4) and the legislative agenda and substantial legislation (Kaunert, 2009; 2010). Kaunert argues that the European Commission has played a very significant role, that of a supranational policy entrepreneur, during the development of a Common European Asylum System (Kaunert 2009: 156–62). In addition, it has been suggested that the European Court of Justice managed to extend its jurisdiction over free movement and asylum cases by using references to 'citizenship' in the Treaty (Lavenex and Wallace, 2005).

Other authors have emphasized the functional pressures originating from the single market and the free movement of persons as drivers for integration in the realm of migration. The free movement of persons principle goes back to the four freedoms inscribed in the Treaty of Rome and has been on the Community agenda more seriously since the 1975 Tindemans report. The adoption of the Schengen Agreement of 1985, the internal market project and the Schengen Convention of 1990 have been viewed as gradually reinforcing the free movement objective and thus the underlying rationale for further cooperation (den Boer, 1997). States are considered unlikely to waive the power of internal controls, unless they can be provided with an equivalent protection with regard to persons arriving at external frontiers. This implies shifting controls to external borders and common migration policies, as otherwise, for instance, the restrictive efforts of one member state would be undermined by liberal policies of another state (cf. Monar, 2001; Turnbull and Sandholtz, 2001; Niemann, 2008). As Monar put it, 'it seems unlikely that without the constraints generated by the internal market programme, the Member States would have been willing to go so far with their co-operation on asylum and policing matters' (Monar, 2001: 754).

Knelangen (2001) and Müller (2003) have reflected on the explanatory potential of several integration theories, including neofunctionalism, at the end of their comprehensive studies on EU JHA, without however, applying it in an in-depth or systematic fashion. Nevertheless, Knelangen comes to the (tentative) conclusion that several important developments of EU JHA cooperation cannot be convincingly explained without recourse to neofunctionalist spillover dynamics (Knelangen 2001: 347).

7.3.4 *Methodological Considerations/Operationalization*

One avenue for evaluating neofunctionalism's explanatory power is to assess the extent to which its sub-concepts/dynamics can account for certain outcomes or developments in EU policymaking. For each neofunctionalist pressure, indicators can be specified in order to operationalize it for empirical research. Given space constraints, the most prominent neofunctionalist dynamic: functional spillover, will serve as an example.

The notion of functional spillover is here operationalized by probing several indicators and mechanisms including: (1) the salience of the original integrative objective, which determines the strength of the functional pressure for further action. (2) The degree of functional interdependence between issue A (original objective) and issue B (requiring further action), that is to say, the extent to which changes/tensions in issue area A (e.g. single market) affect issue area B (e.g. JHA), thus requiring more collective action. (3) The availability of functional solutions. Is further action in a particular issue area necessary to achieve the original integrative goal, or are there alternative solutions? If the initial objective cannot be secured by other means, the functional connection is likely to be a strong one.

7.4 Case Study: Explaining Migration Policy Treaty Revision

To demonstrate how neofunctionalism may be applied to JHA, I have focused on EU migration policy Treaty revision. After the third pillar was established through the Treaty of Maastricht, the subsequent intergovernmental conference (IGC) leading to the Amsterdam Treaty brought visa, asylum, and immigration policy into the community sphere (Title IV TEC). Nonetheless, the decision-making and the institutional set-up remained largely intergovernmental, being only partially reformed by the Treaty of Nice. The Treaty of Lisbon afforded the EU's central institutions a significant increase in powers and introduced the Community Method—qualified majority voting (QMV) in the Council, co-decision of the European Parliament (EP), and full jurisdiction by the European Court of Justice (ECJ)—for nearly all aspects of asylum and immigration policy.[6] The Lisbon provisions on migration thus constitute a remarkable leap forward.

Sections 7.4.1, 7.4.2, and 7.4.3[7] analyse the extent to which the concepts of functional, political, and cultivated spillover may contribute to understanding and explaining the development of migration policy decision rules and institutional aspects, focusing on the 'last' Treaty revision—here understood as the entire process from the Convention to the Treaty of Lisbon. In a departure from the standard method of preparing EU Treaty reforms, the Laeken

European Council decided to form a Convention on the Future of Europe. The Draft Treaty produced by the Convention already included, to a great extent, the substantive changes of the Treaty revision leading to the Treaty of Lisbon.

7.4.1 Functional Spillover

The basic underlying rationale for JHA cooperation is often viewed in terms of functional logics: the establishment of the internal market and the objective of free movement of persons required cooperation in the areas of external border control and other flanking measures to compensate for the elimination of intra-EU borders.[8] States are generally assumed to be reluctant to give up control over their borders without a guarantee of equivalent protection at external frontiers. The risk that the restrictive measures adopted in one member state might be undermined by more liberal policies in another—since 'the free movement of persons also means free movement of illegal immigrants' or rejected asylum seekers—necessitates the adoption of common policies on asylum seekers, refugees, and illegal immigrants (de Lobkowicz, 1994: 104).[9] Similarly, concerns were raised that the abolition of internal borders would lead to 'asylum-shopping' and an uncontrollable influx of illegal immigrants (Achermann, 1995). The Dublin Convention sought to address the question of asylum-shopping by determining that asylum applications had to be dealt with in the state of first entry, but this in turn raised the question of arbitrariness, given member states' differing standards of reception and varying interpretations of the refugee status. Thus some degree of harmonization, for example on the reception of asylum seekers, became necessary. To achieve this objective, and to enact further flanking measures, a greater use of the Community Method was deemed necessary both to expedite cooperation and to enable outcomes above the lowest common denominator. As for the last Treaty revision, this rationale bolstered the case for greater use of qualified majority voting (QMV) in order to overcome decision-making deadlocks in the legislative process.

During the last Treaty revision—spanning from the Convention to the Lisbon Treaty—another source of functional pressure became even more pressing: enlargement. Although an exogenous event, enlargement was gradually internalized as a settled policy goal and thus became an endogenous source of pressure for reform of EU decision-making rules. The establishment of enlargement as an internal objective gave rise to (anticipated) problems/tensions in terms of decision-making and coordination among the member states under the decision rule of unanimity. Even with a mere fifteen delegations many already regarded unanimity as problematic. This logic of impending decision-making gridlock was presented, for example, in Commission papers as early as the Amsterdam IGC (cf. e.g. Commission, 1996). At the time, however, the force of this argument was checked by a perceived 'lack of urgency' since 'no enlargement is foreseen before 2003–2005' (Patijn, 1997: 38; also cf. Devuyst, 1998: 626; Moravcsik and Nicolaidis, 1999: 78, 82). Nonetheless, provisions were made at the Seville European Council of 2002 for signing the Accession Treaty the following year and for enabling the participation of new member states in the 2004 EP elections, so that enlargement became an imminent reality. This put substantial pressure on issue areas that were subject to unanimity, such as migration. Enlargement was to be cited frequently at the Convention as a rationale to substantiate the need for reforming the decision rules of Title IV, i.e. of asylum and immigration policy (cf. Commission, 2002; European Parliament, 2003b).

Although only a brief empirical review could be provided here (for more see Niemann, 2008; 2012), it seems that functional pressures were strong indeed during the last Treaty revision, in three key respects. First, the two original goals were rather salient: (1) the completion and functioning of the internal market and (2) enlargement have clearly been vital EU objectives. Second, the functional interdependences—between (1) the internal market and migration,[10] as well as (2) imminent enlargement and migration/JHA decision rules—have been strong, with original policy objectives clearly impacting on migration policy/decision rules. Third, we can ask whether further legislative actions were necessary to achieve the initial objectives? It seems that some degree of harmonization of migration policies was perceived necessary, and that this objectives and the goal of enlargement were considered achievable only with a reformed institutional set-up (Niemann, 2006: chapter 4).

7.4.2 Cultivated Spillover

The following section turns to the concept of cultivated spillover and the role of supranational institutions. The *Commission* is generally held to have a vested interest in further integration, not least because it is likely to benefit from a more supranational decision-making set-up. In terms of the institutional set-up of EU migration policy, the Commission already acquired an important advantage through obtaining the exclusive right to initiate legislation on asylum and immigration matters after the five-year transitional period following the entering into force of the Amsterdam Treaty. However, the last Treaty revision was also important from the Commission's perspective. QMV and co-decision tend to favour the Commission's legislative preferences, because it reduces the number of (member state) veto players that tend to drive proposals towards the lowest common denominator and it increases the power of the EP, which has (often) tended to be more sympathetic of

Commission proposals on migration policy than the member states (Kaunert, 2009: 151ff; Kaunert and Leonard, 2012: 1405).

The Commission exhibited markedly greater assertiveness in the JHA debate throughout the Convention than at the Nice IGC. The JHA dossier was, in fact, one of the Commission's (strategic) priorities during the Convention (Norman, 2005: 136), and it expended considerable political energy in the cultivation of relations with other actors, both formally and informally. For example, the two Commission representatives regularly attended informal meetings of Convention members, as in the group of so-called 'movers and shakers' that met regularly at the Brussels Hilton to discuss ideas, test positions, and cultivate relations (Norman, 2005: 43). Likewise, the Commission representatives were 'keen contributors to plenary debates' (Kassim and Dimitrakopoulus, 2007: 1255). The Commission actively fostered spillover by making a (more) considerable effort to explain the structural rationales for further integrative steps in the area of visa, asylum, and immigration policy, also by pointing to the inadequacy of current decision rules for a timely implementation or swifter progress of the (Amsterdam and Tampere) policy objectives forums (e.g. Vitorino, 2001).

The negotiating infrastructure suited the Commission. Unlike at an IGC, the convention structure meant its representatives were equal participants. The two Commission representatives, Barnier and Vitorino, were both also 'first-tier' members of the Praesidium with quite some leverage to influence the Convention agenda and negotiations (Beach, 2005: 200). Moreover, the predominantly deliberative decision-making style at the Convention meant that explanations attached to propositions carried greater weight and sound arguments could quickly gain traction with negotiators. The Commission argued forcefully for further Europeanization by pointing to the impending enlargement or the inadequacy of current decision rules for effective implementation of agreed objectives (Vitorino, 2002). The Commission also contributed to the latter rationale by the timely initiation of the required legislative proposals. It was thus up to the Council to find agreement, which further spurred the revelation of problems attached to the unanimity rule.

During the Convention the Commission enjoyed significant informational advantages vis-à-vis other groups (Beach, 2005), possessing a formidable institutional memory and considerable administrative/substantive backing, and readily capitalized on this advantage. The task force established for the Convention consisted of a strong team of experts on the various Convention topics (including JHA) and officials from the legal service, providing sizeable in-house resources to enhance the Commission's presence and to allow its two representatives to shine at the Convention (Kassim and Dimitrakopoulus, 2007: 1255; Norman, 2005: 136). The two Commission representatives had themselves acquired considerable relevant experience—Barnier during the

IGC in 2000 as the Commissioner responsible, and Vitorino representing the Commission in the EU Charter negotiations in 1999–2000. Vitorino's superior expertise and personal reputational capital—together with the remarkable political energy that he and his cabinet brought to bear—allowed him to shape the (JHA) debates in both the working group Freedom, Security and Justice, and in the plenary (Beach, 2005: 198; Goulard, 2003: 374).

Much like the Commission, the *European Parliament* (EP) generally stands to benefit directly from the progression of the integration process. At the last Treaty revision, the potential extension of co-decision to those aspects of migration policy, where the EP until then merely needed to be consulted, clearly constituted an opportunity for Parliament to enhance its competences.

The EP's impact on the last Treaty revision negotiations in the field of migration stands in marked contrast to its lacklustre showing at the Nice IGC. This turnaround may in part stem from the fact that, unlike at Nice, EP representatives at the Convention were fully legitimate and equal participants. Parliament had two delegates in the Praesidium, Klaus Hänsch and Íñigo Méndez de Vigo, affording it some opportunity to shape the Convention agenda and the development of negotiations (Beach, 2005: 199–200). As well as the two members of the Praesidium, the EP sent sixteen representatives (and sixteen alternate members) to the Convention, where considerable coordination among MEPs allowed them to form a comparatively coherent and well organized faction and to exert significant influence over Convention deliberations (Beach, 2007: 1284; Duff, 2003: 4). In addition, EP representatives skilfully cultivated relations with other Convention members. For instance, key MEPs such as Brok and Hänsch, were regular participants in the informal 'movers and shakers' meetings at the Hilton in Brussels where ideas and positions could be ventilated informally (interview NAT-2; EU-4).[11] Moreover, EP members had frequent meetings with national parliamentarians, for example, in the context of COSAC (interview EU-1), or through the European political families. More generally, MEPs proved to be 'especially skilful at building coalitions behind the scenes' (Beach, 2005: 198).

The EP representatives generally felt at home with the negotiation infrastructure of the Convention. Given the parliamentary-like environment and MEPs familiarity with the EU machinery, Convention matters were 'bread and butter' to them (Milton and Keller-Noëllet, 2005: 33) and thus 'privileged the representatives of the EP' (Beach, 2007: 1272). In addition, and as in the case of the Commission (also cf. section 7.4.3), the Convention's more open-ended and deliberative nature (compared to an IGC), meant that good arguments—such as those regarding the reform of migration policy decision rules and institutional issues—could not be rejected out of hand, but were likely to register and shape the direction of negotiations.

EP members were among the most active delegates at the Convention, not least on Title IV issues (visa, asylum, and immigration), frequently intervening in plenary and working group debates and contributing their own papers to the discussion (Brok, 2002; Kaufmann, 2002; Lancker et al., 2002; Mendez de Vigo et al., 2002; cf. Maurer, 2003). Klaus Hänsch (PES), Elmar Brok (EPP), Andrew Duff (Liberals), and Johannes Voggenhuber (Greens), who all supported further communitarization of Title IV, also played a prominent role in their respective political families. With few exceptions, MEPs tended to act in concert with the two Commission representatives, as perhaps the most dedicated proponents of the Community Method concerning asylum and immigration issues. EP members employed the functional rationales to argue for further integration—both those rooted in the internal market and particularly those relating to enlargement and its impact on (JHA) decision rules (European Parliament, 2001: 6, 26; Brok, 2002: 3; Duff, 2003: 2; Mendez de Vigo, 2002: 2; Meyer, 2002: 2)—and thus became active agents of JHA integration. Ultimately, MEPs and the EP more generally were among the strongest, if not the strongest, advocates of the Draft Constitutional Treaty (European Parliament, 2003a; Beach, 2005), thus contributing substantially to its binding strength and endurance.

7.4.3 Political Spillover

The tangibly greater impact of political spillover in terms of socialization, deliberation, and learning processes at the Convention, which also influenced the outcome at subsequent IGCs, was perhaps one of the most significant reversals since the Nice IGC. A number of favourable conditions inherent in the Convention setting may account for this reversal: (1) the initial phase of listening and reflection which preceded negotiations, during which expectations and visions could be freely shared, generated a deeper understanding of other members' ideas and softened pre-conceived opinions (Kleine and Risse, 2005). (2) The quantity of interaction—over fifty sessions of both the plenary and the Praesidium held within eighteen months—fostered the emergence of an *esprit de corps* and a strong sense of responsibility for a successful outcome (Göler, 2003). (3) Convention members enjoyed a remarkable degree of autonomy and were largely unconstrained by governmental briefs (Maurer, 2003: 134; but Magnette and Nicolaïdis, 2004). Moreover, in contrast to the preceding IGCs, domestic bureaucracies could do little to hinder the deliberation process as government representatives were not generally obliged to go through inter-ministerial coordination processes for the formation of national positions (Maurer, 2003: 136). (4) The atmosphere, spirit, and negotiating structure meant that flat rejection of a position was not an option available to members of the Convention, as proposals could not be dismissed without entering into a reasoned discussion where one's arguments would be subject to scrutiny (Closa, 2004: 201). In such an environment, sound arguments, validated on the basis of accepted criteria, carried greater persuasive weight, and were therefore more likely to prevail in the debate.

As a result of this negotiating format, the logic of (strong) functional (and exogenous) rationales for further communitarization was afforded sufficient time to gain traction and eventual acceptance in the minds of actors. In such a deliberative process, negotiators may be expected to concur more fully with the eventual outcome, which would likely emerge through reasoned consensus rather than simple compromise. That the Title IV Convention outcome was indeed largely perceived as such was borne out in interviews (EU-3, EU-6, NAT-1, NAT-4). This same logic applies, albeit to a lesser extent, to the Draft Constitutional Treaty as a whole, lending greater moral weight and authority to the Convention text and problematizing significant departures from this consensus for negotiators at subsequent IGCs (Closa, 2004), not least because member states were very much involved and implicated in its development. Moreover, there was a general feeling that the Convention format had worked well. The dominant policy discourse thus favoured retention of the provisions of the Draft Constitutional Treaty as far as possible (*Guardian* 14/3/03; *Frankfurter Allgemeine Zeitung* 16/6/03). Due to the considerable bonding strength or moral momentum of the Convention text, negotiations on most (non-institutional) issues at the subsequent IGCs came to take it as a starting point. In a way, it turned into the default setting (Beach, 2005: 199). The moral momentum, with regard to migration issues, was such that the Convention text on these issues was not reopened.

The narrative of socialization, deliberation, and learning presented above is difficult to substantiate within given space limitations.[12] Nonetheless, interviewees consistently described the negotiations in terms of arguing and reasoning, either unprompted, or when asked to choose from a range of potential characterizations (EU-7, EU-2; NAT-5, NAT-6). Likewise negotiators generally made little mention of hierarchy, status, qualifications, or other sources of power in their statements, suggesting a reluctance to add non-discursive authority to their arguments. Moreover, there is a remarkable consistence between speakers' utterances in the plenary with statements made in other forums (e.g. Vitorino, 2001; 2002a; 2002b), which is also indicative of 'truthful arguing'. Furthermore, in the absence of persuasive arguments, 'powerful' actors did not prevail in the Convention. For example, the attempts of the German Foreign Minister, the UK government representative, and others to reintroduce unanimity for the (whole) area of immigration (Fischer, 2003; Hain, 2003) eventually succumbed to the powerful rationales for further communitarization described above (interview EU-3, NAT-5). Finally, the successful resolution of issues such as migration—which produced deadlock in a bargaining-like setting of Nice—in the context of the more discursive setting of the Convention, similarly indicates that deliberation and arguing is likely to have played a role (cf. Kleine and Risse, 2010).

7.5 Conclusion

Although neofunctionalists neither devised their theory against the backdrop of developments in JHA, nor focused much on integration in this domain, it seems that neofunctionalist theory adds considerably to our understanding of EU internal security. It seems to do so in a twofold manner. First, neofunctionalism provides us with significant insights into the (still) important question of how decision outcomes in the area of JHA can be explained. Concerning this question, neofunctionalism particularly indicates crucial driving forces and mechanisms of change—such as the various spillover mechanisms introduced and illustrated above—that led to particular decision outcomes. The example of migration-related Treaty revisions suggests that the theory does not only apply to the area of 'low' politics, but also to topics close to the heart of national sovereignty (compare this with the intergovernmental dynamics suggested in chapter 2). Second and closely related, it can thus be argued that neofunctionalism goes beyond mainstream intergovernmentalist conceptualizations of JHA as a purely state-dominated (or government-dominated) process and highlights the involvement of non-state/non-governmental actors across different levels in decision-making processes (in this regard, neofunctionalism shares some analytical affinities with 'governance' approaches discussed in chapter 5). Consequently, neofunctionalism provides a more nuanced picture of the complex reality of EU internal security policymaking.

This chapter has also revealed some limitations of neofunctionalist theory. Most importantly, neofunctionalism (in its conventional version) struggles to account for the limits of European integration. For example, the fact that policymakers did not agree on a full communitarization of asylum and immigration policy during the last Treaty revision cannot be adequately explained by (mainstream) neofunctionalist theory because it lacks an account of disintegrative pressures. Similarly, neofunctionalism may have trouble explaining the disconnect between high-level political agreement and lower-level stagnation on operational cooperation, discussed in several chapters in this volume. However, in this respect is useful to note that some revised neofunctionalist frameworks do not conceptualize integration solely as a dynamic or integrative process, but also consider countervailing forces (Niemann, 2006).

Hence, integration is assumed here to be a *dialectical* process, both subject to dynamics *and* countervailing forces. The latter may induce either stagnation or spillback. Through such a dialectical account the non-linear, stop-and-go nature of the European integration process, and here specifically EU internal security, is thought to be conceptualized more adequately. In this process the strength, variation, and interplay of pressures on both sides of the equation would thus determine the outcome of a particular decision or sequence of decisions.

The latter aspect should, of course, be seen as a shortcoming of neofunctionalism. However, in some sense it may also be seen as a strength that the theory is capable of reformulation. Neofunctionalist theory can thus be seen as still evolving. This should be taken as a challenge rather than an excuse for dismissing neofunctionalism as a framework for conceptualizing EU internal security.

Notes

1. At the EU legislative level—although processes have often been cumbersome and frequently reflected only the 'minimum standards' stipulated in the Treaty (of Amsterdam)—output in quantitative terms has been remarkable (Monar, 2010). The rising importance of this policy field has also found prominent expression at the symbolic level. The Area of Freedom, Security and Justice has been listed as one of the Union's fundamental objectives in the Treaty of Lisbon where it 'ranks' second, ahead of the Single European Market, the Common Foreign and Security Policy, and Economic and Monetary Union.
2. The subsequent case analysis focuses on this aspect of political spillover.
3. While Haas emphasized the role of the High Authority and the European Commission, later on neofunctionalism was often interpreted as viewing the role of supranational institutions, more generally, as an integrative dynamic.
4. Cf. Niemann (2004; 2006) who builds on Habermas (1981), Risse (2000), and Checkel and Moravscik (2001).
5. And arguably even with this set of questions, early/conventional neofunctionalism can only cope with them in an unsatisfactorily manner, as it mainly concentrates on the dynamics of the integration process.
6. However, member states' right to determine access to the labour market by third-country nationals, for example, remains outside the scope of the Treaty.
7. Sections 7.4.1, 7.4.2, and 7.4.3 draw on Niemann (2008; 2012).
8. The principle of free movement of persons goes back to the four freedoms enshrined by the Treaty of Rome. The 1975 Tindemans report first seriously placed its implementation on the Community agenda, and the adoption of the Schengen Agreement of 1985, the internal market project and the Schengen Convention of 1990 gradually reinforced the objective (Den Boer, 1997). The considerable significance that was attached to it was at least in part because, among the four freedoms, the free

movement of persons has the most direct bearing on the lives of individual citizens (Fortescue, 1995: 28). Furthermore, failure to properly ensure this objective risked compromising the efficient working of the internal market (Commission, 1985).

9. To include migration in a paper on 'internal security' is neither meant as a norma-tive, nor as a political statement but reflects the processes of securitization of migra-tion policy, i.e. the tendency of discussing migration primarily as a security issue. In the EU context, the Schengen cooperation is commonly presented as the starting point for an increased linking of security and migration, which resulted in the blurring of different forms of migration and the development of control-oriented, restrictive migration policy. The perceived need of cooperation at the EU level to prevent misuse of free movement by irregular migrants and organized crime tied the debate on migration, refugees, and asylum to the fight against drugs, terrorism, police cooperation and assistance in criminal matters (Huysmans 1995: 53; 2000: 752; 2006: 48, 66; Levy, 2005: 35; Van Houtum and Pijpers, 2007: 299–300).

10. Occasionally, it has been pointed out that the functional link between the single market and migration policy has been exaggerated (Huysmans, 2000). This may be true, but the perception or (discursive) construction of this functional link, and thus its impact on politics, has been very strong indeed (Niemann, 2006).

11. For this empirical investigation, apart from using documentation and secondary literature, I have conducted about twenty interviews. The non-attributable inter-views have been coded as follows: 'EU' refers to interviews conducted in the EU institutions (including the Council Secretariat), and 'NAT' refers to interviews with representatives of national governments/administrations. Most interviews were conducted in Brussels in 2004.

12. But also see the general indications in the literature (Göler, 2003; Maurer, 2003; Closa, 2004; Niemann, 2006). For indicators of communicative action and persua-sion, see Checkel and Moravcsik (2001), Niemann (2004).

References

Achermann, A. (1995) 'Asylum and Immigration Policies', in Bieber, R. and Monar, J. (eds) *Justice and Home Affairs in the European Union*. Brussels: European Interuniversity Press, pp. 127–40.

Beach, D. (2005) *The Dynamics of European Integration*. Basingstoke: Palgrave Macmillan.

Beach, D. (2007) 'The European Parliament in the 2000 IGC and the Constitutional Treaty Negotiations: From Loser to Winner', *Journal of European Public Policy*, 14(8), pp. 1271–92.

Brok, E. (2002) 'What the Constitution of the European Union will need to say on "Freedom, Justice and Security"', CONV 436/02. Brussels.

Checkel, J. T. and Moravcsik, A. (2001) 'A Constructive Research Program in EU Studies?' *European Union Politics*, 2(2), pp. 219–49.

Closa, C. (2004) 'The Convention Method and the Transformation of EU Constitu-tional Politics', in Eriksen, E., Fossum, J., and Menéndez, A. (eds) *Developing a Constitution for Europe*. London: Routledge, pp. 183–206.

Commission of the European Communities (1985) White Paper on the Internal Market, COM(85)331 final.

Commission of the European Communities (1996) Justice and Home Affairs provisions in the EC Treaty—a possible location, CONF/3912/96.

Commission of the European Communities (2002a) Communication from the Commission to the Convention, CONV/229/0222.

de Lobkowicz, W. (1994) 'Intergovernmental Co-operation in the Field of Migration', in Monar, J. and Morgan, R. (eds) *The Third Pillar of the European Union*. Brussels: European Interuniversity Press, pp. 99–122.

den Boer, M. (1997) 'Travel Notes on a Bumpy Journey from Schengen via Maastricht to Amsterdam', in den Boer, M. (ed.) *The Implementation of Schengen*. Maastricht: Institute of Public Administration, pp. 147–54.

Devuyst, Y. (1998) 'Treaty Reform in the European Union: The Amsterdam Process', *Journal of European Public Policy*, 5(4), pp. 615–31.

Diez, T. and Wiener, A. (2004) 'Introducing the Mosaic of Integration Theory', in Wiener, A. and Diez, T. (eds) *European Integration Theory*. Oxford: Oxford University Press, pp. 1–21.

Duff, A. (2003) 'Der Beitrag des Europäischen Parlaments zum Konvent: Treibende Kraft für einen Konsens', *Integration*, 26, pp. 3–9.

European Parliament (2001) 'Report on the Treaty of Nice and the Future of the Union', Committee on Constitutional Affairs. Rapporteurs: Iñigo Méndez de Vigo and António José Seguro, A5-0168/2001 Final.

European Parliament (2003a) 'Resolution on the Draft Treaty Establishing a Constitution for Europe ...', 11047/2003, 24/9/2003.

European Parliament (2003b) 'Background Information: Convention: Area of Freedom, Security and Justice', Brussels, 3/4/2003.

Fischer, J. (2003) 'Suggestion for Amendment of Article III-163 (revised)'. Available at: http://european-convention.europa.eu/pdf/reg/en/03/cv00/cv00727.en03.pdf (Accessed: 24 May 2016).

Fortescue, J. A. (1995) 'First Experiences with the Implementation of the Third Pillar Provision', in Bieber, R. and Monar J. (eds) *Justice and Home Affairs in the European Union*. Brussels: European Interuniversity Press, pp. 19–27.

Göler, D. (2003) 'Die Europäische Union vor ihrer Konstitutionalisierung', *Integration*, 26(1), pp. 17–30.

Goulard, S. (2003) 'Die Rolle der Kommission im Konvent', *Integration*, 26(4), pp. 371–98.

Haas, E. (1958) *The Uniting of Europe*. London: Stevens.

Haas, E. (1964) 'Technocracy, Pluralism and the New Europe', in Graubard, S. (ed.) *A New Europe?* Boston, MA: Houghton Mifflin, pp. 62–88.

Haas, E. (1970) 'The Study of Regional Integration: Reflections on the Joy and Anguish of Pretheorizing', *International Organization* 24(4), pp. 607–44.

Haas, E. (1976) 'Turbulent Fields and the Theory of Regional Integration', *International Organization*, 30(2), pp. 173–212.

Haas, E. (2001) 'Does Constructivism Subsume Neo-functionalism?' in Christiansen, T., Jørgensen, K., and Wiener, A. (eds) *The Social Construction of Europe*. London: Sage, pp. 22–31.

Haas, E. (2004) 'Introduction: Institutionalism or Constructivism?' in *The Uniting of Europe*, 3rd ed. Notre Dame, IN: University of Notre Dame Press, pp. xiii–lvi.

Habermas, J. (1981) *Theorie des kommunikativen Handelns*, 2 vols. Frankfurt/M.: Suhrkamp.

Hain, P. (2003) Suggestion for amendment of Article III-163. Available at: http://european-convention.europa.eu/pdf/reg/en/03/cv00/cv00727.en03.pdf (Accessed: 24 May 2016).

Hoffmann, S. (1964) 'The European Process at Atlantic Cross-purposes', *Journal of Common Market Studies*, 3(2), pp. 85–101.

Hoffmann, S. (1966) 'Obstinate or Obsolete: The Fate of the Nation State and the Core of Western Europe', *Daedalus*, 95(3), pp. 862–915.

Huysmans, J. (1995) 'Migrants as a Security Problem: Dangers of "Securitizing" Societal Issues', in Miles, R. and Thränhardt, D. (eds) *Migration and European Integration: The Dynamics of Inclusion and Exclusion*. London: Pinter, pp. 53–72.

Huysmans, J. (2000) 'The European Union and the Securization of Migration', *Journal of Common Market Studies*, 38(5), pp. 751–77.

Huysmans, J. (2006) *The Politics of Insecurity: Fear, Migration and Asylum in the EU*. London and New York: Routledge.

Jensen, C. (2000) 'Neofunctionalist Theories and the Development of European Social and Labour Market Policy', *Journal of Common Market Studies*, 38(1), pp. 71–92.

Kassim H. and Dimitrakopoulos, D. G. (2007) 'The European Commission and the Future of Europe', *Journal of European Public Policy*, 14(8), pp. 1249–70.

Kaufmann, S. (2002) 'Justiz- und Innenpolitik: Die Gesamte Konstruktion der Dritten Säule Muss Fallen', intervention at the Fifth Plenary Session of the European Convention Held on the 06–07 June. Available at: http://european-convention.europa.eu/docs/speeches/8208.pdf (Accessed: 4 May 2016).

Kaunert, C. (2009) 'Liberty versus Security? EU Asylum Policy and the European Commission', *Journal of Contemporary European Research*, 5 (2), pp. 148–70.

Kaunert, C. (2010) *European Internal Security: Towards Supranational Governance in the Area of Freedom, Security and Justice*. Manchester: Manchester University Press.

Kaunert, C. and Leonard, S. (2012) 'The Development of the EU Asylum Policy: Venue-shopping in Perspective', *Journal of European Public Policy*, 19(9), pp. 1396–413.

Keohane, R. and Hoffmann, S. (1991) *The New European Community: Decision-making and Institutional Change*. Boulder, CO: Westview Press.

Kleine, M. and Risse, T. (2005) 'Arguing and Persuasion in the European Convention: Contribution to the State of the Art Report', Berlin, 28 February 2005.

Kleine, M. and Risse, T. (2010) 'Deliberation in Negotiations', *Journal of European Public Policy*, 17(5), pp. 708–26.

Knelangen, W. (2001) *Das Politikfeld Innere Sicherheit im Integrationsprozess. Die Entstehung einer Europäischen Politik der Inneren Sicherheit*, Opladen: Leske + Budrich.

Lancker, N. M. and Floch, J. (2002) 'Espace comun de liberté, de sécurité et de justice', Working Group X, Working Document 26. Available at: http://european-convention.europa.eu/docs/wd10/5617.pdf (Accessed: 4 May 2016).

Lavenex, S. and Wallace, W. (2005) 'Justice and Home Affairs: Towards a European Public Order?' in Wallace, H., Wallace, W., and Pollack, M. (eds) *Policy-Making in the European Union*. Oxford: Oxford University Press, pp. 457–80.

Levy, C. (2005) 'The European Union after 9/11: The Demise of a Liberal Democratic Asylum Regime?' *Government and Opposition*, 40(1), pp. 26–59.

Lewis, J. (1998) 'Is the "Hard Bargaining" Image of the Council Misleading?' *Journal of Common Market Studies*, 36(4), pp. 479–504.

Lindberg, L. (1966) 'Integration as a Source of Stress on the European Community System', *International Organization*, 20(2), pp. 233–65.

Lindberg, L. and Scheingold, S. (1970) *Europe's Would-Be Polity*. Englewood Cliffs, NJ: Prentice Hall.

Lindberg, L. (1963) *The Political Dynamics of European Integration*. Stanford, CA: Stanford University Press.

Magnette, P. and Nicolaïdis, K. (2004) 'The European Convention: Bargaining in the Shadow of Rhetoric', *West European Politics*, 27(3), pp. 381–404.

Marks, G., Hooghe, L., and Blank, K. (1996) 'European Integration from the 1980s: State-Centric v. Multi-level Governance', *Journal of Common Market Studies* 34(3), pp. 341–78.

Maurer, A. (2003) 'Die Methode des Konvents', *Integration*, 26(2), pp. 130–51.

Méndez de Vigo et al. (2002) Working Group X 'Freedom, Security and Justice'. Working Group X, Working Document 09. Available at: http://european-convention.eur opa.eu/docs/wd10/4572.pdf (Accessed: 24 May 2016).

Meyer, J. (2002)'An Area of Freedom, Security and Justice', CONV 447/02. Available at: http://european-convention.europa.eu/pdf/reg/en/02/cv00/cv00447.en02.pdf (Accessed: 4 May 2016).

Milton, G. and Keller-Noëllet, J. (2005) *The European Constitution: Its Origins, Negotiation and Meaning*. London: John Harper.

Monar, J. (1998) 'Justice and Home Affairs', *Journal of Common Market Studies*, 36(1), pp. 131–42.

Monar, J. (2001) 'The Dynamics of Justice and Home Affairs: Laboratories, Driving Factors and Costs', *Journal of Common Market Studies*, 39(4), pp. 747–64.

Monar, J. (2010) 'Experimentalist Governance in EU Justice and Home Affairs', in Sabel, C., and Zeitlin, J. (eds) *Experimentalist Governance in the European Union*. Oxford: Oxford University Press, pp. 237–60.

Moravcsik, A. (1993) 'Preferences and Power in the European Community', *Journal of Common Market Studies*, 31(4), pp. 473–524.

Moravcsik, A. and Nicolaïdis, K. (1999) 'Explaining the Treaty of Amsterdam', *Journal of Common Market Studies*, 37(1), pp. 59–85.

Müller, T. (2003) *Die Innen- und Justizpolitik der Europäischen Union. Eine Analyse der Integrationsentwicklung*. Opladen: Leske + Budrich.

Mutimer, D. (1989) '1992 and the Political Integration of Europe: Neofunctionalism Reconsidered', *Journal of European Integration*, 13(2–3), pp. 75–101.

Niemann, A. (1998) 'The PHARE Programme and the Concept of Spillover: Neofunctionalism in the Making', *Journal of European Public Policy*, 5(3), pp. 428–46.

Niemann, A. (2004) 'From Pre-theory to Theory? Developing a Revised Neofunctionalist Framework for Explaining EU Decision-making Outcomes', *Dresdner Arbeitspapiere Internationale Beziehungen*, 11, pp. 1–59.

Niemann, A. (2006) *Explaining Decisions in the European Union*. Cambridge: Cambridge University Press.

Niemann, A. (2008) 'Dynamics and Countervailing Pressures of Visa, Asylum and Immigration Policy Treaty Revision: Explaining Change and Stagnation from the Amsterdam IGC to the IGC 2003–2004', *Journal of Common Market Studies*, 46(3), pp. 559–91.

Niemann, A. (2011) 'Conceptualising Common Commercial Policy Treaty Revision: Explaining the Stagnancy and Dynamics from the Amsterdam IGC to the Treaty of Lisbon', *European Integration online Papers*, vol. 15, article 6. Available at: http://eiop.or.at/eiop/ (Accessed: 24 May 2016).

Niemann, A. (2012) 'The Dynamics of EU Migration Policy: From Maastricht to Lisbon', in Richardson, J. (ed.) *Constructing a Policy-making State? Policy dynamics in the European Union.* Oxford: Oxford University Press, pp. 209–33.

Niemann, A. and Schmitter, P. (2009) 'Neo-functionalism', in Wiener, A. and Diez, T. (eds) *Theories of European Integration*, 2nd ed. Oxford: Oxford University Press, pp. 45–66.

Norman, P. (2005) *The Accidental Constitution: The Making of Europe's Constitutional Treaty*, 2nd ed. Brussels: EuroComment.

Nye, J. (1970) 'Comparing Common Markets: A Revised Neo-Functionalist Model', *International Organization,* 24(4), pp. 796–835.

Patijn, M. (1997) 'The Dutch Presidency', in European Policy Centre (eds), *Making Sense of the Amsterdam Treaty.* Brussels: European Policy Centre, pp. 38–9 .

Pierson, P. (1996) 'The Path to European Integration: A Historical Institutionalist Analysis', *Comparative Political Studies* 29(2), pp. 123–63.

Risse, T. (2000) 'Let's Argue! Communicative Action in World Politics', *International Organization*, 54(1), pp. 1–39.

Rosamond, B. (2005) 'The Uniting of Europe and the Foundation of EU Studies: Revisiting the Neofunctionalism of Ernst B. Haas', *Journal of European Public Policy*, 12(2), pp. 237–54.

Sassen, S. (2008) *Territory, Authority, Rights: From Medieval to Global Assemblages.* Princeton, NJ: Princeton University Press.

Schmitter, P. (1969) 'Three Neo-functional Hypotheses about International Integration', *International Organization*, 23(1), pp. 161–6.

Schmitter, P. (2004a) 'A Revised Theory of Regional Integration', in Lindberg, L. and Scheingold, S. (eds) *Regional Integration: Theory and Research.* Cambridge, MA: Harvard University Press, pp. 232–64.

Schmitter, P. C. (2004b) 'Neo-Neofunctionalism', in Wiener, A. and Diez, T. (eds) *European Integration Theory.* Oxford: Oxford University Press, pp. 45–75.

Stone Sweet, A. and Sandholtz, W. (1997) 'European Integration and Supranational Governance', *Journal of European Public Policy*, 4(3), pp. 297–317.

Taylor, P. (1989) 'The New Dynamics of EC in the 1980s', in Lodge, J. (ed.) *The European Community and the Challenge of the Future.* New York: St. Martin's Press, pp. 3–25.

Tranholm-Mikkelsen, J. (1991) 'Neo-functionalism: Obstinate or Obsolete?' *Millenium*, 20(1), pp. 1–22.

Turnbull, P. and Sandholtz, W. (2001) 'Policing and Immigration: The Creation of New Policy Spaces', in Stone Sweet, A., Sandholtz, W., and Fligstein, N. (eds) *The Institutionalization of Europe.* Oxford: Oxford University Press, pp. 194–220.

Van Houtum, H. and Pijpers, R. (2007) 'The European Union as a Gated Community: The Two-faced Border and Immigration Regime of the EU', *Antipode*, 39(2), pp. 291–309.

Vitorino, A. (2001) 'À la Conférence des Présidents des commissions compétentes en matière d'immigration des parlements de l'UE, Sènate belge', Speech/01/608, Brussels, 4/12/2001.

Vitorino, A. (2002b) 'Renforcer l'espace der liberté, de sécurité et de justice', European Convention, Speech/02/261, Brussels, 6/6/2002.

Wiener, A. and Diez, T. (2009) 'Taking Stock of Integration Theory', in Wiener, A. and Diez, T. (eds) *European Integration Theory*. Oxford: Oxford University Press, pp. 241–52.

8

Institutionalism

Shaping Internal Security Cooperation in the EU

Ariadna Ripoll Servent and Dora Kostakopoulou

8.1 Introduction

Internal security cooperation in Europe—defined here in line with the EU's Area of Freedom, Security and Justice (AFSJ)—is one of the most rapidly growing policy areas in the European Union. Since the mid-1990s, it has experienced substantial changes not only in policy but also in institutional structure. However, the institutionalization of the AFSJ remains under-researched and generally disconnected from wider studies of institutional change and development. This chapter offers an overview of the traditional institutionalist approaches available to study this area—namely, rational choice, historical and sociological institutionalism; it unpacks their ontological assumptions and examines their strengths and weaknesses. The chapter then presents a 'constructivist institutionalism' that, while rooted in a sociological approach to understanding institutions, is clearer about the relationship of actors and institutions in the construction of ideas, norms, cognitive templates, identities, and accounts than the three classical institutionalisms. Given the normative character of the AFSJ, a constructivist institutionalism approach reveals how actors produce, construct, change, and transform discursive landscapes (which inform and shape, but do not determine their identities) and helps overcome the structuralist bias inherent in the institutionalist literature. This approach thus opens up space for an actor-based theory of non-linear, incremental, and transformative institutional change and permits us to identify the key variables leading to the institutionalization of the AFSJ. By way of illustration, the chapter then applies this theoretical approach to explain processes of institutionalization and change in the specific area of intra-EU mobility.

8.2 New Institutionalism

Institutionalism is a broad analytical paradigm underlining the importance of institutions for explaining social phenomena. This basic assumption emerged as a direct reaction to the behaviouralist turn of the 1950s and 1960s. Behaviouralism downplayed the importance of rules and organizations and concentrated on aggregated individual actions to explain political outcomes (Powell and DiMaggio, 1991). However, in the 1970s, a variety of voices underlined the necessity to 'bring institutions back in' (Immergut, 1998). Since then, this 'new' version of institutionalism has returned to the idea that 'institutions matter' in shaping social and political outcomes. However, precisely how they matter has become a bone of contention.

For some, institutions are the configuration of rules that constrain the actions of individuals (North, 1990; Ostrom, 1986); for others, it refers to 'symbol systems, cognitive scripts, and moral templates that provide the "frames of meaning" guiding human action' (Hall and Taylor, 1996: 947). One of the main reasons for this eclecticism lies in the origins of the approach. The institutionalist turn evolved from several legislative studies of the American Congress—embedded in the rational choice tradition (Shepsle and Weingast, 1987; Shepsle, 1989)—as well as from organizational studies located in political sociology (Powell and DiMaggio, 1991). Each of these traditions came with very different understandings of institutions and their place in the social world.

As a consequence, classifying institutionalism is not as straightforward as it may seem. There have been many different efforts to label and regroup research which takes institutions as their central point of inquiry. Some scholars have identified up to nine different types of institutionalism (Lowndes, 2010)—and the number keeps growing. However, three different types of institutionalism are generally used as a starting point: rational choice, historical and sociological institutionalism (Hall and Taylor, 1996; Immergut, 1998). We will first examine the main differences between these three types of institutionalisms—their ontological origins, their main assumptions and typical research questions—and explain why we focus on rational choice and sociological institutionalism as the two main theoretical approaches to study EU internal security matters.

8.2.1 Historical Institutionalism

We start with historical institutionalism in order to justify why we have decided to focus on the two other approaches. The main focus of historical institutionalism is its differentiation between short-term and long-term effects of institutions. That is why it emphasizes mechanisms such as path-dependency and the ability that institutions have to produce 'lock-in' effects (Pierson, 1996). The basic point here is that institutions steer and shape action and outcomes over long periods of time. For instance, if we want to study current policy outcomes, we need to look back in time to understand how institutions have shaped the definition of problems and its solutions over time. However, historical institutionalism tends to emphasize stability over change and it does not encompass an explicit ontological choice—especially when it comes to the relative pre-eminence of agency versus structure. This has resulted in a split between scholars using rationalist and those using constructivist 'slants' of historical institutionalism (Jenson and Mérand, 2010; Hall and Taylor, 1996). For that reason—and considering space constraints in this chapter—historical institutionalism has been integrated into the two other approaches.

8.2.2 Rational Choice Institutionalism

Rational choice institutionalism has been the most prominent approach in political science. Its ontology focuses on individual behaviour (Elster, 1986; North, 1990) and how actors can maximize their preferences by calculating the costs and benefits of alternative solutions. Institutions provide the rules of the game, which allow for the stability necessary to make decisions (Katzenstein, Keohane, and Krasner, 1998; Knight, 1992). Thus, although institutions may modify the cost–benefit calculations of specific actors as well as their strategic choices, they do not have an impact on how actors perceive the world or their underlying values and ideas. Actors' preferences are formed exogenously (outside the institutions) and remain stable.

Figure 8.1 summarizes the main elements of a rational choice institutionalism model. This model has to be understood as a heuristic tool and needs to be adapted to specific research questions. In general, however, it shows that rational choice institutionalism is particularly useful to analyse the behaviour of actors in situations of uncertainty, when institutions can provide the necessary information and rules of procedure to facilitate and evaluate costs and benefits. The approach is also particularly suited to explain specific decisions, be they on the creation of new institutional rules or on particular policy outcomes. In line with historical institutionalism, one can emphasize the long-term effects of institutions—understanding them as scope conditions that limit the choices of actors and affect their calculation of costs and benefits.

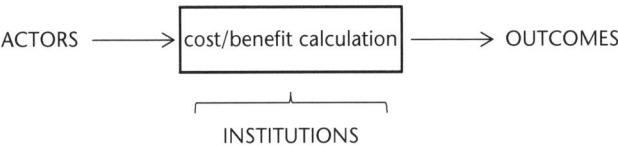

Figure 8.1. Rational choice institutionalism model

8.2.3 *Sociological Institutionalism*

Sociological institutionalism is based on a constructivist ontology, which assumes that social entities do not exist as an external unit but are socially constructed through perceptions, norms, and discourses of social actors. Therefore, institutions (understood as social practices, ideas, and norms) constitute actors and their interests, but the latter can also change and reformulate institutional structures (Checkel, 1999; Wendt, 1998). Sociological institutionalism has stressed the 'logic of appropriateness', namely, the importance of norms and social structures in determining the appropriate behaviour of agents (Olsen and March, 1989). As a consequence, research has generally tried to identify the content of norms and ideas and looked at how institutions shape the preferences of agents—which are susceptible to change as a result of their activities within a specific institutional context.

The structural bias in many sociological institutionalist models has led some authors to emphasize the important role of actors as they operate within socially constitutive settings (Saurugger, 2013). This more recent interpretation of sociological institutionalism is best described as 'constructivist institutionalism' since it emphasizes actors' creative capacities to produce, construct, change, and transform discursive landscapes, which inform and shape, but do not determine their identities (Kostakopoulou, 2005). The aim is, therefore, to go beyond a 'logic of appropriateness' and see actors as reactive and reflexive agents, who are embedded in a given (institutional) context and are capable of developing strategies that are appropriate to a given setting (Hay, 2010; Kauppi and Rask Madsen, 2008; Ripoll Servent and Busby, 2013). Since actors' preferences are formed endogenously, they are susceptible to change and adapt to new (institutional) circumstances. As a result, actors can be acutely aware of the potential consequences of their actions and the expectations generated by them; they can change their thinking and actions while a particular course of action is unfolding; and they can adapt their strategies to mid-term procedural constraints. One should not forget that, at the same time, actors can also easily make errors, adopt flawed strategies, and form and defend fictional goals. Error, confusion, irrational expectations are normal features in human activities. In practice, it means that it is analytically difficult to separate (or 'bracket off') actors and structures as well as their location within a certain spatiotemporal context.

Outcomes, such as specific policy decisions, or processes, such as change or stability, can be thus explained by looking at the interaction between actors and institutions under the shadow of spatiality and temporality. Therefore, institutions are internalized and further reproduced when actors see them as legitimate and incorporate them into their discourses and practices (Nicolini, 2012; Schmidt, 2008). Patterns of smooth reproduction become interrupted when actors contest their logic, practices, and procedures while, on the other hand, the absence of contestation will ensure that they will continue to exist even once the original actors that created them are no longer present. When institutions are contested, actors will need to engage in processes of legitimation to convince others that their understanding is the most adequate in a given institutional context. Through discourses or practices, actors try to legitimize their preferred solution and, by so doing, they may potentially change the institutional context in which they operate. Figure 8.2 proposes a model based on constructivist institutionalism. Here as well, the model is only a heuristic device to guide readers and to underline the most important features of this theoretical approach.

In order to locate the interaction between actors and institutions empirically, it is important to understand who (re-)produces discourses and practices and how the latter are perceived or understood by other actors. This helps to examine to what extent specific actors hold a higher degree of perceived legitimacy and who are the main audiences (either as passive recipients or as sources of contestation). At the same time, it is important to locate the institutional context in order to understand how specific norms, rules, or ideas shape the process of production and legitimation of discourses and practices, for instance by either enhancing or limiting their credibility. This exercise requires often tracing back the origin of discourses and practices and looking at what is said and what is done (and what is not said or not done).

In sum, constructivist institutionalism is a broad-ranging theoretical approach that can be used to study both macro and micro processes in terms of how actors shape—and are shaped by—institutions. In comparison to rational-choice institutionalism, constructivist institutionalism assumes the *relationality* and interlocking nature of all the above-mentioned variables. Certainly, scholars may still choose to understand a complex reality by emphasizing a particular variable, or by focusing on a certain period of change or a particular angle of the agency-structure debate. However, in general, this approach attempts to maintain a more holistic approach where actors and institutions are both equally important to explain processes and outcomes.

Figure 8.2. Constructivist institutionalism model

8.3 New Institutionalism in the AFSJ

It is somewhat difficult to identify the use of new institutionalism in the study of EU internal security cooperation. Often, authors do not explicitly name the theoretical approach that underpins their assumptions and explanation and they can sometimes incorporate elements of various theoretical schools (see Bossong and Rhinard in the conclusion of this volume, chapter 9). This section aims to offer an overview of existing uses of new institutionalism in the study of the AFSJ and also to draw connections and overlaps with other theoretical approaches.

8.3.1 *Rational Choice Institutionalist Approaches to Internal Security Policies*

One of the earliest uses of rational choice aimed to explain the process of integration that led to the gradual *communitarization* of the AFSJ and the distribution of power among intergovernmental and supranational actors. Already in the 1990s, Guiraudon (2000) looked at the behaviour of member states' governments to explain why migration policies had become part of the EU's competences. She argued that governments used the EU level to venue-shop, i.e. to bypass internal domestic veto points that made it difficult to introduce a more control-oriented dimension to these policy issues. Therefore, national governments used the EU venue to maximize their autonomy and obtain policy outcomes closer to their preferences. Institutions are understood in terms of a particular venue or forum that can reduce the uncertainties of the bargaining process and might allow some actors to reduce the costs of policymaking. For instance, if a national venue offers few opportunities to maximize the preferences of some political actors, it might be rational for them to change the venue (e.g. moving migration policies up to the EU venue) so that they can obtain more benefits than if they try to negotiate at home.

Lavenex (2006) broadened the venue-shopping thesis to include instances where actors shifted decision-making laterally, from the 'domestic' community policy realm to the foreign policy realm to escape the weight of institutionalization that came with the gradual supranationalization of the AFSJ. However, the venue-shopping thesis has lost explanatory power after the last treaty reforms, when much of the AFSJ was *communitarized*. A recent comparative analysis has shown how further institutional reforms, such as the empowerment of the European Commission (hereafter, the Commission), the European Parliament (EP) and the European Court of Justice (hereafter the Court), have led to the creation of new veto-points (Bendel, Ette, and Parkes, 2011). Kaunert and Léonard (2012) underlined how the presence of the Court and the European Court of Human Rights

(ECtHR) limited the opportunities for member states to lower the standards of protection in the area of asylum. Looking at the area of skilled-labour migration, Roos (2013) also determined that venue-shopping was not enough to explain why integration was possible in this unlikely policy area and that explanations should also look at processes of lock-in and agenda-framing. The venue-shopping approach shares some similarities with public policy analysis, where the idea of a 'political opportunity structure' is not far from the concept of 'venue'. One of the main differences between the two approaches is that public policy analysis often takes institutions as given and is not interested in examining the institutions that constrain certain decisions. Therefore, it often ignores processes of institutional change and their effect on the policy process and policy change.

Rational-choice institutionalism has also been employed to explain delegation of power to existing or new institutions. Principal–agent models look at how actors (principals) delegate part of their power to other institutions (agents) in order to cut down transaction costs and improve the efficiency of decision-making. Therefore, these models have been mostly employed to explain why member states agreed to *communitarize* internal security policies or why agencies have proliferated in the AFSJ. For instance, Stetter (2000) argued that migration was successfully shifted to the first pillar during negotiations on the Treaty of Amsterdam because member states (as principals) managed to introduce control mechanisms that allowed them to keep oversight of the agent (EU supranational institutions) and the speed of integration. Generally, principal–agency has contributed to the wider literature on agency governance, looking at how and why agencies such as Europol and Frontex have been created and who has control over their activities (Kaunert, Léonard, and Occhipinti, 2013; Léonard, 2009; Trauner, 2012). Finally, principal–agent explanations have also been used to explain changing power relations among the EU institutions, looking, for instance, at how the EP has expanded its control over international negotiations dealing with internal security matters (Ripoll Servent, 2014).

With the 'normalization' (move towards *communitarization*) of decision-making in EU internal security, rational choice has been increasingly used to examine power dynamics and the short- and long-term effects of specific policy solutions and negotiation outcomes. For instance, asylum policies have been analysed as a rational game, where member states cooperate in order to maximize collective goods and share the burden (Noll, 2003; Thielemann, 2003). Coalition-building inside the EP and with the Council is another aspect of EU decision-making that has been examined with rational choice institutionalism. For instance, Hix and Noury (2007) explained how political rather than economic interests (i.e. conflict on the security/liberty dimension rather than restriction/openness of labour markets) led left-wing and liberal groups in the EP to form winning coalitions before the introduction of co-decision. Interestingly, this coalition lost its predominance once the EP became a co-decider of legislation. On that issue, rational choice can show how costs and benefits changed under new formal rules that required from the EP larger majorities and more moderate strategies if it did not want to see a failure in negotiations with the Council. As a result, the EP has accepted more security-oriented outcomes in various internal security matters, such as in irregular immigration, data protection, or asylum (Ripoll Servent, 2015; Ripoll Servent and Trauner, 2014).

However, it has been in the external dimension of the AFSJ that rational choice has dominated the AFSJ research agenda. The relationship between the EU and third countries, especially candidate countries and those at the EU's borders, has prompted analyses based on cost–benefit calculations and the importance of long-term effects and time horizons. There, the concept of 'conditionality' has been used to analyse to what extent the EU has been effective at exporting its own model of internal security and how well its demands have been incorporated in the domestic system of non-EU members (Grabbe, 2000; Trauner, 2009). While 'conditionality' seems to have been effective on enlargement candidates, it has proved less efficient when dealing with countries at the neighbourhood. The lack of enlargement prospects has reduced the EU's leverage, which has substituted its modus of hierarchical policy transfer with 'softer' forms of cooperation based on network governance (Lavenex and Wichmann, 2009).

8.3.2 *Constructivist Institutionalism and Internal Security*

As discussed above, constructivist institutionalism tries to understand the relationship between actors and structures in a given temporal and spatial context. This is important in an area such as the AFSJ, which has been characterized by a very distinct mode of integration due to its inherently sensitive nature. These specificities have led most authors to adopt a longitudinal dimension to study EU internal security policies. The importance of external events, such as the 11 September 2001 attacks or the Arab Spring, has underlined the role of critical junctures and external crises (Den Boer and Monar, 2002). Wolff (2009) used a sociological perspective of historical institutionalism to analyse how different critical junctures helped to mainstream counterterrorism as an EU policy field. This process was helped by the emergence of shared institutional objectives that aimed to create a more 'secure' Europe and to build an area of internal security. Similarly, Argomaniz (2009) looked at key episodes in the construction of EU counterterrorist policies to explain how the choices of particular actors shaped the institutional structure of this area, so that it could not be identified either as a fully intergovernmental or as a fully supranational policy field.

The gradual *communitarization* of the AFSJ has given rise to those studies examining the relationship between actors and institutions in this field and trying to determine how 'normal' they have become in comparison to other (older) EU policy areas. For instance, Adler-Nissen (2009) explored how the UK and Denmark made use of the consensus-oriented culture prevalent in the Council of the EU so as to circumvent their opt-outs from certain internal security policies. Their ability to work within an institutional culture widely accepted by other actors in the Council allowed them to be fully included in decision-making. The role of consensus has indeed become more important, also for inter-institutional relations. Since the generalization of the co-decision procedure, which turned the EP into a co-legislator alongside the Council, we have seen new modes of cooperation emerging and an end to historical conflicts opposing Parliament and member states on matters of liberty and security (Ripoll Servent, 2012; 2015).

New modes of cooperation have become a central focus of constructivist institutionalism and an area of common interest with those using securitization as a theoretical approach (see Balzacq, this volume). Many authors have looked more generally at the origin and development of certain ideas and the role that national and European actors have played in the construction of specific policy rationales. Notably, Bigo (2000; 2002), Geddes (2000), Kostakopoulou (2002a;b), and Huysmans (2006) have examined the role of specific national actors in the framing of immigration and asylum. The changing environment of the post-Cold War and the Balkans wars served to contest the existing understandings of migrants and asylum seekers and allowed for a new discourse linking migration to security. The terrorist attacks of the early 2000s helped to legitimize the discursive link between migrants and security and to create a new normative paradigm that has guided most policy decisions thereafter. Although sharing many assumptions on the importance of discourses and practices, constructivist institutionalism avoids some of the pitfalls of securitization theories by understanding the process of securitization—that is, the tactical transformation of policy issues into security concerns—not as a theoretical given but as a question that needs to be explained empirically. In this line, Kostakopoulou (2015) has observed that the 'security based' frame began losing ground and became supplemented by a 'rights-based' and 'citizen-centred' frame in the area of regular migration and EU citizenship. A 'rights-based' approach characterized the free movement of persons and EU citizenship policy fields and, owing to the policy contiguity between migration and EU citizenship following the partial *communitarization* of Justice and Home Affairs (JHA) in 1997, began to influence the regulation of regular migration.

The effort to problematize and question the production of problems and solutions has led constructivist institutionalists to put more emphasis on the actors responsible for creating, re-producing, legitimizing, and contesting norms, discourses, and practices. This has led to an examination of actors as entrepreneurs, emphasizing their strategic choices in a given institutional setting. Although they have received different names, entrepreneurs are often examined as sources of change or stability, and those who are able to produce legitimate definitions of the policy problem and the institutional rules of the game. For instance, Kaunert (2010) examined the role of the Commission in the process of defining counterterrorism, looking at how the Commission discursively used the attacks of 11 September 2001 in order to accelerate the adoption of the European Arrest Warrant, which, until then, had not been a priority on the policymaking agenda. In this sense, the focus on entrepreneurs goes beyond an examination of coalition-building. It also queries why specific solutions are selected and how they fit with legitimate norms in a given institutional context. For instance, the last years have seen an erosion of data protection standards, especially when specific instruments entered into the realm of counterterrorism. More security-oriented solutions were possible due to the efforts of entrepreneurs, who managed to frame the protection of EU citizens as a more legitimate policy solution than preserving high data protection standards (Ripoll Servent and MacKenzie, 2011; Ripoll Servent, 2013). By focusing on entrepreneurs—whether they are called policy, discourse, or norm entrepreneurs—constructivist institutionalism shares common ground with political sociology, securitization, and certain elements of public policy analysis. All of these approaches are often concerned with how actors frame policies and interact with structural constructs. However, securitization theories and political sociologists put more emphasis on practices and daily interactions between actors. They tend to be more focused on the micro level, examining, for example, the interactions between national border guards and their consequences for our understanding of borders. In comparison, constructivist institutionalism looks also at macro processes, emphasizing the role of political actors and broader policy-making processes, looking both at discourses and practices at the micro and macro level.

Finally, it is important to bear in mind that both institutionalist approaches are often used together to more fully disentangle the logics and dynamics of institutional and policy change in internal security matters (Trauner and Ripoll Servent, 2015; Wolff, Wichmann, and Mounier, 2009). In this sense, both Pawlak (2009) and Ripoll Servent (2015) combined rational choice and sociological/constructivist institutionalism to explore not just how actors maximize preferences in inter-institutional negotiations, but also how these preferences are formed and shaped by broader institutional norms. Thielemann

(2003) also showed how burden-sharing in the area of asylum responded to normative motivations—such as member states' attachment to the single-market programme or international humanitarian principles—rather than cost–benefit calculations. Therefore, in the AFSJ, due to its normative weight and the weight of history, it can prove difficult to enforce a strict division between the different institutionalist approaches.

8.4 Case Studies

The following two case studies will flesh out the differences between rational choice and constructivist institutionalism and reveal the different kinds of insights that we can gain from these theoretical approaches. The first case on irregular migration dissects a particular episode of intra- and inter-institutional bargaining with the help of the rational choice institutionalist model. We then turn to the case of citizenship to highlight more long-term ideational and identity shifts that are better captured with our conceptualization of constructivist institutionalism.

8.4.1 Rational Choice Institutionalism and the Case of Irregular Immigration

This first case study explores the area of irregular immigration and, in particular, the negotiations and outcomes of the Returns Directive (2008/115/EC), a keystone of the EU's immigration policy. The main objective of a 'returns policy' is the harmonization of conditions determining the voluntary or compulsory return of third-country nationals staying irregularly on the territory of member states. This includes a great variety of people; for instance, those who have overstayed their visa or who have had asylum applications rejected. A common returns policy thus touches upon member states' capacity to decide who stays and who leaves their territory.

The Returns Directive was the first occasion in which the EP could co-decide on EU immigration policies. It offers, thus, a good opportunity to examine how the change in institutional rules affected the calculation of cost and benefits during negotiations. First of all, it can be argued that the Returns Directive would probably not have happened without the intervention of the EP. Under consultation, the Council was free to decide alone, even if it had to wait for the non-binding opinion of the EP before reaching an agreement. Member states had no intrinsic interest in a common returns policy (Hailbronner, 2005; House of Lords, European Union Committee, 2006). In contrast, the EP (especially its committee on civil liberties and Justice and Home Affairs—LIBE) had held more liberal approaches on migration (Hix and

Noury, 2007) and was very much in favour of creating some harmonization in this area. This led to the expectation that the EP would make full use of its new power of co-decision and would veto any decision that was not liberal enough or that did not achieve a more integrated policy.

Negotiations were long (2005–8) and the final agreement was eventually found at the earliest possible stage (first reading) of the co-decision procedure. The outcome of negotiations was disappointing for many observers (Acosta, 2009a; Amnesty International, 2008; ECRE, 2008). Acosta (2009b) noted how, out of the six issues that became the focus of debates, four were closer to the position of the Council, while in only two points was the EP partially success-ful in raising standards of protection for third-country nationals. Rational choice can explain why the EP accepted a sub-optimal result at such an early stage of negotiations by looking at the EP's bargaining power, particularly its higher sensitivity to failure and the calculations of some political groups, which wanted to ensure their presence in future coalitions (Ripoll Servent, 2015).

During negotiations, the EP negotiator—known as the *rapporteur*, in this case Manfred Weber, a German Member of the European Parliament (MEP) from the European People's Party (EPP)[1]—realized that there was a good chance that the negotiations might fail. Internally, the uncertainty came from the behaviour of key political groups (the socialists in particular), who changed positions often and made it difficult to evaluate whether certain coalitions would gather sufficient votes in plenary—especially if the EP wanted to go into a second reading. Formal rules require an absolute majority, namely a majority of the members who comprise the EP, and include a short time span before a second-reading vote. In addition, the uncertainty was heightened by the then-Council presidency and most member states, which were still questioning the necessity of a common returns policy and thus were hampering potential inter-institutional agreements. Therefore, most EP polit-ical groups became afraid that, if they pushed the Council further, negoti-ations would fail. Given their preference for more integration, the EP decided that it was better to have some minimum standards rather than to continue with the *status quo*.[2]

The outcome can also be explained by the strategies and calculations of pivotal political groups. The rapporteur used the EP's sensitivity to failure and the shadow of a second reading to secure the support of the liberal group and form a coalition capable of achieving the simple majority necessary to pass legislation at the first-reading stage. The decision of the liberals to support the Christian-Democrats (EPP-ED) can be explained by looking at their short- and long-term time horizons. In the short term, the liberals were keen to have a text which ensured some minimum common standards; therefore, they decided that the best way to maximize their positions was to join the EPP-ED, which meant a shift towards the right side of the political spectrum. In addition, if we look at negotiations not just as a one-shot game but as an iterated game (a repeated game where past decisions affect the behaviour of actors in future games), we can understand that the liberals, being a smaller political group, were afraid of being left out not only on this occasion but also from future coalitions on EU migration policies.[3] From a historical institutionalist perspective, one would say that the liberals were trying to 'lock themselves in' into a long-term exercise of coalition-building.

Therefore, the final coalition of EPP-ED (centre-right) and liberals explains why the eventual outcome was more restrictive and security-oriented than what had been expected at the outset. The fact that the rapporteur was a conservative MEP gave an advantage to the centre-right, since the group's preferences were more similar to the Council's than the EP's position under consultation. Here, a rational-choice institutionalist model helps us to understand not only why the final outcome was biased towards the Council but also why other EP groups accepted this final agreement. The model emphasizes formal motivations: the EP's sensitivity to failure and the pressure to form long-term winning coalitions in an iterated game explain the lower bargaining strength of the EP and the motivations of some political groups to change their position and accept a more restrictive policy outcome than desired.

8.4.2 Constructivist Institutionalism and the Case of Intra-EU Mobility

The case of intra-EU mobility is a good example of how EU supranational institutions can become the main actors behind long-term processes of policy change. A constructivist institutionalist approach can show how the Court and the Commission have acted as legitimating forces behind the policy frames that underpin intra-EU mobility. This principle has always been cherished in EU law and politics, since it constitutes a cornerstone of the internal market as it is one of the four fundamental freedoms.[4] At the same time, the free movement of persons impinges on member states' sovereignty, an institutional norm that encompasses acquired notions about political control over a territory and the provision of security for its citizens. That is why, since the early days of the policy initiative, there has been an enduring battle over the definition of, and limitations to, intra-EU mobility for EU citizens.

We can identify three phases in the definition of this principle: framing, solidification, and contestation. The initial phase shows the efforts of the Commission and the Court to provide a definition that circumscribed the attempts of member states to link free movement of persons with internal security concerns on the basis of the Treaty of Rome. The latter allowed member states to derogate from the free movement provisions on the grounds of public health, public policy, and public security (Article 45(3) TFEU), which were not defined in the treaty. The first framing efforts started with the adoption of Directive 64/221/EEC on the coordination of special measures concerning the movement and residence of foreign nationals which are justified on grounds of public policy, public security, or public health. The directive limited the member states' discretion by stating that these grounds could not be invoked by a member state in order to serve economic ends (Article 2(2)). Instead, they had to be based exclusively on the personal conduct of the individual concerned and may never be imposed automatically. The Court specified further these conditions, stating that national authorities' decisions in this domain must comply with the principle of proportionality[5] and that member states must verify that a Union citizen's personal conduct poses 'a genuine and sufficiently serious threat to the requirements of public policy affecting one of the fundamental interests of society'.[6] Generally speaking, automatic deportations without a careful consideration of personal circumstances became unlawful under EU law. Therefore, during this first phase, the Court successfully framed intra EU-mobility as a rights-based principle that aimed to protect individuals by requiring that policy or security risks must be clearly personified before national authorities decide to take any action. It did so in an incremental and consistent way without encountering 'critical junctures' and the need to alter its normative reasoning.

The second phase managed to solidify and institutionalize these principles developed by the Commission and the Court. In the new millennium, the Citizenship Directive (2004/38/EC), which replaced Directive 64/221/EC, incorporated the Court's case law and stated clearly in Article 27(2) that 'justifications that are isolated from the particulars of the case or that rely on considerations of general prevention shall not be accepted'. Article 28(1) of the directive also incorporated rulings from the ECtHR by stating that:

> Before taking an expulsion decision on grounds of public policy or public security, the host Member State shall take into account considerations such as how long the individual concerned has resided on its territory, his/her age, state of health, family and economic situation, social and cultural integration into the host Member State and the extent of his/her links with the country of origin.

According to the directive, permanent residents, that is, EU citizens resident for five years or more in a host member state, can be ordered to leave only on 'serious grounds of public policy or public security' (Article 28(2)), and permanent resident Union citizens for the previous ten years and minors may not be ordered to leave the territory of a member state, except on imperative grounds of public security (Article 28(3)).

The increased security of residence offered to long-term resident EU citizens and to minors by Article 28(3) of the Citizenship Directive had the effect of 'civilizing' public security (Loader and Walker, 2007) in so far as it accorded priority to the rights and interests of EU citizens over the interests of states. EU citizens were formally recognized as members of their communities of residence and thus protected from deportation. The European Commission (2009) sought to provide an authoritative interpretation of the notion of public security (Article 23) in its guidelines for the better transposition of the Citizenship Directive. It stated that 'public security is generally interpreted to cover both internal and external security along the lines of preserving the integrity of the territory of a Member State and its institutions' (European Commission, 2009). In other words, public security had a state-centric dimension. By contrast, the notion of 'public policy', which provided a less extensive level of protection, referred to 'disturbances of social order'. On this interpretation, public security was seen to cover terrorism and espionage, while criminal offences were seen to fall within the ambit of public policy. The efforts of the Commission to clarify the main terms of the Citizenship Directive solidified the distinction between public security and public policy, which meant that long-term resident EU citizens and minors could only be ordered to leave the territory of the host member state if they posed a very serious risk to the internal or external security of the state and its institutions.

This *status quo* was breached with the emergence of the economic crisis in 2008. The economic difficulties of some member states, coupled with populist discourses and growing Euroscepticism led to a contestation of free movement of people as a core EU principle. Certain national actors, for instance in the Netherlands, Germany, and the UK, started to raise claims about the undesirability of the continued presence of 'foreign criminals' and EU citizens who allegedly had abused the hospitality of the host community. This new counter-frame led to a reconsideration of what public security means in the context of EU law and thus to a reappraisal of the level of protection that could be provided to long-term resident EU citizens who committed criminal offences. This wider political environment of domestic unease was too noisy to be ignored by supranational institutions, which started to use similar arguments to legitimize their decisions. For instance, in the first two cases on the public security exceptions following the entry into force of the Citizenship Directive, namely, Case C-145/09[7] and Case C-348/09,[8] the Court was keen to extend the ambit of 'public security' under Article 28(3) of the Citizenship Directive so as to cover serious criminality, such as dealing in narcotics as part of an organized group. In the latter case, the Court made an even more pronounced widening of the public security derogation: it ruled that it encompasses all criminal offences that 'might pose a direct threat to the calm and physical security of the population' as 'long as the manner in which such offences were committed discloses particular serious characteristics, which is a matter for the referring court to determine' (para. 28). And since all forms of criminality can be seen to 'pose a direct threat to the calm and physical security of the population' (para. 28) of the host member state, the meaning of public security in EU law has shifted away from national security to societal security matters and to conduct which offends 'the particular values of the legal order of the Member State' (para. 29).

This interpretive shift undermines the rights-based approach to mobility that the Court had promoted for several decades and the rationale of the Citizenship Directive. The recent case law creates a clear taxonomy of community membership whereby even very long-term resident EU citizens can easily become 'deportable foreigners' or 'dangerous outsiders' when they break the law. Internal mobility in the EU, thus, becomes infected by the securitization ethos that characterized the regulation of migration in national laws and the AFSJ in the EU. The new frame sits uneasily with the old definitions of intra EU-mobility, thereby leading to a fragile coexistence of security-oriented and rights-based considerations. This can be seen in two recent cases, namely, Onuekwere and M.G.[9] The Court ruled that periods in prison cannot count towards the acquisition of permanent residence or the enhanced protection of Article 28(3) and that the right to permanent residence could not be based on purely formal considerations such as the time physically spent in a member state's territory, but must also take into account 'qualitative elements, relating to the level of integration in the host member state' (para. 25). In practice, this means that, in the context of that overall assessment, national authorities may also take into account other relevant facts relating to the person concerned, for example, that an individual had resided in the host member state during the ten years prior to imprisonment. Although the Court noted that criminal offences committed by an EU citizen show a lack of respect for 'the values expressed by the society of the host member state in its criminal law' (para. 26), both decisions are, nonetheless, reflective of the aim underpinning the Citizenship Directive and in line with the Commission's guidance on the implementation of its provisions (European Commission, 2009). On the one hand, EU citizenship is premised on individuals' participation in societal interactions and their living realities—and not on their isolation from the host society due to criminal activity. On the other hand, the fundamental status of EU citizenship should not be undermined by attempts to 'securitize' intra-EU mobility and to turn EU citizens into foreigners (Kostakopoulou, 2014). As the landscape is changing, one cannot discount the possibility that the Court might find it more difficult to maintain the fundamental status of EU citizenship and to resist the encroaching of the sociopolitical space that has been created by it by national narratives on migration control and societal security.

This case study shows how actors are key in framing, consolidating, and contesting institutional norms and general understandings of problems and solutions. It also explains how a non-majoritarian institution like the Court can profoundly influence long-term policy processes and render certain political decisions or discursive frames unviable. Generally speaking, agents have the capacity to draw on the normative surplus of meaning and the possibilities underlying accepted logics and decisions in order to develop new conceptions, to construct new norms, to alter policy decisions, and to act in complex and unpredictable environments. The constructivist institutionalism model is therefore attuned to nuances in meaning and how it evolves over time as a result of actors' attempts to legitimize certain understandings and institutional practices.

8.5 Conclusion

This chapter has offered a condensed overview of institutionalist approaches to internal security matters. As demonstrated, one of the main advantages of (new) institutionalism is its flexibility and its capacity to take formal and informal institutions seriously—integrating them fully into explanations of many different types of outcomes, such as individual behaviour, policy-making, the creation and evolution of institutions and organizations, legitimating processes, or the emergence and consolidation of discourses and practices. However, institutionalism has also been often characterized by a multiplicity of approaches that have led to fragmentation and undermined theoretical dialogue. That is why, in this chapter, we have concentrated on the two lines of institutionalism that have the most distinct and clearly identified ontological assumptions.

Rational choice institutionalism is based on a rationalist ontology, which sees individuals as cost–benefit maximizers. Individuals will try to evaluate which decision may be most optimal to realize their preferences. In rational choice institutionalism, preferences are exogenous (formed outside the institutional framework) and institutions are intervening variables—they determine the political opportunity structure and therefore affect the calculation of cost and benefits. As seen in the first case study, the formal voting rules in co-decision make it more difficult for the EP to reach a second-reading agreement. Therefore, the procedure increases the cost of continuing negotiations and creates incentives to accept a first-reading deal with the Council, even if the latter is a sub-optimal solution for the EP.

In contrast, constructivist institutionalism is based on a different ontological approach, whereby structures cannot exist independently from actors. Here, actors are responsible for creating, reproducing, and maintaining specific institutions (understood in a broad sense). Institutions can survive their original actors if new actors accept their existence and do not contest their legitimacy. Otherwise, new interpretations of institutions may emerge and actors will have to legitimate any alternative understanding of institutions through discourses or practices. Therefore, we need to look more closely at who (re-)frames discourses and practices and how specific norms, rules or ideas may enhance or limit their credibility and, thus, their ability to be seen as a more legitimate solution. In this sense, the second case study has examined how the Court and the Commission were successful in legitimizing a particular interpretation of intra-EU mobility, which constrained the ability of member states to limit free movement of people through broad notions of public security and public policy, traditionally linked to a state-centred norm of sovereignty. This interpretation was solidified through discursive frames and institutional practices—for instance, through the production of a legal doctrine through case law and its reproduction in EU legislative texts. However, it also examined the instability of these frames and how other actors may make use of external events and changes in the societal context to contest and put into question long-established interpretations of intra-EU mobility.

Institutionalism also offers potential areas of dialogue (or overlap) with other theories. For instance, we can link institutionalism to traditional theories of European integration. Rational choice institutionalism is closely related to (liberal) intergovernmentalism, since they share the same ontological assumptions and often focus on similar phenomena, such as bargaining processes. While liberal intergovernmentalism has often focused on big decisions for European integration, such as treaty reforms, which are characterized by low levels of institutionalization, rational choice institutionalism tends to concentrate on day-to-day policymaking, looking both at formal and informal types of institutions and how they affect the bargaining success of different actors. Constructivist institutionalism shares certain similarities with neofunctionalism (see chapter by Niemann in this volume), particularly its assumptions that actors shape the process of integration through the emergence of internal tensions and contradictions or the assumption that actors' preferences are endogenous are similar to our own understandings of how institutions emerge and change.

Constructivist institutionalism also offers some potential overlap with the field of law (see Mitsilegas in this volume) and governance (see Bossong and Lavenex in this volume). The second case study has shown how legal perspectives can be integrated into constructivist institutionalism, for instance by looking at the role of law as a form of discourse and a potential source of legitimation. As for governance, both approaches focus on how specific understandings of internal security have served to shape the form and functions of the EU's institutional framework and have been used to legitimize certain practices. Therefore, both approaches share an interest in how political norms can have an effect on institutional structures and be used to legitimate the activities of the EU. However, constructivist institutionalism also emphasizes the role of actors in the process of norm production and legitimation.

In sum, institutionalism offers a good starting point to examine key elements of the internal security field. It can focus on institutional dynamics or policymaking; it can trace macro-process of norm production and transfer; and it can examine the micro-behaviour of particular actors. This makes it attractive for researchers and flexible enough to incorporate elements from other theoretical approaches. At the same time, it also underlines how essential it is to narrow down our assumptions and clearly identify one's unit(s) of analysis and level(s) of study. If we want to say more than 'institutions matter', we need to make an effort to move beyond the theoretical debates and start building models that allow us to operationalize our concepts and build on new empirical evidence.

Notes

1. Note that, at that time, the political group was known as the European People's Party-European Democrats (EPP-ED).
2. Green/EFA political adviser, interview, March 2011.
3. Liberal MEP, interview, January 2009; liberal MEP, interview, March 2010.
4. The definition of the internal market is provided by Article 26 TEU (formerly Article 14 TEC). Article 26(2) explicitly refers to the freedom of movement of goods, persons, services, and capital.
5. Case C-100/01, *Olazabal* [2002] ECR I-10981; Joined Cases C-482/01 and C-493/01, *Orfanopoulos and Oliveri* [2004] ECR I-5257.
6. Case C-30/77, *R v Bouchereau* [1977] ECR 1999, para. 35.
7. Case C-145/09, Land Baden-Württemberg v. Tsakouridis, 2010 ECR I-2013.
8. Case C-348/09 Pietro Infusino v Oberbürgermeisterin der Stadt Remscheid [2012].
9. Case C-378/12, *Onuekwere* [2014]; Case C-400/12, *M. G.* [2014].

References

Acosta, D. (2009a) 'Latin American Reactions to the Adoption of the Returns Directive', CEPS Liberty and Security in Europe. Available at: https://www.ceps.eu/system/files/book/2009/11/latin-american-reactions-adoption-returns-directive.pdf (Accessed: 24 May 2016).

Acosta, D. (2009b) 'The Good, the Bad and the Ugly in EU Migration Law: Is the European Parliament Becoming Bad and Ugly? (The Adoption of Directive 2008/15: The Returns Directive)', *European Journal of Migration and Law*, 11(1), pp. 19–39.

Adler-Nissen, R. (2009) 'Behind the Scenes of Differentiated Integration: Circumventing National Opt-Outs in Justice and Home Affairs', *Journal of European Public Policy*, 16(1), pp. 62–80.

Amnesty International (2008) 'EU Return Directive Affects Dignity and Security of Irregular Migrants'. Available at: https://www.amnesty.org/en/latest/news/2008/07/eu-return-directive-affects-dignity-and-security-irregular-migrants-20080704/ (Accessed: 24 May 2016).

Argomaniz, J. (2009) 'Post-9/11 Institutionalisation of European Union Counter-terrorism: Emergence, Acceleration and Inertia', *European Security*, 18(2), pp. 151–72.

Bendel, P., Ette, A., and Parkes, R. (eds) (2011) *The Europeanization of Control: Venues and Outcomes of EU Justice and Home Affairs Cooperation*. Münster: LIT Verlag.

Bigo, D. (2000) 'When Two Become One: Internal and External Securitisations in Europe', in Kelstrup, M. and Williams, M. C. (eds) *International Relations Theory and the Politics of European Integration: Power, Security and Community*. London: Routledge, pp. 171–204.

Bigo, D. (2002) 'Security and Immigration: Toward a Critique of the Governmentality of Unease', *Alternatives: Global, Local, Political*, 27(1), pp. 63–92.

Checkel, J. T. (1999) 'Social Construction and Integration', *Journal of European Public Policy*, 6(4), pp. 545–60.

Den Boer, M. and Monar, J. (2002) '11 September and the Challenge of Global Terrorism to the EU as a Security Actor', *Journal of Common Market Studies*, 40(s1), pp. 11–28.

ECRE (2008) 'Returns Directive: EU Fails to Uphold Human Rights', *Press release*. Available at: www.ecre.org/component/downloads/downloads/165.html (Accessed: 24 May 2016).

Elster, J. (ed.) (1986) *Rational Choice*. Oxford: Basil Blackwell.

European Commission (2009) 'Justice, Freedom and Security in Europe since 2005: An Evaluation of the Hague Programme and Action Plan', Communication from the Commission to the Council, the European Parliament, the European Economic and Social Committee and the Committee of the Regions.

Geddes, A. (2000) *Immigration and European Integration: Towards Fortress Europe*. Manchester: Manchester University Press.

Grabbe, H. (2000) 'The Sharp Edges of Europe: Extending Schengen Eastwards', *International Affairs*, 76(3), pp. 519–36.

Guiraudon, V. (2000) 'European Integration and Migration Policy: Vertical Policy-making as Venue Shopping', *Journal of Common Market Studies*, 38(2), pp. 251–71.

Hailbronner, K. (2005) 'Refugee Status in EU Member States and Return Policies', Study for the Civil Liberties, Justice and Home Affairs Committee of the European Parliament.

Hall, P. A. and Taylor, R. C. R. (1996) 'Political Science and the Three New Institutionalisms', *Political Studies*, 44(5), pp. 936–57.

Hay, C. (2010) 'Ideas and the Construction of Interests', in Béland, D. and Cox, R. H. (eds) *Ideas and Politics in Social Science Research*. Oxford: Oxford University Press, pp. 65–82.

Hix, S. and Noury, A. (2007) 'Politics, Not Economic Interests: Determinants of Migration Policies in the European Union', *International Migration Review*, 41(1), pp. 182–205.

House of Lords, European Union Committee (2006) 'Illegal Migrants: Proposals for a Common EU Returns Policy', 32nd Report of Session 2005–06, HL Paper 166. London: House of Lords.

Huysmans, J. (2006) *The Politics of Insecurity: Fear, Migration and Asylum in the EU.* London: Routledge.

Immergut, E. M. (1998) 'The Theoretical Core of the New Institutionalism', *Politics & Society*, 26(1), pp. 5–34.

Jenson, J. and Mérand, F. (2010) 'Sociology, Institutionalism and the European Union', *Comparative European Politics*, 8(1), pp. 74–92.

Katzenstein, P. J., Keohane, R. O., and Krasner, S. D. (1998) 'International Organization and the Study of World Politics', *International Organization*, 52(4), pp. 645–85.

Kaunert, C. (2010) *European Internal Security: Towards Supranational Governance in the Area of Freedom, Security and Justice*, Manchester: Manchester University Press.

Kaunert, C. and Léonard, S. (2012) 'The Development of the EU Asylum Policy: Venue-shopping in Perspective', *Journal of European Public Policy*, 19(9), pp. 1396–413.

Kaunert, C., Léonard, S., and Occhipinti, J. D. (2013) 'Agency Governance in the European Union's Area of Freedom, Security and Justice', *Perspectives on European Politics and Society*, 14(3), pp. 273–84.

Kauppi, N. and Rask Madsen, M. (2008) 'Institutions et acteurs: rationalité, réflexivité et analyse de l'UE', *Politique Européenne*, 25(2), pp. 87–113.

Knight, J. (1992) *Institutions and Social Conflict*. Cambridge: Cambridge University Press.

Kostakopoulou, D. (2002a) 'Floating Sovereignty: A Pathology or a Necessary Means of State Evolution?' *Oxford Journal of Legal Studies*, 22(1), pp. 135–56.

Kostakopoulou, D. (2002b) 'Long-term Resident Third-Country Nationals in the European Union: Normative Expectations and Institutional Openings', *Journal of Ethnic and Migration Studies*, 28(3), pp. 443–62.

Kostakopoulou, D. (2005) 'Ideas, Norms and European Citizenship: Explaining Institutional Change', *The Modern Law Review*, 68(2), pp. 233–67.

Kostakopoulou, D. (2014) 'When EU Citizens Become Foreigners', *European Law Journal*, 20(4), pp. 447–63.

Kostakopoulou, D. (2015) 'Citizenship and Integration: Contiguity, Contagion and Evolution', in Trauner, F. and Ripoll Servent, A. (eds) *Policy Change in the Area of Freedom, Security and Justice: How EU Institutions Matter*. London: Routledge, pp. 153–77.

Lavenex, S. (2006) 'Shifting Up and Out: The Foreign Policy of European Immigration Control', *West European Politics*, 29(2), pp. 329–50.

Lavenex, S. and Wichmann, N. (2009) 'The External Governance of EU Internal Security', *Journal of European Integration*, 31(1), pp. 83–102.

Léonard, S. (2009) 'The Creation of FRONTEX and the Politics of Institutionalisation in the EU External Borders Policy', *Journal of Contemporary European Research*, 5(3), pp. 371–88.

Loader, I. and Walker, N. (2007) *Civilizing Security*. Cambridge: Cambridge University Press.

Lowndes, V. (2010) 'The Institutional Approach', in Marsh, D. and Stoker, G. (eds) *Theory and Methods in Political Science*, 3rd ed. Houndmills: Palgrave Macmillan, pp. 60–79.

Nicolini, D. (2012) *Practice Theory, Work, and Organization: An Introduction*. Oxford: Oxford University Press.

Noll, G. (2003) 'Risky Games? A Theoretical Approach to Burden-Sharing in the Asylum Field', *Journal of Refugee Studies*, 16(3), pp. 236–52.

North, D. C. (1990) *Institutions, Institutional Change and Economic Performance*. Cambridge: Cambridge University Press.

Olsen, J. P. and March, J. G. (1989) *Rediscovering Institutions: The Organizational Basis of Politics*. New York: Free Press.

Ostrom, E. (1986) 'An Agenda for the Study of Institutions', *Public Choice*, 48(1), pp. 3–25.

Pawlak, P. (2009) 'The External Dimension of the Area of Freedom, Security and Justice: Hijacker or Hostage of Cross-pillarization?' *Journal of European Integration*, 31(1), pp. 25–44.

Pierson, P. (1996) 'The Path to European Integration: A Historical Institutionalist Analysis', *Comparative Political Studies*, 29(2), pp. 123–63.

Powell, W. W. and DiMaggio, P. J. (eds) (1991) *The New Institutionalism in Organizational Analysis*. Chicago, IL: University of Chicago Press.

Ripoll Servent, A. (2012) 'Playing the Co-Decision Game? Rules' Changes and Institutional Adaptation at the LIBE Committee', *Journal of European Integration*, 34(1), pp. 55–73.

Ripoll Servent, A. (2013) 'Holding the European Parliament Responsible: Policy Shift in the Data Retention Directive from Consultation to Codecision', *Journal of European Public Policy*, 20(7), pp. 972–87.

Ripoll Servent, A. (2014) 'The Role of the European Parliament in International Negotiations after Lisbon', *Journal of European Public Policy*, 21(4), pp. 568–86.

Ripoll Servent, A. (2015) *Institutional and Policy Change in the European Parliament: Deciding on Freedom, Security and Justice*. Houndmills: Palgrave Macmillan.

Ripoll Servent, A. and Busby, A. (2013) 'Introduction: Agency and Influence inside the EU Institutions', *European Integration online Papers (EIoP)*. Available at: eiop.or.at/eiop/pdf/2013-003.pdf (Accessed: 24 May 2016).

Ripoll Servent, A. and MacKenzie, A. (2011) 'Is the EP still a Data Protection Champion? The Case of SWIFT', *Perspectives on European Politics and Society*, 12(4), pp. 390–406.

Ripoll Servent, A. and Trauner, F. (2014) 'Do Supranational EU Institutions Make a Difference? EU Asylum Law before and after "Communitarization"', *Journal of European Public Policy*, 21(8), pp. 1142–62.

Roos, C. (2013) 'How to Overcome Deadlock in EU Immigration Politics', *International Migration*, 51(6), pp. 67–79.

Saurugger, S. (2013) 'Constructivism and Public Policy Approaches in the EU: From Ideas to Power Games', *Journal of European Public Policy*, 20(6), pp. 888–906.

Schmidt, V. A. (2008) 'Discursive Institutionalism: The Explanatory Power of Ideas and Discourse', *Annual Review of Political Science*, 11(1), pp. 303–26.

Shepsle, K. A. (1989) 'Studying Institutions: Some Lessons from the Rational Choice Approach', *Journal of Theoretical Politics*, 1(2), pp. 131–47.

Shepsle, K. A. and Weingast, B. R. (1987) 'The Institutional Foundations of Committee Power', *The American Political Science Review*, 81(1), pp. 85–104.

Stetter, S. (2000) 'Regulating Migration: Authority Delegation in Justice and Home Affairs', *Journal of European Public Policy*, 7(1), pp. 80–103.

Thielemann, E. (2003) 'Between Interests and Norms: Explaining Burden-Sharing in the European Union', *Journal of Refugee Studies*, 16(3), pp. 253–73.

Trauner, F. (2009) 'Deconstructing the EU's Routes of Influence in Justice and Home Affairs in the Western Balkans', *Journal of European Integration*, 31(1), pp. 65–82.

Trauner, F. (2012) 'The European Parliament and Agency Control in the Area of Freedom, Security and Justice', *West European Politics*, 35(4), pp. 784–802.

Trauner, F. and Ripoll Servent, A. (2015) *Policy Change in the Area of Freedom, Security and Justice: How EU Institutions Matter*. London: Routledge.

Wendt, A. (1998) 'On Constitution and Causation in International Relations', *Review of International Studies*, 24(5), pp. 101–18.

Wolff, S. (2009) 'The Mediterranean Dimension of EU Counter-terrorism', *Journal of European Integration*, 31(1), pp. 137–56.

Wolff, S., Wichmann, N., and Mounier, G. (2009) 'The External Dimension of Justice and Home Affairs: A Different Security Agenda for the EU?' *Journal of European Integration*, 31(1), pp. 9–23.

Part III
Concluding Remarks

9

Next Steps in Theorizing Internal Security Cooperation in the EU

Raphael Bossong and Mark Rhinard

9.1 Introduction

This volume assembled a number of prominent scholars to contribute to our understanding of the emergence and dynamics of cooperation in EU internal security. If there was any doubt before, European responses to the influx of migrants since 2013 has underlined the growing centrality and political salience of integration in the Area of Freedom, Security and Justice (AFSJ). At the same time, we need to consider the theoretical directions of the longer-term evolution of this field. Fundamental questions—such as: Why has internal security cooperation proceeded in the pattern that it has? What is the meaning of 'security' and how are different conceptions deployed in language and action? Why is implementation difficult in certain policy areas of AFSJ? What should be the proper balance between 'freedom and security', e.g. the rule of law and the pursuit of security?—continue to be asked and demand both up-to-date and theoretically informed answers.

As the introduction to this book set out, a wide range of vibrant research agendas has emerged in this dynamic area of European integration, but they remain fairly fragmented and isolated. The time is right for reflection and more conscious theoretical debate to help a maturing field consolidate developments, illuminate gaps and overlaps, and identify opportunities for dialogue. The contributions in this volume provide a crucial foundation for this endeavour and offer a basis for broader reflections on possible ways forward, which we take up in this chapter. (See Table 9.1 below for a summary presentation of the theoretical contributions in this book, including their central propositions, main foci, and connections to broader theoretical debates.)

Table 9.1. Theoretical contributions in this book

	Central proposition	Application in context of EU internal security cooperation	Connections to broader theoretical debates
Securitization	Inherent logic and discursive dynamics of security politics set it apart from regular policy analysis.	Critical analysis of EU security discourses and practices, either in specific instances or in aggregated form. Limited theoretical focus on the nature of the EU as such.	Relations between discourse and practice, nature of evidence in critical security studies, and definition of *governmentality*.
Int. political sociology	Fundamental importance of professional fields and related beliefs and practices for policy outcomes.	Emergence, positioning, and intermingling of European professional communities for internal security. EU provides background for critical analyses of professional influence.	Post-structuralism in international politics, practice and reflexivity as linked to deep epistemological or methodological stances.
Governance	Significant stakeholder networks and coordination processes beyond formal legal and institutional structures.	Comparison of EU internal security with governance of other policy areas, as well as over time. General analysis of coordination challenges for security issues across borders.	Nature of statehood and the legitimate bases for authority; potential to provide public goods in transnational and complex settings.
Law	Importance of judicial controls and legal standards vs. executives and policymakers.	Evolution of legal oversight system for EU internal security; normative assessment with regard to fundamental legal norms.	Pluralist and path-dependent international legal orders, political role of courts.
Neofunctionalism	Functionalist and related political and institutional pressures that can advance formal EU integration.	Expansions of EU competences in internal security affairs, in connection with (spillovers) regarding other policy fields and general interests of EU institutions.	Persistence of grand integration theory (e.g. 'new intergovernmentalism'); role of crises for the EU; possible disintegration dynamics.
Institutionalism	Deep influence of formal and informal institutions on policy actors and outcomes.	Policy decisions and sequential developments in EU internal security cooperation; attention to changing inter-institutional relations in this policy area.	Institutionalism as an overarching paradigm in the social sciences; rationalist or constructivist (interpretivist) bases for cooperation.

For the rich and nuanced presentation of each approach, we can only refer to the individual contributions to this volume, whereas the remainder of this conclusion will seek to draw out some wider themes and open areas for further research. To repeat, we do not want to lay any claim towards an authoritative synthesis, let alone exclude the wide range of alternative perspectives that could be brought to bear in this area. The variety and diversity of social science paradigms and range of sub-disciplines simply could not be adequately covered in a single volume. As outlined in the introduction, theoretical diversity is compounded by the breadth of policies that can be subsumed under the heading of European internal security. For instance, one could delve further into anthropological perspectives on migration and EU borders, or employ criminological research techniques on the evolving patterns of transnational crime. Moreover, we are presented with ever more growing and diffuse topics that are added to the policy agenda, such as critical infrastructure protection, emergency management, or cybersecurity, each of which may benefit from specific theoretical angles. Thus, the menu of hypotheses or analytical pathways in this area is bound to expand. At the same time, it is precisely the strength and purpose of theorizing to reach a more generalized plane of reflection that distils core questions and cross-cutting concerns, in order to avoid excessive fragmentation or tendencies to fall back on overly descriptive accounts of new developments.

In that sense, this volume and the following concluding reflections should be read as an invitation for more sustained debate and reflection. We begin by teasing out connections and contrasts amongst the theoretical approaches presented in this book. Looking across the chapters to identify interconnections is a risky endeavour, not least because each is positioned in a particular ontological and epistemological stance. Nor are we inclined to preach theoretical orthodoxy since, as mentioned, a degree of eclecticism is necessary to capture the complex dynamics underpinning this field and to enhance the sophistication of various theories. However, we are keen to pinpoint where different theoretical approaches 'speak' to one another and highlight what can be gained from identifying mutual strengths and weaknesses. We opened this volume by organizing existing literature in three broad categories— approaches focused on politics, policy, and polity—partly to encourage a reflection of commonalities amongst disparate perspectives. Those commonalities can be further highlighted if authors are open and explicit about their scholarly ambitions, assumptions, and scope conditions. Such questions include: In which aspect of European cooperation on internal security are scholars interested (for instance: integration and cooperation broadly speaking, institutional change dynamics, or policy outcomes)? Does a study aim to understand internal security as a particular form of cooperation or one of many kinds of cooperation?

Answers to these questions may then be integrated into bigger ideas or debates for a sustained critical dialogue between theoretical approaches. In particular, we suggest two such organizing ideas. The first is the potential 'normalization' of European internal security as an object of study, which can denote, somewhat paradoxically, both the increasing regularity with which decisions are taken along 'Community' lines, and the increasing level of politicization or open contestation of this policy area. Another organizing idea for dialogue between theoretical perspectives is the 'big' question about the possible trajectory or 'finalité' of EU integration in this area, even if it raises thorny secondary questions on the status of theorizing or deeper relations between structure and agency.

We also want to highlight and stimulate further possible research avenues in the field, both within the discipline of EU studies and beyond. Some suggestions and ideas, such as reinvigorating intergovernmental theorizing and developing more coherent approaches to studying the role of crises in driving change, are thus outlined in the final parts of this chapter. The conclusion summarizes the discussion and draws the volume to a close.

9.2 Normalization: A Policy Field like any Other?

As discussed in the opening chapters of this volume, the 'special' status of EU policymaking in the internal security domain—with its intergovernmental modes of cooperation and lack of strong legal instruments to bind cooperation—has long been up for debate. Since the Lisbon Treaty and the shift of internal security policymaking towards the more mainstream Community Method, one may work with the hypothesis of a possible 'normalization' of internal security decision-making. At an empirical level, this is justified by treaty changes that normalized the decision-making process of internal security cooperation in the EU. The Amsterdam Treaty (1999), in addition to the Lisbon Treaty (2009), subjected AFSJ policy to the Community Method, thereby enhancing the role of supranational bodies like the Commission, Parliament, and Court of Justice. Yet as argued by Monar in this volume, suggestions of normalization run counter not only to habitual arguments by policy experts about the 'specificities of the field', but may also be questioned due the nature of the public good in question, its potential impact on individual rights and the increasing operational dimension of cross-border cooperation for internal security.

Reflecting further on the normalization or remaining specialization of EU internal security cooperation can help us to make more nuanced or reflective assessments about the fruitfulness or desired leverage of different theoretical perspectives. Clearly, if one is to regard internal security as a field that can be readily compared to other EU policy fields, the range of theoretical tools that can be borrowed from mainstream political science and EU studies is bound to expand. As elaborated at several points in the remainder of this chapter, however, this should be accompanied by a subtler and more precise specification of what each approach specifically brings to the table of EU internal security cooperation and what we can learn in return for other policy fields, rather than only replaying theoretical debates about 'fitting' general purpose approaches to policymaking and EU integration.

In contrast, non-EU-centred approaches to internal security analysis continue to highlight the specific nature of the field and unique dimensions of security as a policy domain. Yet, also here, we can note subtle differences that shape the potential for comparative research. For instance, the approaches by Bigo (political sociology) and Balzacq (securitization) stem from different academic disciplines (sociology and security studies, respectively) but take a familiar ontological stance and seek to illuminate the construction of discourses and practices of officials and stakeholders closely involved in security cooperation. They are not, in the first instance, concerned with explaining specific policy outcomes but rather wider logics of governmentality. Thus, they tend to regard EU cooperation as only a sub-set or manifestation, if highly pertinent one, of wider trends in contemporary security provision. Furthermore, both approaches are ontologically conscious, and aim to overcome both the structure–agency divide and abstract notions of the meaning of security by a theoretically rich understanding of the meaning of practices by socially embedded, and usually creative or entrepreneurial, actors. Thus, Bigo, in this volume, offers intriguing details on the interplay of different 'guilds' in internal security that can be likened to communities of practice (while not adopting the dominant interpretation of the latter concept in international relations). This interplay often yields illiberal and control-oriented policies outside the gaze of democratic actors. Securitization, for its part, also suggests the emergence and legitimation of practices of security that conflict with, or undermine, conventional notions of democratic politics as open-ended contests among alternative values and elites.

It would be a mistake, however, to glide too easily between the aforementioned takes on EU internal security. Despite its increased sensitivity to context and practices beyond a binary vision of the 'state of exception', securitization remains interested in teasing out a central 'logic' or 'governmentality' as a historical vector or normative criterion. Political sociology is arguably more broadly interested in the emergence, definition, contestation, and practice of power and distinction in various social and political fields. Following Foucault, one may, of course, see security and discipline as particularly central to more 'modern' forms of power that link the 'state' more deeply with (seemingly liberal) society. Still, political sociology, in itself, cannot clearly resolve the question of whether contemporary internal security cooperation constitutes a special set of practices and distinctions for European societies, or rather should be seen as a general manifestation of societal and political differentiation. So there may be no deep theoretical difference between the field of European internal security and other transnational fields, such as European law (Mudge and Vauchez, 2012)—even if close engagement with securitization has predisposed scholars from the PARIS school to highlight the dominance of security professionals, or the expansive nature of the (internal) security field. An appreciation of the more contingent relevance of the 'field of internal security' may be detected among more recent contributions from the PARIS school (see the contribution by Bigo, in this volume), but could be sharpened and used to generate more comparative research on the centrality of security logics, professionals, and their practices for the overall trajectory of contemporary societies.

Theoretical approaches that are more intimately connected with the EU as a 'unique' kind of polity raise other questions about the priorities and comparability of explanatory factors in the context of internal security. To be precise, neofunctionalism (Niemann in this volume), new institutionalism (Ripoll Servent and Kostakopoulou), and governance (Bossong and Lavenex) developed in relation to the wider discipline of political science, but the approaches also bring a particular agenda to interpreting the EU integration process. They may see it, for instance, as a particularly strong case of endogenous cooperation dynamics, of the deep effects of institutional change, or of a breeding ground for diverse modes and patterns of policymaking.

These perspectives imply a certain degree of normalization with regard to the substance of internal security cooperation, i.e. the comparability of various EU policy fields and the general relevance of other explanatory factors. In fact, all three 'mainstream' approaches assembled in this volume address this question. More contemporary readings of neofunctionalism have transcended the categorical heuristic distinction between 'high' and 'low' politics, and rather emphasize more contextual conditions for the unfolding, or resistance to, spillover dynamics.

New institutionalists, for their part, tend to recognize the particular normative sensitivity of internal security issues, thus suggesting that rationalist models of institutional competition or principal agent dynamics may need to be modified. This directs attention to, but does not necessarily demand, more constructivist variants of institutionalism for understanding internal security cooperation fully. Indeed, sociological or constructivist institutionalism have much broader scope conditions. Thus, the 'constructivist institutionalism' advocated by Ripoll Servent and Kostakopoulou gives prominence to wider normative dynamics than purely process-based socialization, which may deserve further attention in other policy areas than internal security.

Governance approaches are more ambivalent with regard to comparability. On the one hand, governance is an approach focused on generalized forms of interaction amongst actors, institutions, and ideas, forms which shift and move across different venues, structures, levels, and policy goals. This explains why, in EU studies, there is considerable variation of governance forms across different policy goals and levels/mechanisms of governance through which policy outputs are generated and managed. This relates to the wider debate on the transferability of standard EU governance approaches, such as mutual recognition or negative integration, to the case of EU internal security. On the other hand, the chapter by Bossong and Lavenex points to a more specific debate on security governance that seeks to distil some shared patterns and problems on the basis of a *domain-driven* rather than institutionalist logic. Thus, there are differences amongst governance scholars regarding the significance of the domain of application. But these differences should not be exaggerated. The overarching components of a governance approach— dispersion of public authority, increased involvement of private actors, and the heightened complexity of social coordination processes—also apply to other thematic issue areas such as environmental or economic policy. Despite the specific label of 'security governance', therefore, theoretical concepts and questions remain comparable across policy fields.

There is a different angle on the 'normalization' debate in internal security cooperation that appears in several of the contributions of this volume. That angle reflects a wider, more normative, concern regarding the trajectory of EU politics. Some view the field of international security cooperation as following the trajectory of other fields of European integration, which are increasingly losing their technocratic and consensual character and exhibiting more intense political contestation—as is normal in national democratic arenas (De Wilde, 2011). If anyone doubted this or marvelled at previous periods of 'integration by stealth' during the 1990s and 2000s (Herrschinger et al., 2013), the recent migration crisis has underlined how traditional visions about the nation state and its responsibilities for the provision of internal security remain very much alive. Similarly, with regard to other issues such as PNR or data retention, there has been fierce debate amongst EU institutions and EU member states.

However, we have few theoretical orientations to help assess these developments, be it at the EU level, or more generally in the area of internal security. What might, in fact, be a 'normal' degree of politicization in matters of internal security? Is it not true that issues such as migration controls, the fight against terrorism or the management of crime and deviance are highly vulnerable to polarized party competition or, at least, erratic 'morality politics' (Akkerman, 2015; Euchner et al., 2013; Neal, 2012; Gurowitz, 2008)? Are there good reasons to insulate large parts of these issues away from the swings of majoritarian decision-making, to ground it in civil rights and negative freedoms of the individual, and to place it in the hands of judicial and professional actors? Or should we avoid falling back into the 'trap' of technocracy? The existing literature on EU internal security cooperation arguably has still to develop a more systematic debate on such questions.

9.3 Finalité: The Big Questions of European Integration

Another major theme touched upon in the chapters and central to many analytical approaches in EU studies (if not always explicitly acknowledged), as well as to various strands of critical security studies, is the 'big question' on the future direction of cooperation and integration in matters of internal security and its likely effect on politics and society. Proclamations about the 'finalité' of integration or the drift of historical forces have long been unfashionable, considering the predictive errors by traditional political theorizing about the EU as a whole, and, indeed, about other macro-historical political developments. Nevertheless, we would argue that some degree of comment and reflection is desirable—and unavoidable—and plays an important role in informing the choice of alternative theoretical approaches. For instance, approaches from critical security studies and political sociology are inclined towards self-perpetuating or structural cooperation dynamics that privilege security considerations—which, unsurprisingly, constitute their core research interest (see section 9.2). The theoretical reference to practices and construction of norms and discourses seems to provide for an escape from the overwrought structure/agency debate. In practice, however, much of the research in this vein tends towards the assumption of a security-driven governmentality that transcends countervailing actions. For instance, why are there still very few studies on dynamics of de-securitization (Hansen, 2012) in the context of the EU's AFSJ (Schwell, 2009)? Could the increased political contestation of EU internal security policy be read in this light, since normative arguments on the need to respect the rights of migrants are increasingly brought to the fore? Or is the political drama surrounding the refugee crisis yet another indicator of the widespread securitization of EU borders? And how does this square with readings of securitization as more depoliticized practices of security professionals? Related dilemmas are also evident with regard to the repressive policy effects that the PARIS school explains by the interactions of security professionals. None of this is meant to imply that these approaches are factually or analytically incorrect. But considering their assumptions, the approaches provide little space for alternative perspectives on the historical trajectory of EU internal security cooperation, with no serious consideration of drivers and trends toward a less security-oriented transnational regime.

Conversely, other political science or legal approaches tend to support a progressive perspective on the interplay between different institutions, power logics, and normative orders with regard to internal security policy-making at the EU level. The governance perspective may be most ambivalent in this regard, as there is no postulated theoretical mechanism about a likely move from negative integration and soft coordination, which tends to privilege security-oriented executives, towards more 'positive' standard-setting in matters of civil rights or more equal political participation. An empirically guarded but progressive counterpoint is provided by legal theorizing that suggests a growing role for *ex ante* and *ex post* rule-of-law controls on EU internal security. Substantial practical barriers to the realization of a dogmatically more consistent legal regime for EU internal security remain in place, including the dominance of different legal traditions, deeply embedded ideas of 'correct' procedural norms, and reliance on national courts—none of which are perfectly aligned with transnational cooperation realities (but see Mitsilegas in this volume). Nevertheless, many legal scholars tend to remain animated by the notion that legal norms for civil or human rights can, over time, be anchored in transnational settings, especially in the EU as an advanced project of legal integration.

Further reflection on the notion of 'justice' in relation to internal security cooperation, along with related notions of constitutional stability, are certainly necessary (Herlin-Karnell, 2014; Murphy and Arcarazo, 2014). Can such an order be achieved by a standard, liberal model of defence of universal rights and civil rights, underscored by the Charter of Fundamental Rights and the EU's (eventual) accession to the ECHR? Or would it also involve more contentious, substantive choices with regard to the criminalization of certain offences, which are still relatively limited at the EU level? Legal analyses would also have to address the possible tensions between general standards for freedom of movement, the comparability of civil rights across member states, and questions of social cohesion. This mirrors the classic debate on the Court of Justice as an advocate of market freedoms that do not sit easily with national welfare states (Scharpf, 2010). In the area of internal security, such questions are increasingly evident in the debate over migration and asylum. Utilitarian models for 'burden-sharing' based on GDP, territory, and unemployment rate cannot be easily reconciled with other legal concepts or rights for individuals, such as family reunification.

To return to a more general plane of theoretical reflection, it is, thus, difficult to think of and use different paradigms in the study of internal security without a background vision of its structural drift, be it progressive or dystopian. This could be seen as a contentious claim, as explicitly predictive and macro-level theorizing has long been widely criticized. But it must be asked: what do alternative approaches offer when it comes to genuinely contingent and open-ended narratives about the further course of EU internal security cooperation? Political scientists have underlined the role of supranational policy entrepreneurs, in particular, the European Commission and the Council Secretariat (Kaunert, 2010; Kaunert and Giovanna, 2010; Bossong, 2013), in using security crises and windows of opportunity for shaping policy in this issue area. Yet even if policy entrepreneurship should, in principle, be open to varying outcomes, to date we have a dominant narrative of *more* integration and new policy agendas after every major crisis and window of opportunity. This made sense in order to account for the rapid rise of EU internal security cooperation over the last two decades, but may have become outdated in the light of recent developments.

From a purely empirical perspective, contingency and uncertainty over the next possible stage in EU cooperation in matters of internal security are clearly pressing concerns. Aside from the dynamics of the migration crisis, one could point to a longer-brewing sense of strategic confusion and a lack of 'vision' during the so-called post-Stockholm debate and against the minimalist 'strategic guidelines' for the ASFJ that were issued by the European Council guidelines in June 2015 (Bossong and Rhinard, 2013b). From a theoretical perspective, scholars could, therefore, extend their reach into the wider literature on public policy analysis that deals with the erratic patterns of stability and change in more 'mature' policy fields. This can, in part, already be detected in a recent innovative volume (Trauner and Ripoll Servent, 2014) that seeks to assess the degree of policy change in European internal security cooperation since the Lisbon Treaty. Fruitful avenues that can be deepened in this respect might include punctuated equilibrium theory (Baumgartner and Jones, 2005), competing advocacy coalitions (Sabatier, 1998) or, more broadly, more rigorous applications of path-dependency (Pierson, 2004; Capoccia and Kelemen, 2007) that provide more detail on feedback loops and critical junctures in policy developments.

At the same time, this avenue of inquiry needs to connect to the different theoretical perspectives assembled in this volume. To assess the maturity of the policy field of EU internal security cooperation, one can, for instance, gather sociological data on the density of the transnational field of security professionals. Alternatively, one can focus on textual or discursive evidence to gauge the degree of institutionalization or legal development. One would need to grapple with the fact that it is unclear what could count as empirical evidence for a mature 'equilibrium' of governance arrangements in a given policy area—in contrast to the assumption of a gradual move from soft to harder forms of governance to resolve transnational collective action problems.

Finally, when pondering the maturity and finalité of European cooperation, we also need to think more seriously about disintegration—or at least increasing fragmentation. Repeated initiatives of differentiated integration in internal security cooperation and the very real possibility of the UK's 'permanent opt-out' underlines that we need to pay more attention to this prospect. One could reach back to classic theories of EU integration such as neofunctionalism, which treats the question of 'spill-back' as a familiar research question (Schmitter, 1970). One may also build on abstract rationalist (institutionalist) approaches to international cooperation, where selective cooperation 'à la carte' may even be desirable, including in the EU (Majone, 2014). The general debate on disintegration in the face of crises (Webber, 2014; Vollaard, 2014; Lefkofridi and Schmitter, 2015), but also more multidimensional fragmentation and power dispersion (Jensen et al., 2014), is currently gathering speed in EU studies and should be brought into dialogue with theorizing on internal security cooperation.

9.4 Connecting to Research on the EU

Beyond the themes of normalization and finalité discussed above, we see a number of other approaches from EU studies, and political science more generally, that may usefully be applied to EU internal security cooperation. First, contrary to scholarly tendencies to use constructivist variants of institutionalism, other approaches could be used in a more explicit and ambitious manner; these include: rationalistic tools of negotiation theory, veto player analysis, and principal–agent approaches. Complex principal–agent analyses have gained an increasing foothold in the analysis of EU agency governance (Dehousse, 2008; Rittberger and Wonka, 2011). And the AFSJ is, in fact, the EU policy area with the largest number of agencies (Kaunert et al., 2013), several of which have seen substantial increases in budgets and statutory powers in recent years (Busuioc and Gronleer, 2013).

The dynamics of institutional competition could be studied further, including agenda-setting by the Commission and the bi-cameral interaction of the Parliament and Council. Research could elaborate on ongoing discussions over whether the 'normalized' decision process makes the European Parliament more or less of a cooperative partner with the Council (Ripoll Servent, 2015), which could be explored via general normative orientations as well as a focus on specific power-political alliances and institutional positioning. The power of the Commission becomes relevant here, too, in that the Commission is purportedly in decline (but see Nugent and Rhinard, 2016). If one can find evidence of Commission influence (as has been done in some studies, see Bossong and Rhinard, 2013b) in this 'hard case', it would go far in improving our understanding of policy and integration dynamics. Finally, the Court of Justice still has to define a more regular and predictable role in internal security, so that it should not only be approaches from the perspective of general legal doctrine and precedent, but also from the perspective of explicit political manoeuvring and its impact on integration, as has been long discussed in other policy areas (Burley and Mattli, 1993; Conant, 2007).

Building on the coherence of the EU legal and institutional order, another aspect that deserves a closer look in the study of EU internal security cooperation is policy implementation. It has been repeatedly criticized in the pre-Lisbon period that the rapid growth of policy instruments at the political level strongly diverges from the reality of cooperation or implementation on the ground (Argomaniz, 2010; Bures, 2011; Block, 2011). The EU previously lacked enforcement mechanisms to ensure legal transposition, and few observers had a clear sense of the actual take-up and use of various instruments. In the area of migration research, this has partially been addressed by comparative quantitative research of clearly identifiable numbers, such as asylum claims and acceptance rates (Toshkov and de Haan, 2012). In other areas of internal security, however, we have only isolated attempts to move beyond general critiques of weak implementation and towards more systematic data (Block, 2011). Thus, as internal security becomes subject to more institutional oversight and compliance monitoring—and generates related official data—mainstream implementation and transposition research (Börzel et al., 2011; König and Mäder, 2014) could better test the presumed gap between political decisions and operational realities.

The debate on the EU's 'executive order' (Trondal, 2010; Curtin and Egeberg, 2013) could also be connected more closely with internal security cooperation. As just mentioned, we already have a growing literature on the governance of agencies in this area. To date, this literature has largely focused on normative questions of accountability and power relations between agencies and member states (Pollak and Slominski, 2009; Trauner, 2012; Carrera et al., 2013). The question of 'effectiveness', or the centrality of EU agencies, in the implementation of EU internal security cooperation, is less well understood (Bures, 2008; Horii, 2012). There are good reasons for this, including the fundamental methodological and conceptual challenges to assessing effectiveness in transnational settings (Hegemann et al., 2012) and internal security affairs (van Dongen, 2011; Manksi, 2011); the tension between policy oversight and effectiveness (McGinley and Parkes, 2007); and more pragmatic challenges regarding access to data. Nevertheless, there seems to be room to develop a more fine-grained picture of the impact of internal security policy across the states, which not only relates to the willingness or capacity of member states to transpose these policies, but also to the managerial and executive capacities of EU actors. As touched upon above, greater depth of empirical and theoretical research on migration policies in Europe can serve as an inspiring ideal for other aspects of internal security cooperation.

Yet the most glaring gap in the current academic literature on EU internal security cooperation is the lack of renewed intergovernmental approaches. In this respect, one might draw a comparison between studies on the AFSJ and on the Common Foreign and Security Policy (CSFP). The latter has displayed a persistent strand of modified intergovernmental theorizing since its inception (Bickerton et al., 2011; Howorth, 2012), while there are only isolated, theoretically self-conscious applications with regard to internal security issues (Friedrichs, 2008; Lorenz, 2011). This also relates to an emerging and important research agenda within EU studies—the 'new intergovernmentalism'— which concerns the relation between the formal/legal or discursive framework for policymaking (communitarization) and the actual practice of European political cooperation. At the heart of the new intergovernmentalism is the suggestion that, since the Maastricht Treaty, there has been a 'tendency towards European integration without supranationalism...predicated on an increasingly deliberative and consensual approach to EU decision-making [by the representatives of member state governments]' (Bickerton et al., 2015: 1). Proponents argue that the emergence of deliberation and consensus as the 'dominant behavioural norms' have resulted in EU policymaking, at all stages, becoming more Council based. Moreover, the European Council has emerged as 'a centre for governing major new areas of EU activity and crisis management' with a corresponding decline in the use of the Community Method (Bickerton et al., 2015a: 2). At first sight, new intergovernmentalism may find an 'easy case' in internal security cooperation. If one supports the approach's basic premise, it could be that other EU policy fields are becoming, from a procedural perspective, more like internal security cooperation pre-Lisbon, when cooperation was more inter- or trans-governmental and conducted in semi-transparent, deliberative forums rather devoid of supranational actors.

However, the increasing degree of contestation in EU politics may resemble more familiar formulations of intergovernmentalism—and related, rationalist hard-bargaining dynamics—instead of deliberation (Schimmelfennig, 2015). Yet in contrast to areas related to economic integration, there are no sophisticated models of national preference formation and bargaining strategies—as in the much-criticized, but still useful perspective of liberal intergovernmentalism and two-level games (Moravcsik, 1997). Much research on internal security cooperation contains vague references about the importance of 'national sovereignty' (however that may be defined) in this area, while a direct, national electoral impact on different policy alternatives in EU internal security cooperation is not easy to discern—at least until the recent migration crisis drove the issue to the top of national agendas.

The lack of a theoretical orientation on national preferences in intergovernmental bargaining is aggravated by the distinctiveness of *internal* security cooperation, whereby it is at least problematic to resort to more general IR theories on preference formation with regard to security issues. This is not to say that we have no plausible candidates or hypotheses for a more general theory of intergovernmental preference formation in internal security cooperation. At least from a rationalist or public choice perspective, one could point to: differential adaptation costs regarding implementation and Europeanization; a number of collective action problems with regard to different security challenges, which—in turn—are either more or less amenable to cooperation (Bossong and Rhinard, 2013a); or straightforward economic calculations of 'burden-sharing'. Again, the current migration crisis provides ample material for analysis, and already exhibits many classic coordination problems, such as 'beggar-thy-neighbour' politics.

Yet given the symbolic nature of many security issues or the role of nationally specific 'security cultures' (Burgess, 2009), other, less rationalistic approaches are surely needed. For instance, one could draw upon broad empirical research on public opinion and Euroscepticism, and explore its complex intersection with different issues that fall under the remit of the ASFJ. There is initial evidence that higher levels of migration correspond to higher levels of Euroscepticism (Toshkov and Kortenska, 2015)—though not necessarily to anti-migration attitudes in general—whereas poll data (e.g. European Commission, 2011) otherwise suggests considerable public support for European cooperation on organized crime and terrorism.

Finally, one should not forget about the component of bargaining theory in classic intergovernmental theories of EU integration. Here it is again reasonable to argue that the field of internal security may merit closer attention beyond simple assumptions about preference intensity and the voting power of governments. The EU has now moved to a more generalized regime of qualified majority voting, albeit with complex reservations, while the threat of alternative options and preference intensity is complicated by multiple and realistic options for flexible integration and transgovernmental cooperation beneath and beyond the EU. Of course, outside options have always been an option in EU integration and intergovernmental bargaining, as underlined by the response to the euro crisis and supplementary instruments or treaties beyond EU law. However, it is clear that differentiated integration, opt-outs, and experimentation between smaller sets of member states is particularly pronounced in the case of internal security cooperation, which may make this option more pertinent than in other policy areas. So we have yet to develop a more complex, if necessarily partial, theorizing on preferences, intergovernmentalism, and bargaining dynamics in internal security cooperation. A recent suggestive approach has been to compare related integration dynamics in areas of so-called core state powers (Genschel and Jachtenfuchs, 2016), which includes coercive force, public finance, and the use of substantial public administration capacities, and where the potential tensions between public issue salience and different state elite interests could help to explain highly variegated outcomes. However, this very high-level perspective needs to be specified further and critically tested with regard to the various sub-areas where 'coercive force' is implicated, or more generally, the diversity of the ASFJ.

This could be done in parallel to further research on the role of private actors, which—alongside security professionals and state elites—remain relevant to the mediation or accentuation of national preferences in internal security cooperation. While classic business interest groups can occasionally shape migration and border security policy, the fields of critical infrastructure protection or cybersecurity centrally revolve around the role of private businesses, be it as vulnerable actors, producers of 'security solutions', or regulatory counterparts for policymakers. As touched upon by Bossong and Lavenex in this volume, the notion of security governance can provide a fruitful entry point to tease out related complex coordination dynamics between public and private actors. Neofunctionalism also highlights the possible role of societal interest groups, like advocacy groups, lawyers, and other epistemic communities. Sociological approaches, such as the PARIS school, provide another fruitful take on capturing the disposition or epistemic baggage of private actors that increasingly interact in shared fields with public institutions. However, other perspectives from EU studies and political science on the dynamics of contemporary regulation (Brown and Marsden, 2013) and emerging global regimes (Jakobi and Wolf, 2013) should be used to trace the role of private actors with regard to the technological aspects of internal security.

9.5 Connecting to Research on Internal Security

This leads us to perspectives that reach beyond the remit of the EU, its particular history, and the likely trajectory of integration in the area of internal security. For instance, internal security cooperation continues to take place through many other transnational channels (Jakobi, 2013; Bowling and Sheptycki, 2012), be it through mini-lateral cooperation (e.g. Anglo-Saxon countries' homeland security), regional initiatives (e.g. the 'North American Security Perimeter'), or like-minded informal groupings inside the EU (Bures, 2012). To understand normative and interest-based incentives to cooperate across borders, or to explore illustrative communities of practice across borders, we may need to turn to theories more broadly pitched at inter-state cooperation. This suggests general theories from the field of IR, and not just variants adapted to study endogenous dynamics within the EU. The focus on 'global public goods' offers some purchase on state incentives and disincentives for cooperating across borders to produce different goods linked to internal security (Bossong and Rhinard, 2013a). That said, many of the theories outlined in this book operate at a meta- or macro-level of explanation and are thus also suitable for analysing phenomena outside the EU.

Similarly, the formative effects of 'crises' in shaping cooperation, policy change, and elite interaction is not limited to EU internal security cooperation—particularly as one should move away from the aforementioned tendency to equate crisis with subsequent 'advances' in EU integration. The role of crises in history is the theme of a long line of theorizing in general political science literature (Allison, 1971; for a review of that literature, see Boin, 2004). Crises have an effect at both cognitive levels (shaping how decision-makers act and how they construct their interests when under pressure), normative levels (shaping the resolution—or not—of different value claims when a crisis hits), and in terms of shaping outcomes (symbolic instrument usage in the absence of reasoned thinking). Governments around the globe have been studied in terms of the effects of crises on process and outcomes, ranging from the US post-September 11 to the EU during the Ash Cloud crisis. In each event, the nature of behaviour (whether in single states or in multilateral organizations) was critically altered by the pressures exhibited by crises. This links to the associated literature on 'sense making' during crises, which in the EU tends to conflate situation assessment with opportunities for integrative solutions (usually benefitting EU institutions and agencies; see Boin et al., 2013; 2015), and the search for better methods of forecasting impending crises, which also place more competences and control opportunities in the hands of policymakers (Meyer and de Franco, 2011). Using not only a 'crisis' perspective in the EU setting, but also looking across regional cases to understand the effect of crises on internal security cooperation, should prove fruitful.

Finally, aside from taking a crisis as the starting point of analysis, we should not ignore more radical takes on the question of who or what constitutes an actor or vector for political developments. This mainly alludes to the profound role that technology, or rather technological environments and systems, may exercise in this regard. The more recent concern with cyber issues, border security, and critical infrastructures has reemphasized this much older debate, which can be traced all the way back to historical materialism and the role of technological and economic modernization for political mobilization and conflict (Habermas, 1975). From a post-structuralist perspective, critical security studies have increasingly sought to highlight complex *assemblages* of practices and technologies of control (Amicelle et al., 2015; see also Bigo in this volume). Moreover, one could point to the growing popularity of sociological 'science and technology studies', and, in particular, the 'actor-network-theory' of Bruno Latour (2005) that seeks to eradicate the conventional distinction between human actors and passive technological artifacts. The latter should rather be understood as embedded 'actans' that shape human actions and relations just as much as humans shape their technological environment (Sayes, 2014). Whether one wants to build on either of these specific academic literatures or not, it is, thus, essential to expand our range of questions and theoretical toolkit beyond conventional political institutions or the role of human security professionals, and to arrive at richer understandings of the ever-growing scope and salience of technological factors and instruments for the provision of internal security.

9.6 Conclusions

This book originated from the observation that the study of internal security cooperation in the EU has reached a milestone in its evolution, with a slow but advancing march towards more developed, advanced applications of theory. The results of those applications have been exciting and influential, not only within this particular field but further afar as well. Yet considering the relative youth of the discipline, we argued that the time was right to take stock of theoretical achievements, to spark a wider debate on theorizing in the field, and to illuminate ways forward. The questions we hoped to answer were: Where do we stand? What has been accomplished? Where might the field be going? This volume has taken a first cut at answering those questions but the debate must continue. The health of an academic discipline is measured largely by the robustness of debate taking place within it and the degree to which findings can be communicated to a broader (academic) audience. Both of those features are facilitated by meta-reflection on theoretical approaches since those approaches are constituted by different key terms, underlying assumptions, and basic goals. This book thus hopes to mark the start—not the end—of a sustained meta-reflection and debate on the theoretical constitution of the field as it moves forward.

References

Akkerman, T. (2015) 'Immigration Policy and Electoral Competition in Western Europe: A Fine-grained Analysis of Party Positions over the Past Two Decades', *Party Politics*, 21(1), pp. 54–67.

Allison, G. T. (1971) *Essence of Decision: Explaining the Cuban Missile Crisis*. Boston: Little, Brown.

Amicelle, A., Aradau, C., and Jeandesboz, J. (2015) 'Questioning Security Devices: Performativity, Resistance, Politics', *Security Dialogue*, 46(4), pp. 293–306.

Argomaniz, J. (2010) 'Before and after Lisbon: Legal Implementation as the "Achilles heel" in EU Counter-terrorism?' *European Security*, 19(2), pp. 297–316.

Baumgartner, F. B. and Jones, B. D. (2005) 'A Model of Choice for Public Policy', *Journal of Public Administration Research and Theory*, 15(3), pp. 325–51.

Bickerton, C., Hodson, D., and Puetter, U. (2015) 'The New Intergovernmentalism and the Study of European Integration', in Bickerton, C., Hodson, D., and Puetter, U. (eds) *The New Intergovernmentalism: States and Supranational Actors in the Post-Maastricht Era*. Oxford: Oxford University Press, pp. 1–50.

Bickerton, C. J., Irondelle, B., and Menon, A. (2011) 'Security Co-operation beyond the Nation-State: The EU's Common Security and Defence Policy', *JCMS: Journal of Common Market Studies*, 49(1), pp. 1–21.

Block, L. (2011) *From Politics to Policing: The Rationality Gap in EU Council Policy-making*. The Hague: Eleven Publishing.

Boin, A. (2004) 'Lessons from Crisis Research', *International Studies Review*, 6(1), pp. 165–94.

Boin, A., Ekengren, M., and Rhinard, M. (2013) *The European Union as Crisis Manager: Problems and Prospects*. Cambridge: Cambridge University Press.

Boin, A., Ekengren, M., and Rhinard, M. (2015) *Making Sense of Sense-Making: The EU's Role in Collecting, Analysing, and Disseminating Information in Times of Crisis*. Stockholm: Swedish National Defence College, Acta B Series.

Börzel, T. A., Hofmann, T., and Panke, D. (2011) 'Caving in or Sitting it out? Longitudinal Patterns of Non-compliance in the European Union', *Journal of European Public Policy*, 19(4), pp. 454–71.

Bossong, R. (2013) *The Evolution of EU Counter-terrorism: European Security Policy after 9/11*. London, Routledge.

Bossong, R. and Rhinard, M. (2013a) 'European Internal Security as a Public Good', *European Security*, 22(2), pp. 129–47.

Bossong, R., and Rhinard, M. (2013b) 'The EU Internal Security Strategy: Towards a More Coherent Approach to EU Security?' *Studia Diplomatica*, LXVI(2), pp. 45–58.

Bowling, B. and Sheptycki, J. W. E. (2012) *Global Policing*. Los Angeles, CA: and London: Sage.

Brown, I. and Marsden, C. T. (2013) *Regulating Code: Good Governance and Better Regulation in the Information Age*. Cambridge, MA: MIT Press.

Bures, O. (2012) 'Informal Counterterrorism Arrangements in Europe: Beauty by Variety or Duplicity by Abundance?' *Cooperation and Conflict*, 47(4), pp. 495–518.

Bures, O. (2011) *EU Counterterrorism Policy: A Paper Tiger?* Farnham and Burlington, VT: Ashgate.

Bures, O. (2008) 'Europol's Fledgling Counterterrorism Role', *Terrorism and Political Violence*, 20(4), pp. 498–517.

Burgess, J. P. (2009) 'There is No European Security, Only European Securities', *Cooperation and Conflict*, 44(3), pp. 309–28.

Burley, A.-M. and Mattli, W. (1993) 'Europe before the Court: A Political Theory of Legal Integration', *International Organization*, 47(1), pp. 41–76.

Busuioc, M. and Groenleer, M. (2013) 'Beyond Design: The Evolution of Europol and Eurojust', *Perspectives on European Politics and Society*, 14(3), pp. 285–304.

Capoccia, G. and Kelemen, R. D. (2007) 'The Study of Critical Junctures: Theory, Narrative, and Counterfactuals in Historical Institutionalism', *World Politics*, 59(03), pp. 341–69.

Carrera, S., den Hertog, L., and Parkin, J. (2013) 'The Peculiar Nature of EU Home Affairs Agencies in Migration Control: Beyond Accountability versus Autonomy?' *European Journal of Migration and Law*, 15(4), pp. 337–58.

Conant, L. (2007) 'Review Article: The Politics of Legal Integration', *JCMS: Journal of Common Market Studies*, 45(s1), pp. 45–66.

Curtin, D. and Egeberg, M. (2013) *Towards a New Executive Order in Europe?* London: Routledge.

Dehousse, R. (2008) 'Delegation of Powers in the European Union: The Need for a Multi-principals Model', *West European Politics*, 31(4), pp. 789–805.

De Wilde, P. (2011) 'No Polity for Old Politics? A Framework for Analyzing the Politicization of European Integration', *Journal of European Integration*, 33(5), pp. 559–75.

Euchner, E.-M., Heichel, S., Nebel, K., and Raschzok, A. (2013) 'From "Morality" Policy to "Normal" Policy: Framing of Drug Consumption and Gambling in Germany and the Netherlands and their Regulatory Consequences', *Journal of European Public Policy*, 20(3), pp. 372–89.

European Commission (2011) 'Internal Security', *Special Eurobarometer* 371. Brussels.

Friedrichs, J. (2008) *Fighting Terrorism and Drugs: Europe and International Police Cooperation.* London and New York: Routledge.

Gurowitz, A. (2008) 'Policy Hypocrisy or Political Compromise? Assessing the Morality of US Policy toward Undocumented Migrants', in Price, R. M. (ed.) *Moral Limit and Possibility in World Politics*. Cambridge, Cambridge University Press, pp. 138–64.

Habermas, J. (1975) 'Towards a Reconstruction of Historical Materialism', *Theory and Society*, 2(1), pp. 287–300.

Hansen, L. (2012) 'Reconstructing Desecuritisation: The Normative-political in the Copenhagen School and Directions for How to Apply It.' *Review of International Studies*, 38(3), pp. 525–46.

Hegemann, H., Heller, R., and Kahl, M. (eds) (2012) *Studying 'Effectiveness' in International Relations: A Guide for Students and Scholars*. Opladen: Budrich.

Herlin-Karnell, E. (2014) 'Europe's Area of Freedom, Security and Justice through the Prism of Constitutionalism: Why the EU Needs a Grammar of Justice to Improve Its Legitimacy', Discussion Paper Wissenschaftszentrum Berlin für Sozialforschung SP IV 2014–801.

Herschinger, E., Jachtenfuchs, M., and Kraft-Kasack, C. (2013) 'Transgouvernementalisierung und die ausbleibende gesellschaftliche Politisierung der inneren Sicherheit', in Zürn, M. and Ecker-Ehrhardt, M. (eds) *Die Politisierung der Weltpolitik. Umkämpfte internationale Institutionen*. Berlin: Suhrkamp, pp. 190–212.

Horii, S. (2012) 'It Is about More than just Training: The Effect of Frontex Border Guard Training', *Refugee Survey Quarterly*, 31(4), pp. 158–77.

Howorth, J. (2012) 'Decision-making in Security and Defense Policy: Towards Supranational Inter-governmentalism?' *Cooperation and Conflict*, 47(4), pp. 433–53.

Genschel, P. and Jachtenfuchs, M. (2016) 'More Integration, Less Federation: The European Integration of Core State Powers', *Journal of European Public Policy*, 23(1), pp. 42–59.

Jakobi, A. P. (2013) *Common Goods and Evils? The Formation of Global Crime Governance*. Oxford: Oxford University Press.

Jakobi, A. P. and Wolf, K. D. (2013) *The Transnational Governance of Violence and Crime: Non-state Actors in Security*. Basingstoke: Palgrave Macmillan.

Jensen, M. D., Koop, C., and Tatham, M. (2014) 'Coping with Power Dispersion? Autonomy, Co-ordination and Control in Multilevel Systems', *Journal of European Public Policy*, 21(9), pp. 1237–54.

Kaunert, C. (2010) 'The area of Freedom, Security and Justice in the Lisbon Treaty: Commission Policy Entrepreneurship?' *European Security*, 19(2), pp. 169–89.

Kaunert, C. and Giovanna, M. D. (2010) 'Post-9/11 EU Counter-terrorist Financing Cooperation: Differentiating Supranational Policy Entrepreneurship by the Commission and the Council Secretariat', *European Security*, 19(2), pp. 275–95.

Kaunert, C., Léonard, S., and Occhipinti, J. D. (2013) 'Agency Governance in the European Union's Area of Freedom, Security and Justice', *Perspectives on European Politics and Society*, 14(3), pp. 273–84.

König, T. and Mäder, L. (2014) 'The Strategic Nature of Compliance: An Empirical Evaluation of Law Implementation in the Central Monitoring System of the European Union', *American Journal of Political Science*, 58(1), pp. 246–63.

Latour, B. (2005) *Reassembling the Social: An Introduction to Actor-Network-Theory*. Oxford: Oxford University Press.

Lefkofridi, Z. and Schmitter, P. C. (2015) 'Transcending or Descending? European Integration in Times of Crisis', *European Political Science Review*, 7(1), pp. 3–22.

Lorenz, A. (2011) 'Cooperation, Integration, Europeanisation? National Governments' Interests in European Justice and Home Affairs', in Bendel, P., Ette, A., and Parkes, R. (eds) *The Europeanization of Control: Venues and Outcomes of EU Justice and Home Affairs*. Berlin: LIT Verlag, pp. 77–115.

Majone, G. (2014) 'Policy Harmonization: Limits and Alternatives', *Journal of Comparative Policy Analysis: Research and Practice*, 16(1), pp. 4–21.

Manski, C. (2011) 'Policy Choice with Partial Knowledge of Policy Effectiveness', *Journal of Experimental Criminology*, 7(2), pp. 111–25.

McGinley, M. and Parkes, R. (2007) 'Rights vs. Effectiveness? The Autonomy Thesis in EU Internal Security Cooperation', *European Security*, 16(3), pp. 245–66.

Meyer, C. O. and de Franco, C. (2011) *Forecasting, Warning and Responding to Transnational Risks*. Basingstoke: Palgrave Macmillan.

Moravcsik, A. (1997) 'Taking Preferences Seriously: A Liberal Theory of International Politics', *International Organization*, 51(4), pp. 513–53.

Mudge, S. L. and Vauchez, A. (2012) 'Building Europe on a Weak Field: Law, Economics, and Scholarly Avatars in Transnational Politics', *American Journal of Sociology*, 118(2), pp. 449–92.

Murphy, C. C. and Arcarazo, D. A. (eds) (2014) *EU Security and Justice Law:After Lisbon and Stockholm*. Oxford and Oregon: Hart Publishing.

Neal, A. W. (2012) 'Terrorism, Lawmaking, and Democratic Politics: Legislators as Security Actors', *Terrorism and Political Violence*, 24(3), pp. 357–74.

Nugent, N., & Rhinard, M. (2016) 'Is the European Commission Really in Decline?' JCMS: Journal of Common Market Studies, 54(5), 1199–1215.

Pierson, P. (2004) *History, Institutions, and Social Analysis*. Princeton, NJ and Oxford: Princeton University Press.

Pollak, J. and Slominski, P. (2009) 'Experimentalist but not Accountable Governance? The Role of Frontex in Managing the EU's External Borders', *West European Politics*, 32(5), pp. 904–24.

Ripoll Servent, A. (2015) *Institutional and Policy Change in the European Parliament: Deciding on Freedom, Security and Justice*. Basingstoke: Palgrave.

Rittberger, B. and Wonka, A. (2011) 'Introduction: Agency Governance in the European Union', *Journal of European Public Policy*, 18(6), pp. 780–9.

Sabatier, P. A. (1998) 'The Advocacy Coalition Framework: Revisions and Relevance for Europe', *Journal of European Public Policy*, 5(1), pp. 98–130.

Sayes, E. (2014) 'Actor–Network Theory and Methodology: Just What Does It Mean to Say that Nonhumans Have Agency?' *Social Studies of Science*, 44(1), pp. 134–49.

Scharpf, F. W. (2010) 'The Asymmetry of European Integration, or Why the EU Cannot Be a "Social Market Economy"', *Socio-Economic Review*, 8(2), pp. 211–50.

Schimmelfennig, F. (2015) 'What's the News in "New Intergovernmentalism"? A Critique of Bickerton, Hodson and Puetter', *JCMS: Journal of Common Market Studies*, 53(4), pp. 723–30.

Schmitter, P. C. (1970) 'A Revised Theory of Regional Integration', *International Organization*, 24(4), pp. 836–68.

Schwell, A. (2009) 'De/securitising the 2007 Schengen Enlargement: Austria and "the East"', *Journal of Contemporary European Research*, 5(2), pp. 243–58.

Toshkov, D. and de Haan, L. (2012) 'The Europeanization of Asylum Policy: An Assessment of the EU Impact on Asylum Applications and Recognitions Rates', *Journal of European Public Policy*, 20(5), pp. 661–83.

Toshkov, D. and Kortenska, E. (2015) 'Does Immigration Undermine Public Support for Integration in the European Union?' *Journal of Common Market Studies*, 53(4), pp. 910–25.

Trauner, F. and Servent, A. R. (2014) *Policy Change in the Area of Freedom, Security and Justice: How EU Institutions Matter*. London: Routledge.

Trauner, F. (2012) 'The European Parliament and Agency Control in the Area of Freedom, Security and Justice', *West European Politics*, 35(4), pp. 784–802.

Trondal, J. (2010) *An Emergent European Executive Order*. Oxford: Oxford University Press.

van Dongen, T. W. (2011) 'Break It Down: An Alternative Approach to Measuring Effectiveness in Counterterrorism', *Journal of Applied Security Research*, 6(3), pp. 357–71.

Vollaard, H. (2014) 'Explaining European Disintegration', *JCMS: Journal of Common Market Studies*, 52(5), pp. 1142–59.

Webber, D. (2014) 'How Likely Is It That the European Union Will Disintegrate? A Critical Analysis of Competing Theoretical Perspectives', *European Journal of International Relations*, 20(2), pp. 341–65.

Name Index

Subject Index

Printed and bound by CPI Group (UK) Ltd, Croydon, CR0 4YY